COLORADO ARTIST
JACK ROBERTS
· Painting the West ·

F. DARRELL MUNSELL

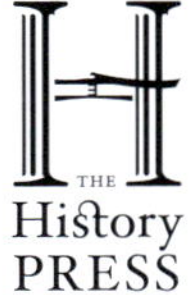

THE
History
PRESS

Published by The History Press
Charleston, SC 29403
www.historypress.net

First published 2015

Manufactured in the United States

ISBN 978.1.46711.845.3

Library of Congress Control Number: 2015946483

Notice: The information in this book is true and complete to the best of our knowledge. It is offered without guarantee on the part of the author or The History Press. The author and The History Press disclaim all liability in connection with the use of this book.

COLORADO ARTIST
JACK ROBERTS

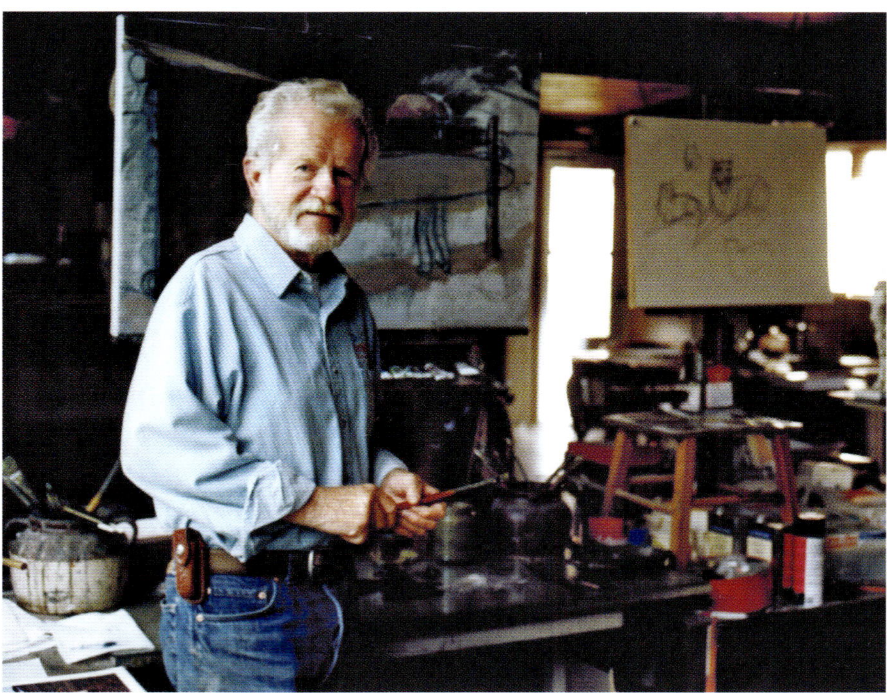

A 1997 photograph of Jack Roberts in his Redstone studio. *Photo credit: Bob Louden.*

CONTENTS

FOREWORD

Opening the door to Jack Roberts's studio opens the door to his life. Situated in the picturesque Crystal River Valley south of the village of Redstone, Colorado, the cabin edges against sheer sandstone cliffs. Here, spring water runs pure and sweet, and when the sun hits the south-facing porch, the rooms mellow with warmth and light. This was Jack's home for thirty-one years. He chose the site with particular care, and in this setting, he found inspiration to create an average of forty paintings a year.

The great front room that served as his studio still exudes his presence. His easel, brilliant flakes of color intact, stands next to a crock holding a variety of brushes. On a cluttered table nearby, photos, sketches and handwritten notes document the progress of various paintings. Imagination pictures him working here, the canvas framed in light from the huge north window behind him, his brush crafting a detail with meticulous care. Yet the colors and intensity suggest the other side of his nature—the flamboyant, adventuresome and passionate essence of creativity.

Chronologically, his paintings reveal changes in his lifestyle and philosophy, as well as in subject matter and style. He often drew from his own experiences, but when a historical subject caught his fancy, he researched it fully, sketching, thinking and expanding his image until it came to life on his canvas. And whether depicting bar scenes, cowboys, Indians, pioneers, newspapermen or noted expeditions, he approached each subject with dedication and accuracy. He was a major illustrator of the American West.

Jack never lost his passion for painting. Throughout his life, he was driven by the need to fulfill himself as an artist, not only to make a living but also to create lasting works that reflected true character and historical significance. The paintings he left behind are a testimony to his success.

JANE R. MUNSELL

ACKNOWLEDGEMENTS

The first Jack Roberts painting I saw was in the Buffalo Valley Inn south of Glenwood Springs, Colorado, in the early 1970s. It was his famous *Saturday Night*, the depiction of a cowboy taking a bath in a washtub. I bought a postcard of it. My next encounter with Jack's painting occurred during a visit to the Leanin' Tree Museum and Sculpture Garden of Western Art in Boulder, Colorado, more than two decades later. There, in the Jack Roberts Room of the gallery, I marveled at the way he portrayed cowboys working in the high country of western Colorado. My curiosity about this talented artist was enhanced by this experience.

Although we lived within a few miles of each other during the last three years of his life, I never had the opportunity to meet him. A few years ago, I visited his studio in Redstone, Colorado. There, I met Jack's son, Gary Miller, who generously offered to let me browse through his father's papers, letters and other memorabilia. I am grateful to Gary for that opportunity.

The search convinced me that Jack's life story should be told. But letters and newspaper cuttings could take the story only so far. The information derived from interviews, telephone conversations and e-mail correspondence with nearly fifty people provided the heart and soul of the story of this flamboyant and creative artist. Although there are too many people to thank here, special thanks are extended to Gary and Monica Miller, Don and Angela Parkison and Bartlett for their perceptive and personal family accounts. I am also indebted to Steve and Joan Benson and Lanny Grant for their valuable insights into Jack's life and career. A general thank-you is extended to all who have come forward eagerly to share their stories about Jack.

I am delighted to be able to include over sixty photographs of Jack's paintings in this book. Each painting helps to tell his story. I am indebted to Darlene Dueck, curator of the American Museum of Western Art, and Tim Trumble of Leanin' Tree for providing photographs of paintings in their collections and allowing me to use them for this publication. For granting me permission to include photographs from their collections, I thank the following: Alpine Bank, Rifle; Bruce and Joe Carlson; Glenwood Hot Springs, Glenwood Springs; Judith Hayward, Grand Valley Historical Society; Ken Johnson; Manor Vail, Vail, Colorado; Scott and Lori McInnis; Gary and Monica Miller; David Bailey of the Museum of Western Colorado, Grand Junction, Colorado; Sue Anschutz Rodgers; and the U.S. Bank, Grand Junction, Colorado. Additionally, I thank Deanna Musgrave Corn, Hope Kapsner, Bob Louden, Greg McKennis, Angela and Don Parkison, Kathy and Duane Piffer, Troy and Gloria Pollard and Mike Waski for their permission to include photographs of Jack's paintings in their possession. I am grateful to Beth White for photographing several of the paintings presented in this book and to Alyssa Ohnmacht for preparing the photographs for publication.

For her expert editorial help, I thank my wife, Jane. Her constructive criticism and suggestions were most helpful, and her encouragement made this a joyful journey through the life and career of a remarkable man.

ONE OF DUNN'S BOYS

Jack Roberts was a frustrated and angry man when he arrived in western Colorado in 1947. In Colorado, he sought liberation from a marriage he found stifling and an infant son he did not want. He also sought inspiration for his stalled career as an illustrator and artist. Divorced from his wife and free from domestic responsibilities, Jack devoted the rest of his life to studying the history and exploring the culture of Colorado. In doing so, he found the subject matter that inspired and motivated him to become a professional artist of considerable distinction.

Born on April 1, 1920, in Oklahoma City, Jack was the son of Jasper and Elsie Myrtle McMurray Roberts. Jasper, a lawyer in Oklahoma City, was actively involved in politics. He held public office in Oklahoma County as assistant county attorney and as secretary of the county election board, a position in which he managed local and state political campaigns. Jack described his father as an intellectual who enjoyed classical music and literature. Although he admired his father, he was much closer to his mother. He spent considerable time with her after she moved to Albuquerque, New Mexico, following her divorce from Jasper and her remarriage. He adored his two elder sisters, Cosette Evelyn and Mary Elizabeth, and remained in contact with them throughout their lives.

Jack's paternal grandfather was Creed Fulton Roberts, a Methodist minister and circuit rider for the Indian Mission Conference in the Oklahoma Territory. Early in his career, Creed helped to bring an end to the Indian raids against white settlers in Montague County, Texas, by

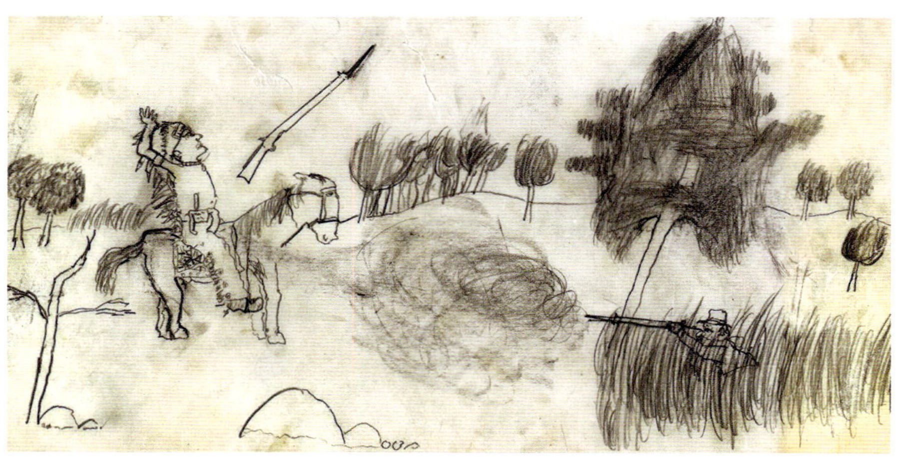

Jack Roberts, at the age of eight, drew this illustration of his grandfather Creed Roberts killing an Indian chief. *Courtesy of Gary Miller.*

converting some of the Indian chieftains to Christianity. As a young boy, Jack was enthralled by the stories of his grandfather's adventures with the Indians. One incident in particular captured his imagination: the story of Creed shooting and killing the chieftain leader of the Indian raids against the white settlers in 1872. At the age of eight, he illustrated the story in a series of pencil drawings, showing how Creed shot the chieftain in self-defense and escaped the other members of the raiding party. With evident pride, Jack noted that his grandfather was held in high esteem by members of the white community as well as by some of the Indian leaders, who later brought him a hatchet and scalping knife and declared, "As white man say, 'We bury them!'"[1]

The Creed drawings are only a small part of the extant collection of early illustrations and cartoons that Jack spent hours imaginatively creating. In addition, he drew sketches of his favorite heroes and cast them in handwritten stories. There was Tom Mix in "The Vanishing Rider" and "Hello Cheyenne," Jack Hoxie in "The Western Whirlwind" and Hoot Gibson in numerous stories, including "The Danger Rider" and "Clearing the Trail." Buster Keaton and "Tarzan the Mighty" also had starring roles in long and well-conceived accounts of adventure.

From an early age, he felt somewhat outside the mainstream. "Something sort of set me on the track of a misfit," he recalled years later. "I was always the very last kid chosen for ball teams. Pretty soon drawing pictures was something that was an outlet for me, and I was good at it so I just went on down the course to become an artist."[2] As a young man, he dreamed of joining the ranks of the prominent magazine illustrators who were his idols.

With this ambition, he enrolled after graduation from high school in classes at the University of Oklahoma to study art. He was, by his own admission, "a top student" at the university, but he found the experience too limiting. "I don't think you need a college degree to become an artist," he later explained. "The best place to learn is a good art school." Therefore, he packed his bags and brushes and headed for the American Academy of Art in Chicago, where, he said, "the action was."[3]

With obvious understatement, Jack said he was a "nobody" at the academy. More than likely, he felt out of place there. Many of his colleagues, he later related, were "excellent technicians" but devoid of any "spiritual aspects" of painting. Having nothing to say in their work, they trained to become commercial artists who used other people's ideas. To Jack, this approach to painting was too mechanical, too lacking in personal emotion and meaning. Techniques were important, Jack conceded, but only as a vehicle to convey the story of the painting. "My career," he explained years later as his work gained recognition, "is based on the principle of painting what I like and finding someone who likes the same thing."[4] He held true to this principle throughout his career.

Although disappointing in some respects, his experience at the academy proved to him that he had the talent to match his passion for painting, and he was eager to find new inspiration. With family resources at his disposal, he joined the acclaimed Art Students League in New York City. These were anxious times for the country, as international tensions and conflict predicated war. These were also anxious times for Jack, who, with his restless spirit, never felt comfortable in a large urban setting. Although "a dedicated city-hater,"[5] the move was the most fortuitous one of his early life and educational career. It was at the Art Students League that he met the renowned artist and teacher Harvey Dunn.

Dunn, a native of South Dakota, had, like Jack, left his home as a young man to study at the Chicago Institute of Art. A period of study with Howard Pyle, the foremost illustrator of the period, influenced his view of art, and after serving in World War I, he focused much of his attention on teaching. He was selective in his choice of students and demanding of their talents, and his ability to inspire and befriend those who studied with him had established his reputation as one of the most inspirational teachers of art in the United States.

In 1941, at age twenty-one, Jack entered the Grand Central School of Art under Dunn's tutelage. "By a magnificent stroke of good fortune, I was one of the art students selected for study in New York under the great Harvey Dunn during his twilight years,"[6] Jack observed in 1971, when his career was finally beginning to flourish. "I'm proud to be one of 'Dunn's boys,'" he added. Jack, along with such notable artists as Dean Cornwell, John Clymer, Gerard Delano, Arthur Mitchell, Bert Proctor, Harold Von Schmidt and Frank Street, was the beneficiary of Dunn's program of selecting elite students from art academies and schools for his classes at the Grand Central School of Art. The students he chose to tutor already had mastered the techniques of painting. When they came to him, Dunn stressed, they needed to be taught the "essential spirit" of painting.[7]

The lesson consisted more of a philosophy of life than of the art of painting. Art, both Dunn and Pyle believed, could not be taught any more than life could be taught. Simplicity and directness of approach were Dunn's standards. The artist must discover his inner self and "paint more with feeling than with thought."[8] Additionally, the artist must find worthwhile subjects to illustrate, paint the epic rather than the incident and let the composition tell the story.

Dunn also thought it important to impress on students that being an artist was not easy. Discouragement served a purpose, for real artists could not be discouraged. In one of his most quoted admonitions to students, Dunn said:

> *There are 10,000 people in the United States who can paint and draw to beat the band. You have never heard of them, and you never will. They have thoroughly mastered their craft and that is all they have—their craft. Merely knowing your craft will never be enough to make a picture. If you ever amount to anything at all, it will be because you were true to that deep desire or ideal which made you seek artistic expression in pictures.*[9]

Jack never forgot what Dunn taught him. "I still think of my mentor, Harvey Dunn, almost every day," he wrote to his son in 1998 in the twilight of his career. "I wonder if he would approve of my work today. He has been such a powerful, significant influence on my life."[10] In nearly every interview or conversation regarding his work in later years, Jack alluded to his study with Dunn as the pivotal point in his career.

Yet upon leaving Dunn's tutelage in 1943, Jack was not sure he could have a career in fine arts or even become an artist. Like many young men of his generation, he found his goals challenged by a world at war. He served briefly in the Marine Corps as a ranger, but an injury kept him stateside. After his discharge in 1944, he was employed as a production illustrator for Douglas Aircraft in Oklahoma City. He painted nights after work, and by June 1945, he had completed a series of eight oils titled *The Fighting Marines*. The paintings, along with pen-and-ink sketches, were exhibited at the Oklahoma Art Center. Five of the most gripping canvases were withdrawn from the show for a week and displayed in the office windows of Halliburton to boost sales of a special E War Bond drive. The *Airview News* observed that they were "thought-provoking studies of fierce fighting action or its grim results."[11]

Although Jack's first exhibition was a success, dark clouds were forming over his private life. His return to Oklahoma was a journey into disillusionment. He seldom mentioned this phase of his life in later years, guarding the memories from even those closest to him. Encouraged by Dunn about his career in art, but at the same time warned about the pitfalls for young artists, Jack slipped into the grasp of alcoholism. Lost in the drink-induced illusions of failure and captured by a marriage he regretted, he sought refuge elsewhere. "There have been many American artists who have found enough inspiration in their own native environment for a lifetime of painting pictures. Such has not been the case with me," he said in explaining his decision to leave Oklahoma. "I failed to discover any degree of inspiration from a childhood in the Oklahoma dust bowl during the Great Depression. It has taken the rugged charm and rich history of the Rockies to awaken any creative urge in me."[12] "Were it not for Harvey Dunn," he stated, "I would never have come to western Colorado to explore and examine the subject matter here."[13] For Jack, the move was the beginning of a liberated love affair with Colorado and the West.

2

A DRUNK COWBOY AND A DRUNK ARTIST

Desperate for inspiration and new experiences, Jack headed to Colorado. He arrived in Grand Junction and for several months drifted from job to job until he found employment during the next four years as a carpenter for the Denver and Rio Grande Western Railroad Bridge Gang out of Glenwood Springs during the winters and as a ditch rider cowboy during the summers. Both employments were life-altering experiences that influenced his artistic career. "The Bridge Gang experience was unforgettable," he told a client, Al Dunton, on August 5, 1992. "That Gang was composed of eight men that were the salt of the earth—hard-working, hard-drinking, big-hearted and loyal beyond measure." He thought about the gang of eight again in 1997 when he wrote notes for his painting *Mother Machree.*

I was on Don Robinson's bridge gang in Glenwood Springs during the winter of 1949. It was pay day and Don told his men that they could quit for the day with a full day's pay when they finished a certain part of the mainline bridge. It was a full day's work by any calculation but it was completed in four hours and the entire gang of eight men retired to the old Glenwood bar [Glenwood Café].

By 4:00 P.M. it was a wild and boisterous party in that old saloon. The bartender, Jack Osburn, was standing at the end of the bar talking to foreman Don. I was standing next to Don and I heard this conversation—

"Don, this sure is a hard-drinking gang you have here."

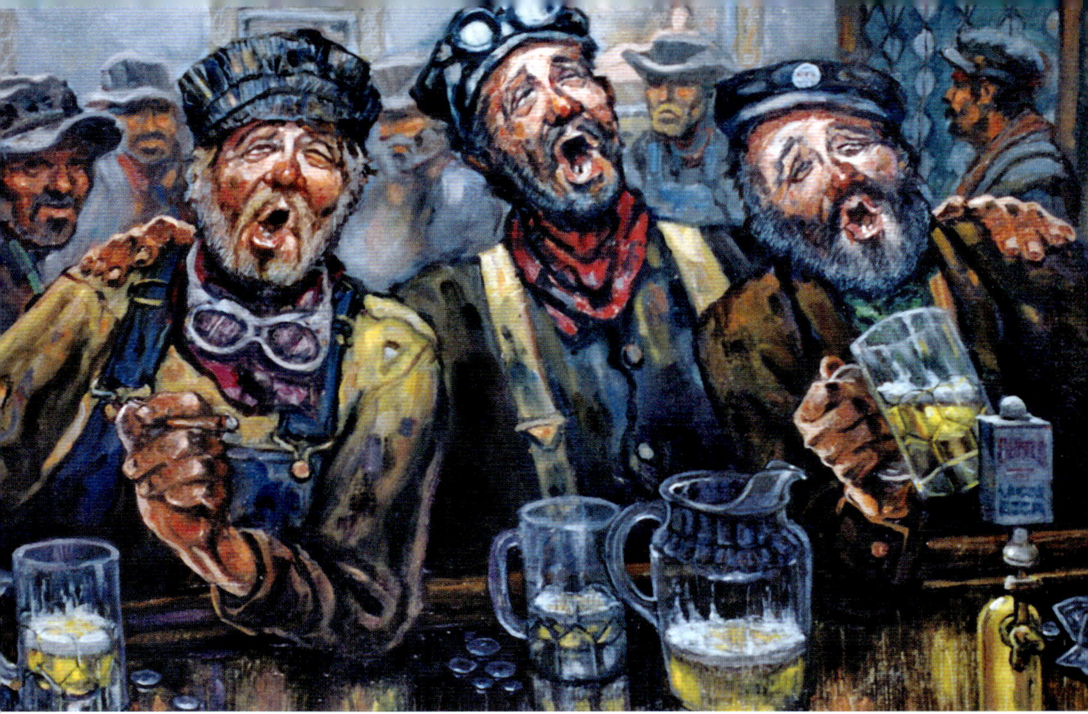

Three Bridge Men. Railroad bridge gang workers sing the old sentimental song "Mother Machree." *Courtesy of Bob Louden.*

"Well, Jack, I guess you're right. Maybe they are a bunch of drunks, but let me tell you something—give me another gang just like this one here and we could go into Hell and put out the fire!"

Jack easily fit in with this group of hard-drinking and rowdy men, and one can be certain he joined them as they tried to harmonize on the sentimental old song about motherhood—"Mother Machree." From this association and many more like it, he began to form character sketches in his mind for future paintings. He also sank deeper into alcoholism.

His main inspiration, however, came from his cowboy days. In the summer of 1948, Jack landed a job as a ditch rider for the Benton Land and Livestock Company, a member of the Burns Cattle Association. For three years, he rode the Flat Tops in the Derby Ridge area near Burns, Colorado, during the summer months for the Albertson, Gates and Benton ranching families. Finally, his search for a meaningful life experience from which he could draw inspiration was successful, as he explained in a letter to Carolyn Benton on July 6, 1971:

It was the summers of 1948 and '49 that I rode the ditch up on the Derby and I assure you that I will never forget it. My experiences up there served as an inspiration to me for many years and do so even yet. Your late husband, Harry, is enshrined forever in my memory for his kindness and consideration in giving me that job and taking a chance on such a green hand as I was then. He was certainly a prince of a fellow.

The thing that made it so extraordinary was the contrast it offered to the way of life I had known in New York City. Every day was an adventure. Every day was filled with colorful and exciting things that I never knew existed. The pictures I painted during those beautiful days were lousy but at least I was being exposed to the way of life I believed was worth portraying. Many times since then I have publically admitted that I was an incompetent cowboy but I still loved every minute of it. I desperately needed the experiences I gained up there and I suspect Harry realized this and therefore tolerated my mistakes.

Although Harry Benton hired Jack, it was the responsibility of Andrew "Mac" McCall, Benton's foreman, to train him. Consequently, he became an unforgettable icon in Jack's life. Mac liked very few people, Jack noted, "but he liked me…partly because Harry Benton liked me." Mac taught Jack the cowboy way of life, including the cowboy way of cooking. And following his recipes, Jack became a great cook. Living such an isolated and lonely life, he enjoyed the occasions when people stopped by, especially when he was preparing a meal. Clifford Neil, another cowboy friend, warned Jack to be careful when strangers appeared at his cabin's door. Few strangers ever did, but it was Jack's nature to extend

The Headgate. Cowboy ditch worker adjusts irrigation gate. *Courtesy of the Alpine Bank of Rifle, Colorado.*

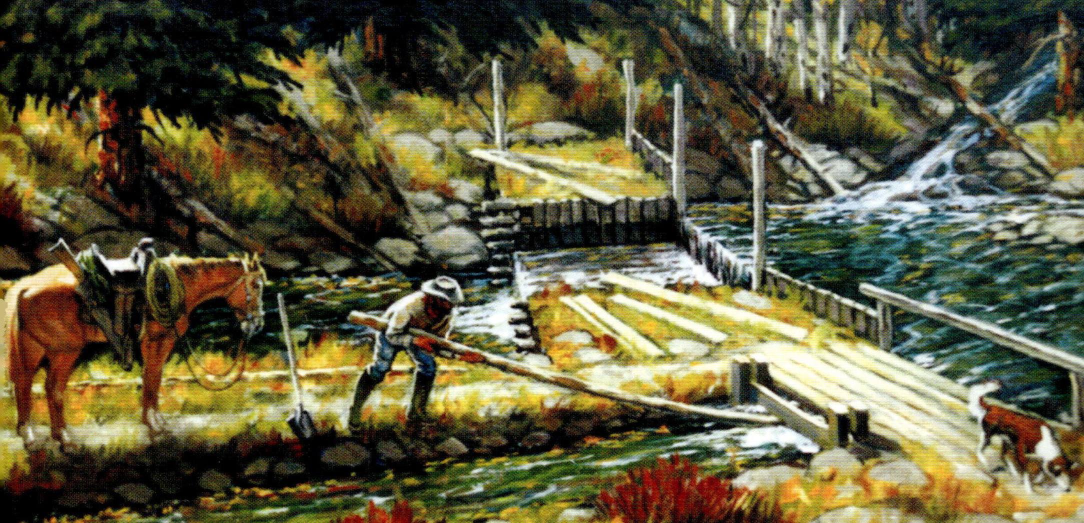

hospitality to anyone who happened by. When two men knocked on his door one day, Jack graciously invited them in. "Come on in," he offered. "I've got an elk steak on the stove. Come in and help me enjoy it." He soon discovered that one of the men was a game warden, who promptly fined him for shooting an elk out of season.[14]

Jack was a very agreeable person who made friends easily, even though some of his cowboy cohorts found him an "odd sort." Henry "Blackie" Daniels was one of his closest friends and drinking buddies during the ditch camp days. They spent hours playing cards at the ditch camp cabin, and occasionally, Mac McCall loaned Jack money so the two could make a trip to the bars in Glenwood Springs. Jack and Blackie remained close friends after both moved to the Hanging Lake Resort in the 1950s. Blackie took tourists to Hanging Lake on horseback, and Terles Daniels, his wife, cooked and ran the café at the resort. During their long friendship, Jack used Blackie as a model for many of his paintings, the most popular of which was the one of a cowboy taking a bath in a tub in front of a wood cookstove that hung in the Buffalo Valley Inn in Glenwood Springs for many years.[15]

"Those were wonderful, wild, romantic days," Jack fondly described the summers he rode the ditch at Derby Creek. The existence of the ditch rider was lonely and filled with hard work, but he saw the romantic side of the cowboy's life in the cow camps of the remote high country. "Living up there and painting pictures in the wilderness and also working as a cowboy was my inspiration," he noted, and from that experience, he learned to appreciate the cowboy and his way of life as an important part of the American heritage. But being a cowboy, he later confided, "was a tough life," and after a few years as a ditch rider, he decided that he would rather paint cowboys than be one.[16]

Although he was never proud of the paintings he produced during and immediately after his ditch-riding days, his heavy drinking presented a way to get them out where they could be seen and purchased. Gregarious and fun-loving, Jack relished telling stories in the bars he frequented, buying for or receiving drinks from those who listened. "I'd run up a terrible tab buying for friends," he confessed. "I was lucky when I could settle my bar bill with a painting…The Glenwood Café…got a whole series of my paintings."[17] So did the Buffalo Valley Inn south of Glenwood Springs. In this way, Jack began to sell paintings. More precisely, the owners of bars and restaurants sold the paintings that Jack left with them to pay his bills.

Despite Harvey Dunn's warning that making a living by painting pictures was difficult, Jack launched a professional career in 1952. Dub Danford, operator of

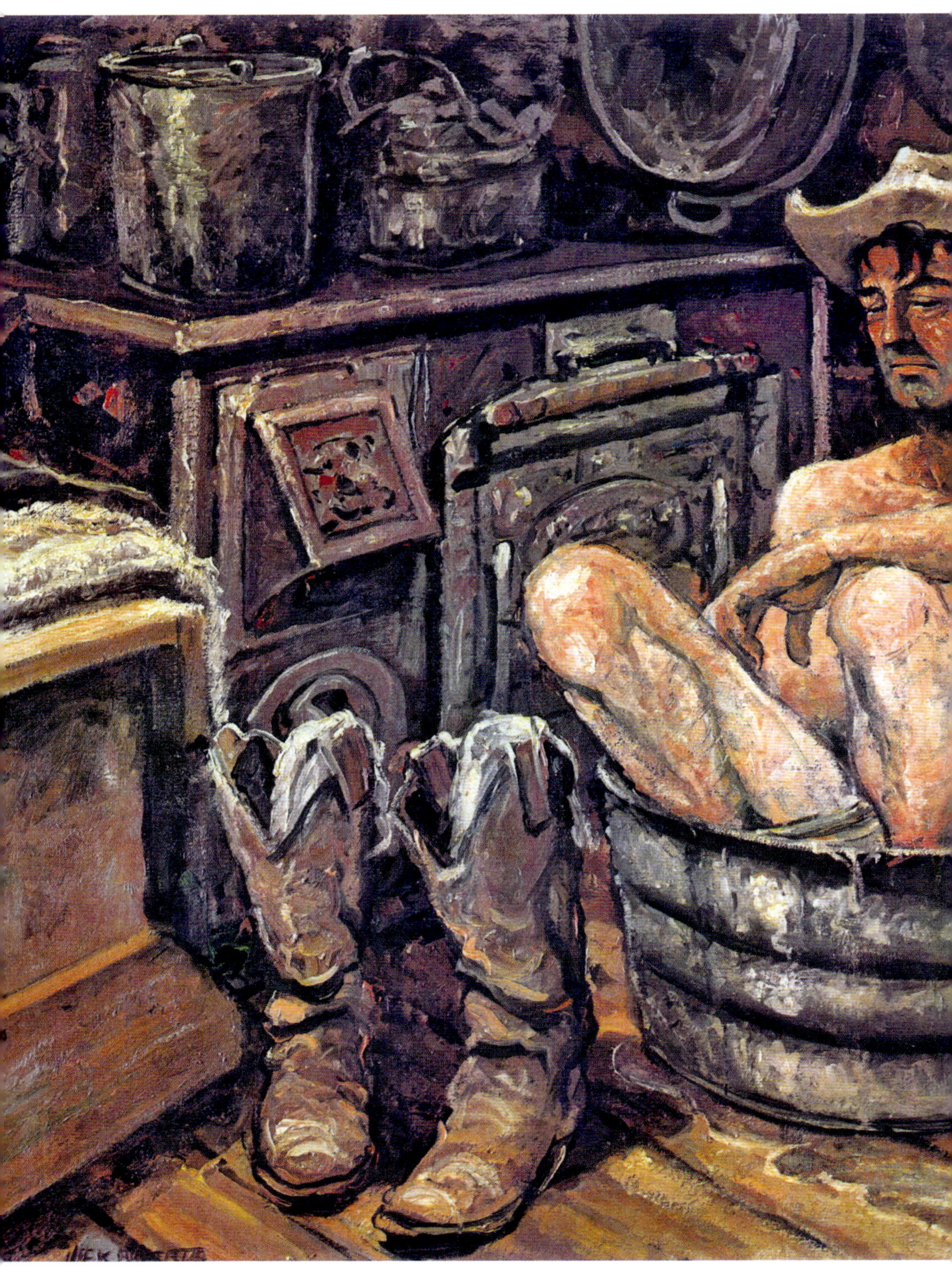

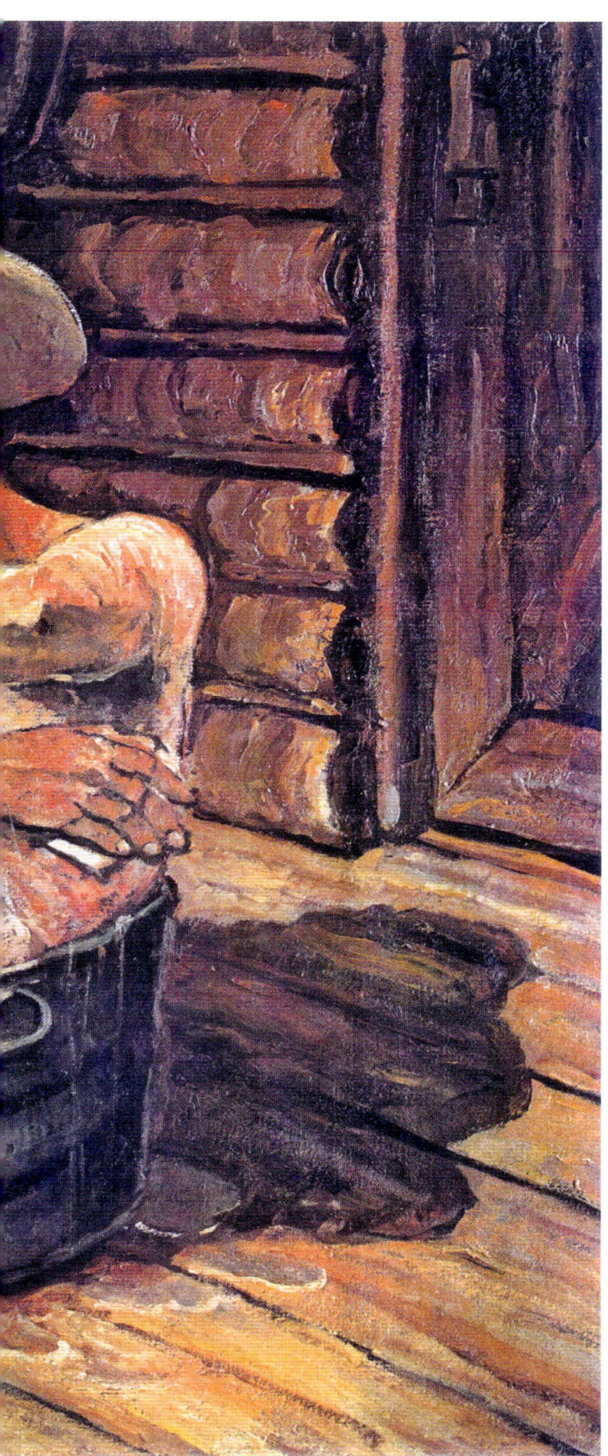

the Hanging Lake Park Resort in Glenwood Canyon near Glenwood Springs, hired him as a guide and wrangler. The new employment opportunity allowed Jack to establish a studio at the resort, and for several years, he was both guide and resident artist. As a guide, he took visitors on horseback up the steep path to Hanging Lake. He was popular with his clients, who clung to every word of his many tall tales.

One of his favorites that he told to test the gullibility of the tourists was about an old man who lived in a cave on the canyon rim high above the resort. "Look up there," Jack would instruct his listeners as he pointed to a pair of blue jeans he had hung on a line to mark the cave. "An old man lives up there, and if you listen closely on Saturday night, you'll hear his beer cans hitting the cliff." If they shouted his name loud enough, Jack told them, he might come out of the cave and wave at them. Falling for the trick, they would

Saturday Night. This painting hung in the Buffalo Valley Inn in Glenwood Springs, Colorado, for many years. It is one of Jack's most popular early paintings. *Courtesy of Gary Miller.*

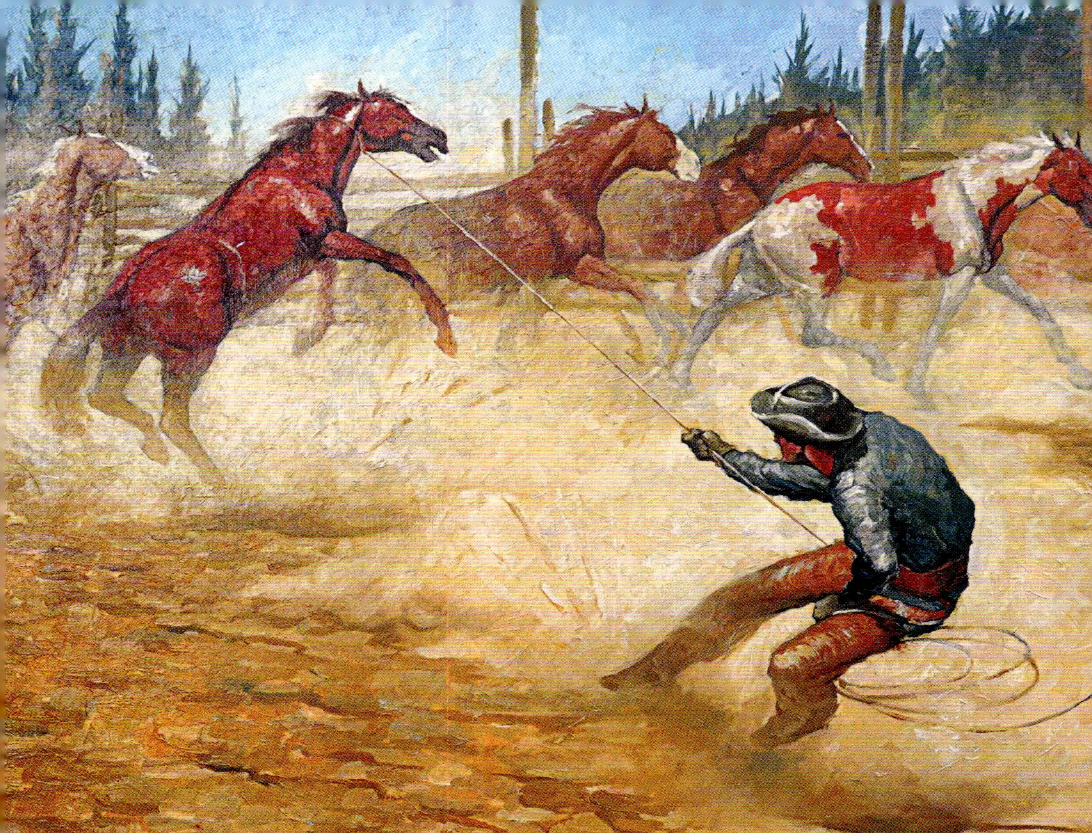

Jack Roberts painted this untitled corral scene around 1950. *Gary and Monica Miller Collection. Courtesy of Gary Miller.*

Opposite, bottom: Friendship. Musgrave Collection. Courtesy of Deanna Musgrave Corn.

shout, "Lucifer, Lucifer," but to no avail. Feigning resignation, Jack would observe, "I guess he's not coming out tonight."

He could not believe how credulous some of the tourists were. "They never asked me how he got up there," he related years later. "I guess they leave their brains at home. Now, I'm kind of sorry I did that." Yet the story was too good to let die, and he climbed to the rim again in the mid-1980s to rewire the jeans, "bleached white from years in the sun."[18]

With a studio of his own, he began to paint in earnest. The popular rustic café at the resort was an ideal place to show his paintings, and he was able to make a modest living selling sketches and paintings to tourists and a few locals who were becoming acquainted with his work. He described himself during those years as a "blood and guts" painter who painted only what interested him. Besides pictures of cowboys, his most popular paintings depicted the bawdy revelry of old-time saloon characters: rowdy men and full-bodied women, all hilariously enjoying drink and song. These were

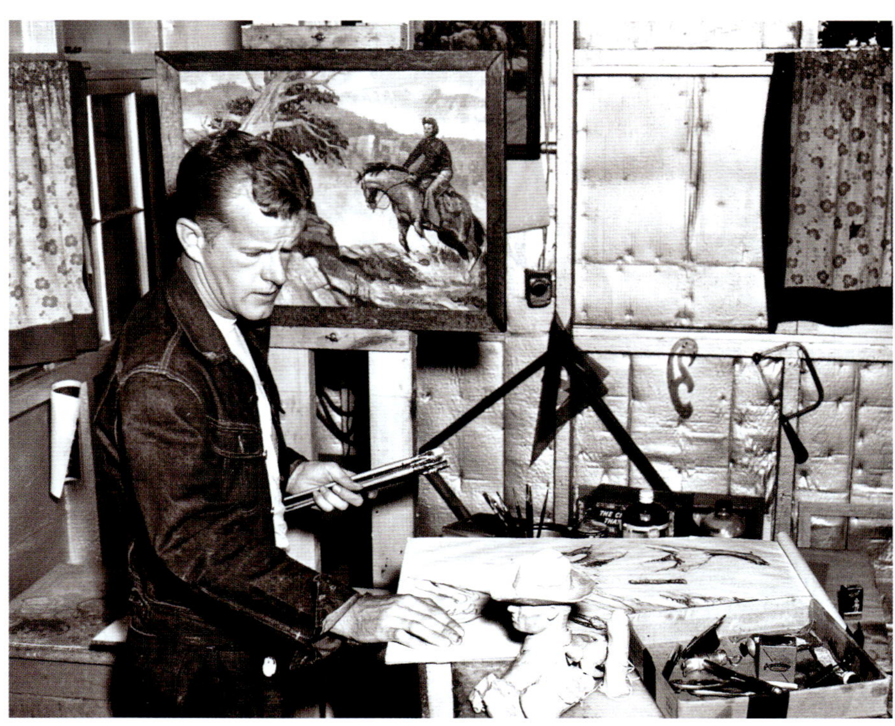

Jack Roberts in his Hanging Lake studio. *Courtesy of Gary Miller.*

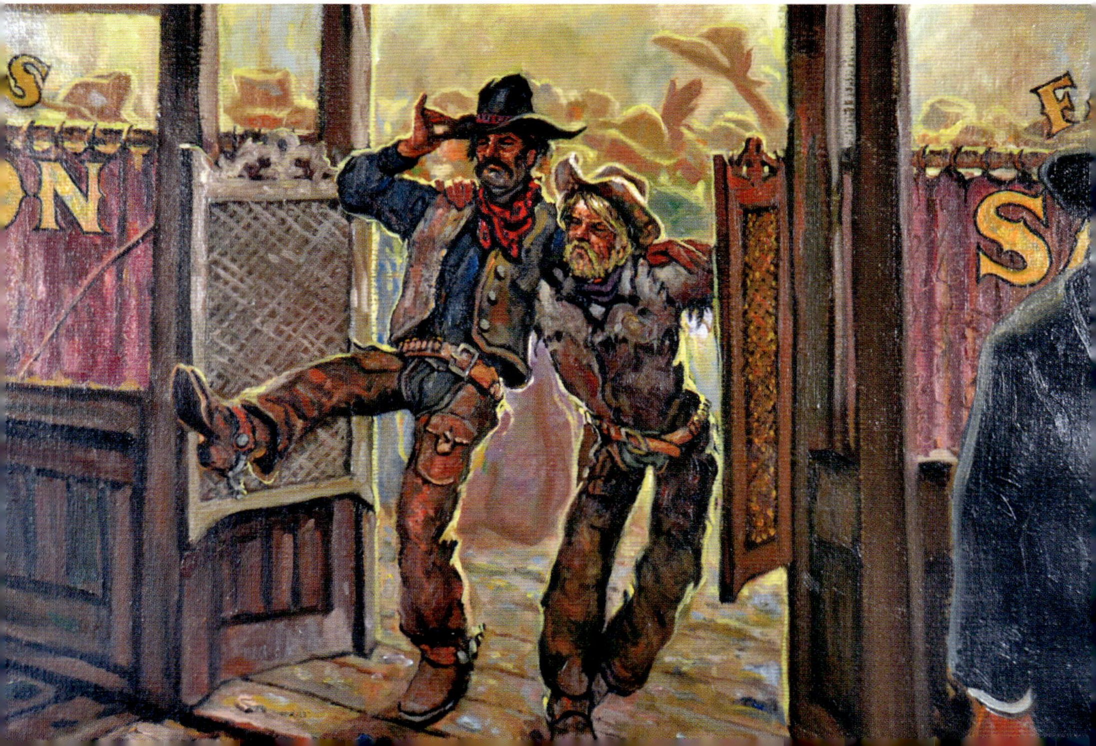

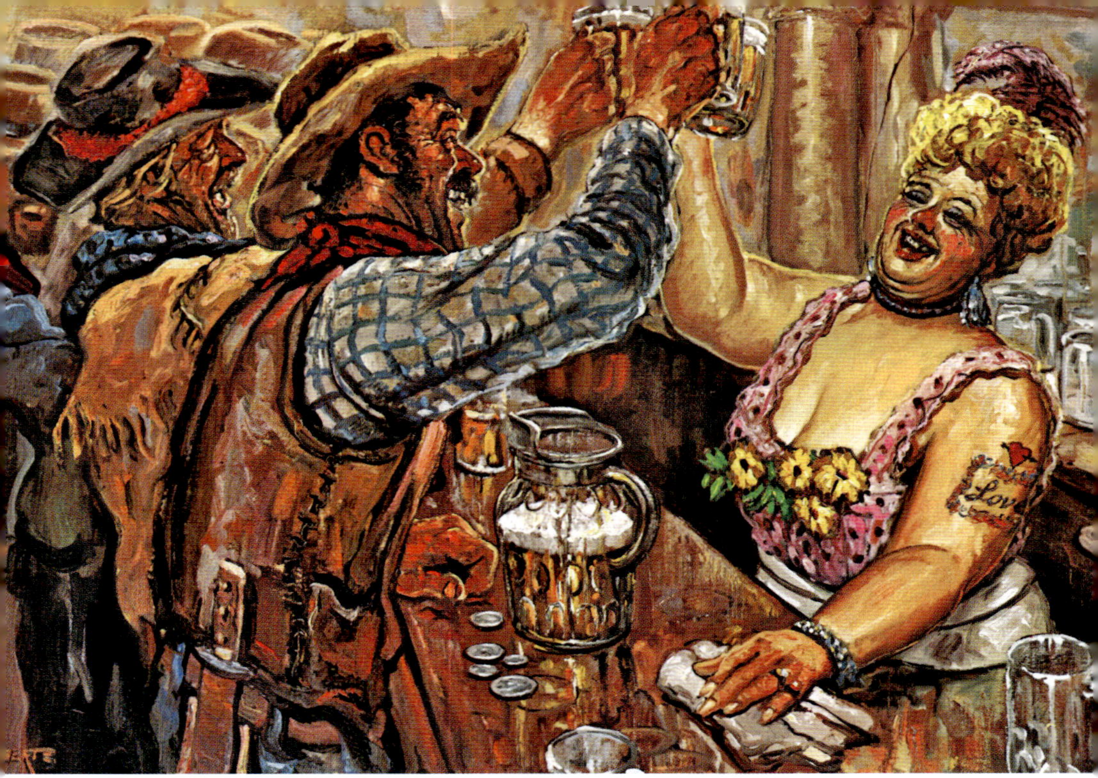

Above: *The Toast*. Photo Credit: *Leanin' Tree Museum and Sculpture Garden of Western Art, Boulder, Colorado.*

Below: *Problems. Musgrave Collection. Courtesy of Deanna Musgrave Corn.*

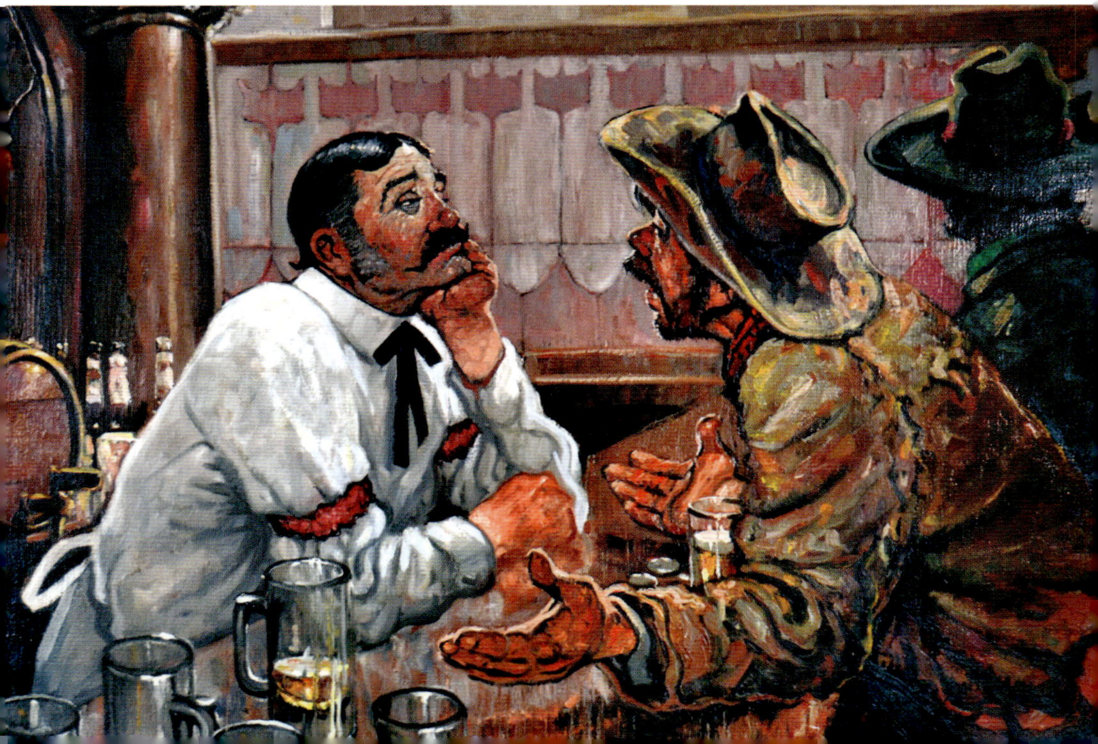

caricature-like depictions that took on a cartoonish element. There was an excellent market for that kind of work, and he gleefully noted that he did "pretty good on drunkards, whores and that whole seamy way of life." Although his paintings were becoming progressively better, Jack admitted that his heavy drinking during this period of his career affected his work. "[B]ut," he was quick to note, "I was painting saloon scenes then, anyway, so what's the difference? I made a lot of money painting drunks." At least he made enough money to live on the fringe as a professional artist, and through his humorous paintings of saloon characters and roughhewn cowboys, he clearly indicated that he was having a good time being, as he said, "a drunk cowboy and a drunk artist."[19]

3

DEFEATING THE GUY IN THE MIRROR

Alcohol was the ruling force over Jack's life during his Hanging Lake days of the 1950s. Yet despite the agony wrought by alcohol, there was fun to be had at his favorite drinking establishments. On weekends, Jack and his friends went to Glenwood Springs to patronize bars and spend their money. The Glenwood Café—a popular haunt for cowboys, ranchers and workers of all kinds—and Doc Holidays were two of their favorite places. During their lengthy sessions there, Jack and Charlie Cousins, a drinking buddy and fellow prankster, took turns telling stories for drinks. At the right time, they teamed up to relate varying episodes involving the Apple sisters, Peely, Seedy and Corey, and their little brother Seedless, who all worked with Goober Gaylord for their boss, Kil Frickens, at the feather factory. It was, of course, a canard from Jack's fictitious world that could be embellished when the interest was there and the drinks kept coming. When the listeners at the bar slowed down in buying rounds, Jack and Charlie stopped the narrative and would not begin again until more drinks were forthcoming. Jack admitted he got the idea for the gig from Samuel Clemens (Mark Twain), who obtained free drinks in San Francisco during the 1860s by telling tall tales.[20]

Jack's favorite trick at the Glenwood Café involved a lithograph of Otto Becker's rendition of Cassilly Adams's famous painting *Custer's Last Fight*. The large Budweiser advertisement featuring the print hung in a prominent place behind the bar. Jack was fond of relating this story, which followed a set pattern. He and his friends, all regulars at the bar, waited for a stranger, usually a tourist, to come into the café and sit at the bar. Then Jack or one of his buddies would nonchalantly mention to the stranger how great the painting was. If the man gave a quick look at it and somewhat disinterestedly agreed, the perpetrators knew they had a prospective victim for their scheme. When the man became distracted or went to the restroom, the bartender quickly exchanged the print with a duplicate that Jack had substantially altered. Now the picture showed airplanes dropping bombs on Custer and his Seventh Cavalry troops and tanks coming up over the hill in pursuit of the battle. The flashes of light from the exploding bombs splashed all over the scene.

When the man returned or his attention was regained, Jack or one of his buddies pointed out to him how faithful the artist had been in depicting the Battle of the Little Bighorn. The victim generally reacted in total bewilderment, questioning the modern intrusion of tanks and planes. "Come on, fella," Jack and his friends cajoled. "There are no tanks and planes in that painting. What do you mean?" In the best scenario, the victim, totally confused, would go outside to find someone he could bring in to verify his perception of the picture. While he was gone, the bartender would switch the scenes again. "Let me show you those bombs and planes," the man would tell his new witness, but of course, they were no longer there. Everyone in the bar participated in the stunt. "What are you talking about? There are no planes and bombs in that painting," they chimed in. And when the man was distracted again, Jack's version of the print was put back on the wall. Despite the victim's protestations that the anomalies were there, no one paid any attention, and when the thoroughly befuddled man left—probably thinking it was time to quit drinking—all had a good laugh. Jack was proud that he and his fellow pranksters never got caught in pulling off the stunt countless times. They were true professionals.[21]

There was an arrogance and growing sense of entitlement in Jack's behavior during those days. On one occasion, he was incensed when he received a parking ticket for parking in a restricted zone in Glenwood Springs. There should be no restricted parking zones, he fumed. Besides, he argued, he should have the right to park wherever he wanted. Losing his plea, Jack brought in a jar of pennies soaked in honey to pay his fine.[22]

Jack had many companions during his "drunk years," but Ben Turner, who had earned recognition as an artist in Taos and Santa Fe, was his favorite. Jack admired Turner and referred to him as the leading landscape painter in America. The two had much in common, including past art training in Chicago and an appreciation for the vast western scene. Through their bond of friendship, the two artists reinforced each other in their painting and drinking. Turner was a binge drinker, and Jack was more than happy to accompany him drink for drink through the bars they frequented.

"Ben and I used to go into Denver on some real benders," Jack related in an interview in the 1970s. "I remember one time we saw a poor down-and-out fellow, sleeping on a pile of rags in a doorway on Larimer Street. Ben took a look at him and gave him a 50-cent piece and told him to go and get a good drink and quit trying to paint pictures. Ben figured that anyone that was down and out and drunk was an artist." It might have been true, Jack added, for artists had a high rate of alcoholism. "There are lots of screwballs and alcoholics in this profession. Creative work is…well, that's why we're all nuts."[23] As for himself, Jack conceded that he was neither capable of living in the mainstream nor able to make a living at anything other than painting.

When both were sober enough to paint, Jack spent many hours in Turner's Redstone, Colorado studio learning what "Benny" had to teach him about painting. After Harvey Dunn, Jack noted, Turner was the greatest influence on his work. He adopted both artists' method of applying paint thickly on the canvas, using broad, bold brush strokes and occasionally a palette knife to spread it out. Turner was especially good at achieving a three dimensional look by varying surface textures. He used thin paint for objects in the background to make them look distant and thick paint and darker colors for objects in the foreground to make them stand out. Jack became accomplished in this technique as well. He also mastered the technique of scratching, using the tip of a brush or knife or piece of wire to achieve a tactile effect that gave authenticity to details like branches of trees or cracks in logs.

Turner also taught Jack about framing. He stressed that since a frame was just the transition from the canvas to the outside world, it must work with the painting. Never let the frame be a distraction, he instructed. To accomplish this, Jack almost always painted his frames to match the tone of his paintings. He frequently applied a neutral gray paint thinly enough to allow some of the original color to show through. He also used a neutral paint to subdue the whiteness of the linen frame and painted the attached picture lights a similar tone to achieve a unified appearance. Ben taught him that light, by accenting texture and intensity, was an important part of the presentation. Therefore, Jack seldom sold a painting without a light.[24]

With few exceptions, both Ben and Jack disliked painting formal portraits. Those requesting portraits expected a photographic likeness, indeed a flattering one. "It isn't possible to paint a commissioned portrait and have a work of art as well," Turner advised. Instead, both artists loved doing character portraits—old Mexicans and Indians for Ben and cowboys and saloon figures for Jack. To be successful, the faces of the characters had to tell a story or express an emotion, not portray a physical reality. After much persuading, Jack finally painted a portrait of his mother, Myrtle. She liked it. He hated it.[25]

As his paintings improved and his reputation as an artist spread in the Glenwood Springs area during the late 1950s and early 1960s, Jack's work became increasingly popular. Most of the paintings during this time were a mixture of cowboy and saloon scenes. Because they were popular and sold well, Jack concentrated on these subjects and painted variations of the most popular scenes. Consequently, cowboys appeared in varying poses while enjoying themselves in the saddle shed, baking or serving biscuits, participating in poker games, taking a bath in a tub, sewing or writing letters or singing and laughing in saloons. A comparison of similar "proposition"

Baking Powder Biscuits is one of the paintings in the Equitable Life Assurance Society's 1965 calendar. *Gary and Monica Miller Collection. Courtesy of Gary Miller.*

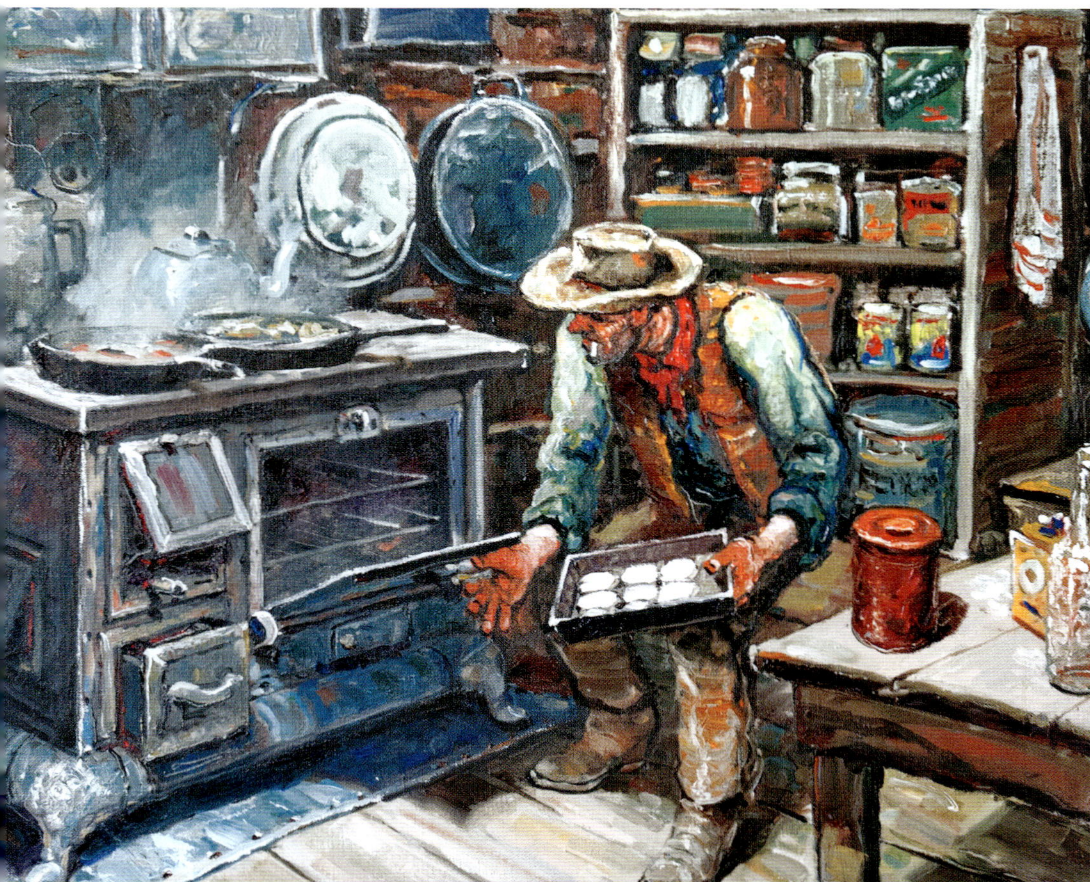

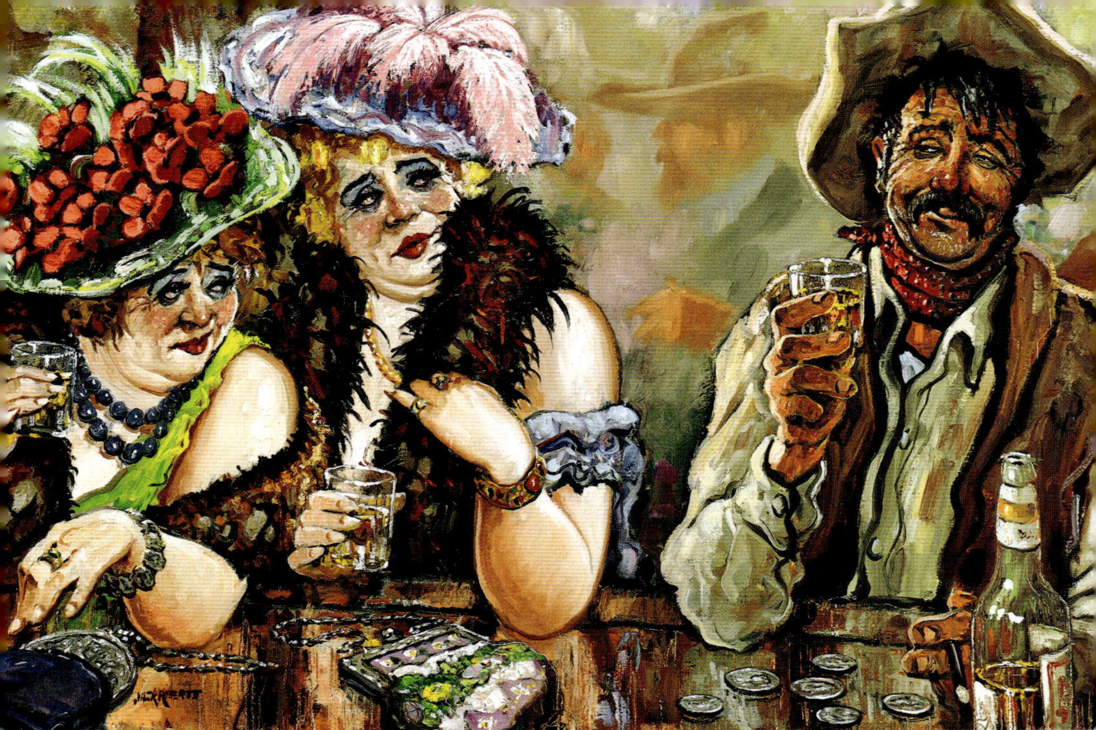

The Appraisal. Photo credit: Leanin' Tree Museum and Sculpture Garden of Western Art, Boulder, Colorado.

paintings demonstrates Jack's ability to restage a scene by altering details. The settings, cowboys humorously conversing with luxuriously dressed women in saloons, are similar. But the women's reactions to the men's advances differ in each composition, so that each can be seen as a separate story, or viewed together as an ongoing sequence. Characterization was Jack's specialty, and he captured diverse personalities again and again in the boisterous paintings of this period.

Through his early paintings, Jack had discovered a successful formula for his work that matched his theory of art with his life experiences. He had articulated his views in a letter to his father, Jasper, on November 3, 1950. Jasper hoped to fulfill his own creative aspirations and interest in history through the publication of a novel based on his personal legal and political experiences entitled *Man of Clay*. Jack proposed a sketch for the cover of the novel, in which he intended to capture the story's theme of a man struggling in a world of political machinations and intrigue. "I believe people are tired of seeing good looking things," he wrote. Instead, he insisted, they wanted paintings that expressed the reality of life and told a story of human endeavor. With disheveled hair and "the weight of hard years showing on his pre-mature face," the man in the sketch, Jack observed, was "a man with character in his face." This was what Jack liked to paint—"men for whom life was a battle."[26] He found these men, and women, in the bars and restaurants he frequented and in his mind's images of those with whom he had worked as a cowboy and railroad bridge gang member.

Although his career was finally progressing by the early 1960s, his life was still filled with anguish. More than ever, alcoholism cast a dark shadow of doubt and disillusionment over him that threatened his sense of self-fulfillment. For days on end, he found it difficult to paint. He admitted that he was getting into trouble, and nearly drowning after driving drunk into the Colorado River was a major wake-up call.[27] One morning, he said, "I woke up…looked in the mirror…and saw the son of a bitch causing all the trouble. I took a good look at him." It was July 27, 1961, his "dry day," when Jack decided to see if he had the strength of character to find a new life, free from the burden of alcohol. He saw that alcoholism, "the disease of artists," as he called it, was destroying the life and cutting short the brilliant career of his friend Ben Turner, and he feared the same would happen to him. Through his own firm commitment and the help of Alcoholics Anonymous, Jack defeated "the guy in the mirror." He never took another alcoholic drink during the rest of his life.[28]

Sobriety helped him meet the growing demand for his paintings. At one time, he had twenty-two paintings hanging in the lobby of the Hotel Colorado. They sold like "hot cakes," he proudly proclaimed in an interview with Heather McGregor in 1999. From 1961 to 1964, the Denver Art Galleries, whose director, Lemon Saks, discovered Jack through the display at the Hotel Colorado, sold over two dozen of his paintings on commission. During the same period, the Buffalo Valley Inn sold nearly as many.

With his paintings in demand, Jack welcomed a series of new local commissions and patrons. Francis and Bertha Christensen, owners of the Buffalo Valley Inn, commissioned twelve paintings commemorating the cowboy and his lifestyle to hang permanently in the restaurant. Jack could not have asked for a better place to display them. The building's wonderful rustic setting and interior proved a most fitting background, and Jack directed prospective clients to the inn to view them.

Henry "Hank" Williams Jr., a local rancher and owner of the Rock-N-Pines Ranch and popular Rock-N-Pines Den restaurant west of Glenwood Springs, was another of Jack's major patrons. Jack was a frequent visitor to the ranch, particularly for the famous barbecues, and a regular customer at the restaurant. Hank helped Jack out tremendously during his difficult years by purchasing at least fifty of his oil paintings, many of which he displayed

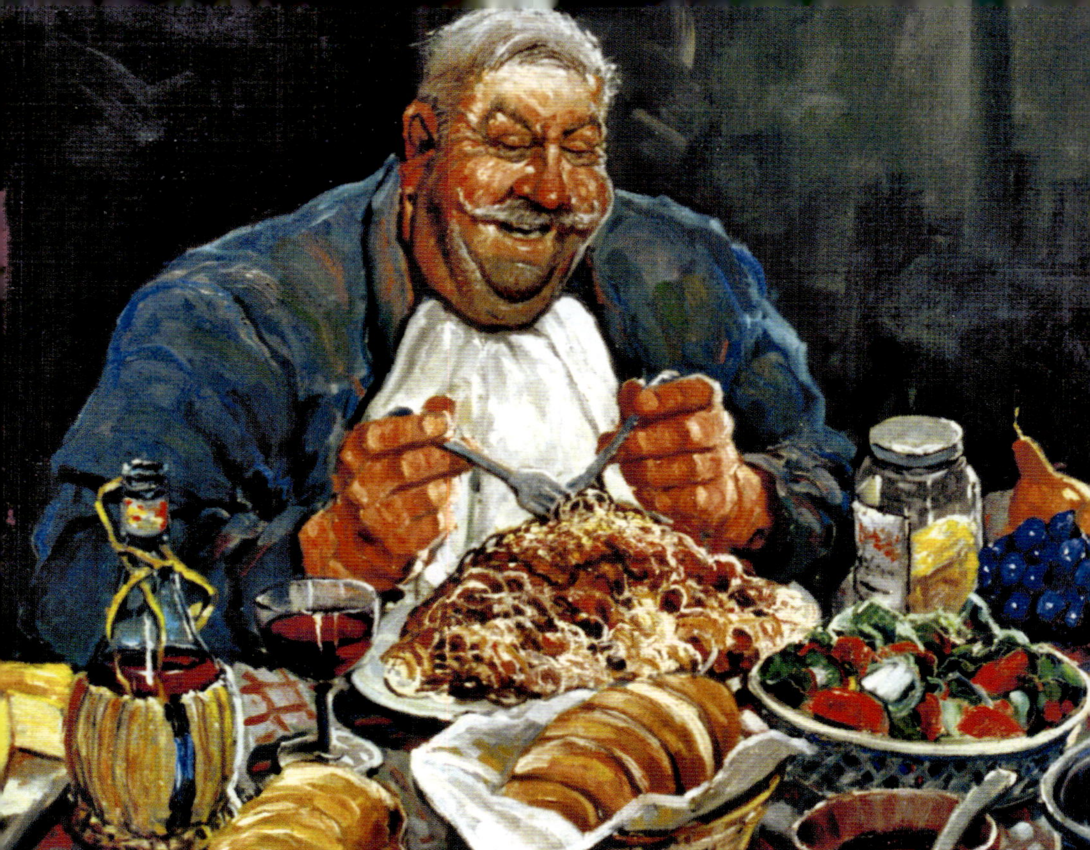

Angelo Rapisardi. This 1963 painting of a 450-pound sheep rancher from New Castle, Colorado, hung in the Rock-N-Pines Den restaurant. It was a local favorite. *Hank Williams Collection. Courtesy of Greg McKennis.*

at the restaurant, and by employing him to draw advertisement illustrations for his various business enterprises.

Russ Osburn, owner of the Glenwood Café, also purchased several of Jack's paintings for display in his establishment. Unfortunately, they met a tragic fate. On January 15, 1967, Glenwood Springs fireman Larry Velasquez helped to fight the out-of-control flames that destroyed the Glenwood Café. As he stood on the roof with a water hose spraying the interior of the building through a hole, he saw the oil paint streaming from about thirty of Jack's canvases.[29] They, as well as the rest of the building, were rendered to ashes. A similar fate awaited several of Jack's paintings in the Williams collection when fire destroyed the Rock-N-Pines Den restaurant on December 23, 1972. Although sick about losing his work, Jack was more determined than ever to establish a legacy as a great western artist.

There were many others who helped Jack through the "rough patches," as he called these difficult times. "When the beans get scarce you look to whoever you can to get through," he observed. Brinkley "Buster" Brown was one of them. A Texas industrialist turned Colorado rancher, Buster purchased several paintings over the years when Jack desperately needed money. "Paint me another picture," Buster instructed Jack on those occasions.[30]

Few were more helpful to him than Marge and Ernest "Ernie" Gerbaz, president of the First National Bank in Glenwood Springs. After the bank quit loaning Jack money, Ernie and Marge personally helped him for many years through the 1960s and much of the 1970s. At first, Jack secured the personal loans with paintings that the Gerbazes kept until he paid off the loans. Eventually, however, Ernie loaned Jack money on an unsecured basis but required him to sign promissory notes. Even though it was difficult for him at times, Jack always found the money to pay off the loans. In 1969, he finally secured a mortgage through the First National Bank to build his studio/cabin in Redstone. During Jack's more solvent days, the Gerbazes visited his studio many times and purchased several of his paintings. "Jack was more than an acquaintance—he was a real friend to us," Ernie said. Helping him find a way to a better and more enriched life was a reward the Gerbazes cherished.[31]

Cleaning up his life also meant cleaning up the mess he had made behind his studio at the Hanging Lake Resort. Jack loved to tell the story of the "great cleanup," which he related many times in a humorous way that only he could. For many years during his drinking days, he discarded his empty cans and bottles by throwing them out of an open window at the rear of his studio into the gap between the building and a rock bank. The pile became enormous. When it came time to remove the rubbish, Jack chose a most unusual, and most likely illegal, way of doing it. He raked the cans and bottles from behind his studio and hauled them trip after trip in a wheelbarrow to the side of U.S. Highway 24, which ran past the Hanging Lake Resort. With a snowplow, he then pushed the mountain of cans and bottles across the highway into the Colorado River. It took several "pushes" to complete the task, but finally all the containers were in the water "twinkling in the sun" as they spread out in the calm waters of Lake Shoshone above the dam and Shoshone Power Plant.

Jack always became more animated as he finished telling the story. With obvious embellishment, he described how a friend on duty at the plant that day screamed, "Oh my God! Oh my God!" as he jumped from his chair when he saw the flotilla of "twinkling" cans and bottles slowly moving toward the diversion tunnel for the hydro plant. Alarmed that the debris would get into the plant's turbines, he immediately called Jack. "Damn it, Jack," he shouted. "I know you put those cans and bottles in the river. Get down here now and help me clean this mess up." Jack sheepishly complied and helped fish the cans and bottles out of the river and put them in plastic bags. "We worked all day getting that stuff out," he noted with understated amusement. "We were exhausted."[32]

Jack's decision to conquer alcoholism came at a most fortuitous time in his career, for several people outside the local area were becoming interested in his work. These included Lemon Saks of Denver Art Galleries; Edward Trumble of Leanin' Tree Publishing Company; Charles Gersbach of the Lord Gore Club of Vail, Colorado; and Philip Anschutz of the Anschutz Corporation. All entered Jack's life during the 1960s not only as major patrons but also as friends. At this very time, the exposure Jack received from the Equitable Life commission brought national interest in his work. It was a pivotal moment in his career that greatly magnified his opportunities for obtaining important commissions and establishing lasting friendships.

4

EQUITABLE LIFE AND LORD GORE

In 1963, John Bershenyi, the Equitable Life agent in Glenwood Springs, visited Jack in his Hanging Lake studio to sell him a life insurance policy. Although John was familiar with Jack's work, he was especially impressed by a series of paintings Jack was currently working on that depicted the range life of cowboys. Several of the finished canvases hung on the walls of the studio. After a long conversation about the meaning of the paintings, John encouraged Jack to submit a photo portfolio to the Equitable Life Assurance Society's office in New York City as a proposal for the company's annual calendar.[33] Jack agreed, although he could not have known that by doing so, he would dramatically change the course of his life and career.

Each year, the society published a calendar with twelve paintings illustrating various aspects of American heritage. In 1963, the calendar featured National Parks, and the 1964 calendar portrayed reproductions of great works owned by American museums. For its 1965 calendar, the society chose to portray some traditions of the West and commissioned Jack to paint twelve paintings on cowboy life to convey that theme. Jack immediately accepted the commission and set aside everything else to complete a series of paintings that he entitled *Life on the Range*.

For this commission, Jack relied on his experience of living at his cowboy friend Bill Schum's Grizzly Creek Cow Camp cabin and riding with him on the range during the summer of 1963. The paintings expressed his interpretation of the cowboy way of life, which began with the cowboy himself, as he explained in the narrative for the calendar: "The American cowboy…is a raw-boned outdoor man and a self-confessed maverick in today's civilization. Only a good saddle horse, the wide-open range and the high wind can satisfy his restless spirit. He is not to be pitied, indeed he has a life that is the envy of millions."[34] The twelve paintings the society selected for the calendar represented aspects of a cowboy's life during each month of the year. In explaining what he wanted to convey, Jack wrote:

> *I choose to portray those aspects of a cowboy's life that have not changed in 75 years, and I see that he still lives in a log-cabin-type cow camp without electricity or plumbing. He still takes a bath in a washtub. He still makes use of a pack horse to make temporary camp in an area that would be inaccessible by other means. He still goes horseback wherever he goes and he still carries a rifle for predators. He is an important part of the American heritage.*[35]

The twelve original paintings featured in the calendar were publicly displayed in various banks and galleries throughout the nation during 1965. They were exhibited at the Central Bank and Trust Company in Denver in January and the First National Bank in Colorado Springs in March. The *Rocky Mountain News* reviewed them at length in its January 16, 1965 issue, favorably noting the artist's attention to characterization and authenticity:

> *Roberts uses the approach of the timeless cowboy choosing to depict in his works the never changing facets of the man and his way of life. His figures are for the most part hard-bitten, homely men, weather-worn, saddle-shaped and often seedy…*[His attention to detail] *displays a thorough knowledge of the men, their lodgings and their day-to-day way of life.*

Equitable Life distributed 750,000 copies of the calendar internationally and estimated that 100 million people saw them.[36] The society also printed 150,000 copies of the calendar's cover painting entitled *Rimrock* as birthday cards for clients. The commission was, as Jack noted, the "biggest turn" of his career.[37] No longer just a popular local painter, he now was a nationally acclaimed artist.

In 1970, Lemon Saks, owner of the Denver Art Galleries, said of Jack that he was "one of the five artists in Colorado whose work sells anywhere in the world." He was in a position to know, for over the years he sold many of Jack's paintings to customers on both sides of the Atlantic Ocean. The Equitable Life exhibit in Denver in 1965 gave him the opportunity to

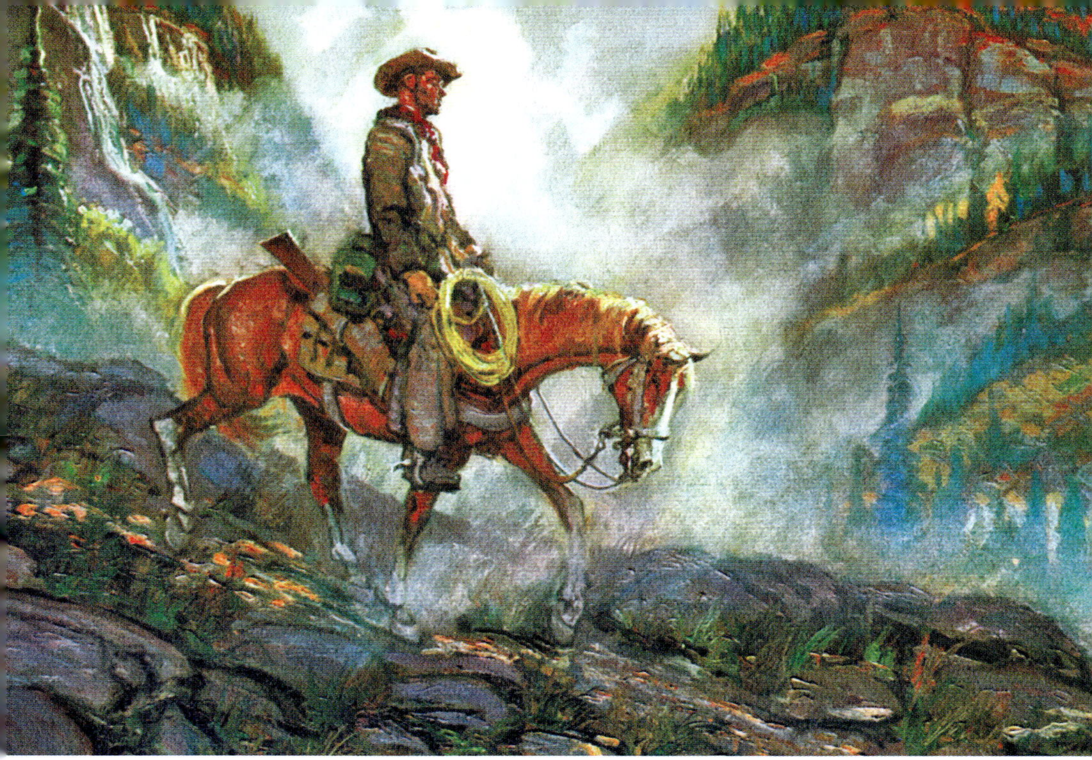

Rimrock. Cover and September painting for the Equitable Life Assurance Society's 1965 calendar. Photo is taken from the calendar. *Courtesy of Steve Bershenyi.*

place twenty-two of Jack's paintings on consignment at his gallery at 1635 Broadway. Most were on the same theme as the calendar illustrations. In advertising the show, Saks noted, "There is an ever-growing interest and demand for paintings by Jack Roberts who has established the reputation of a Western artist who transcends time through the magic of his brush."[38]

The paintings sold quickly, and Lemon encouraged Jack to paint more pictures of like manner for his gallery. But Jack was already off on another tangent. In November 1964, Charles Gersbach telephoned Jack to inquire if he would be interested in painting a series of pictures depicting the Lord Gore expedition of 1854–57 through the American West. Gersbach was a representative of a Denver investment company that planned to build a condominium and private club in the new ski resort of Vail, Colorado, and the investors wanted the paintings to hang in the club. Although he knew very little about the Gore expedition, Jack was intrigued by the idea. After years of painting cowboy and saloon scenes, he was eager to move on to other themes. The images of an English baronet roaming the Rocky Mountain West on an extended expeditionary hunt were too vivid in his mind to allow him to reject the offer without further research. He immediately visited the Denver Public Library to conduct his investigation.

What he found, extremely sketchy as it was, piqued his interest further. His research produced two stories that seemed strangely incongruous. The first, inscribed on the plaque located on the summit of Gore Pass, told that Sir St. George Gore, Eighth Baronet of Manor Gore in Ireland, guided by Jim Bridger and "accompanied usually by forty men, many carts, wagons, hounds and unexampled camp luxuries," hunted in Colorado, Montana and Wyoming for three years, killing more than two thousand buffalos, 1,600 elks and deer and one hundred bears. The second story was that Lord Gore destroyed all of his possessions, including the "unexampled camp luxuries," and lived with the Hidatsa Indians in an earthen lodge for six months during the winter of 1856–57 at the end of his three-year adventure. This was an incredulous contradiction, Jack believed, as he noted:

> *At the outset, it is doubtful if Lord Gore could have established any clear identity with the Indians, and vice versa. He was a class-conscious, feudal superior from the opposite end of the earth, and they were the Spartan disciples of nature. And yet, after two and one-half years of stilted co-existence, the baronet destroyed his "unexampled camp luxuries" and adopted the Indian way of life. What caused this unprecedented change? I called Charles Gersbach and told him I wanted the job. And so it began.*[39]

It began with two portraits, one of Lord Gore and the other of Jim Bridger, the legendary mountain man the baronet selected as head guide of the expedition. Jack used an old photograph to paint Bridger's portrait, but for Gore, it was an entirely different and difficult matter. Without the benefit of pictorial evidence, Jack used contemporary accounts to construct the baronet's physical description. "Very few characters in Western history left so much legend with so little fact," he explained. "But a painter must work with whatever material he has, so I attempted to capture on canvas the image I had of Lord Gore."[40] He admitted that he took "some liberty as an artist" in painting Gore and the rest of the paintings in the series. But after doing extensive research, he had a good feeling about his portrayal. Besides, he rationalized, he knew more about the baronet than anyone else. But agreeing to do the two portraits was only the beginning. He visualized a series of paintings that would document the entire hunting episode.

The Gore project was another turning point in Jack's life and career. He became so involved in the story of Gore and Bridger that he wanted to do more than just paint scenes—he wanted to put them in a framework of history. After completing the two portraits for Charles Gersbach, he found the thought of returning to painting cowboys and saloon characters "prosaic." When approached to do cowboy paintings, he answered, "No, I'm not doing them anymore."[41] Instead, he vowed to devote the rest of his career to researching and painting historical events and themes. As a result, he became both historian and artist, the combination of which made him one of the foremost illustrators of the western frontier.

With his extensive research into and almost excessive thought about the historical events and themes that interested him, Jack believed he was able to establish the right historical perspective and knowledge to bring the events and characters to life on canvas. This was certainly true of the Gore expedition, to which Jack dedicated his life from 1966 to 1971 researching and illustrating. He continued to be intrigued by the incongruous nature of the story—why the aristocratic gentleman destroyed most of his possessions, including the vehicles that had carried them, and lived with the Hidatsa Indians for six months before returning to St. Louis and eventually to England.

As he collected every piece of evidence he found about the Gore expedition in books, manuscripts, letters, government documents, periodicals, private journals and a multitude of other sources, Jack painted scenes that he believed told the story of the saga. Originally, he had a series of twelve paintings in mind. Although he did not have a commission, he was committed to the task. He had six of the canvases completed when Philip Anschutz appeared at his studio in October 1967. Anschutz liked the paintings and was ready to buy them on the spot. But Jack wanted a single purchaser for the entire series, as he explained in his letter to Anschutz on November 7, 1967:

> *This is just a note to let you know that I certainly do appreciate your visit of a month ago here at my studio, and I am pleased that you have such an interest in the Lord Gore paintings.*
>
> *At this time there is not much that I can add to the conversations we had. There are six paintings here that you saw, and there are six more that are yet to be painted to make the complete series. Considering the amount of research involved, the manuscript, the maps and so forth, it will probably be about nine months before this project is completed. It is too soon now to make a definite decision on who will be the owner of the paintings. I am sure that the complete series will have some historic value and I believe that they should all be kept together. It is not the type of thing that will simply be sold to the highest bidder.*

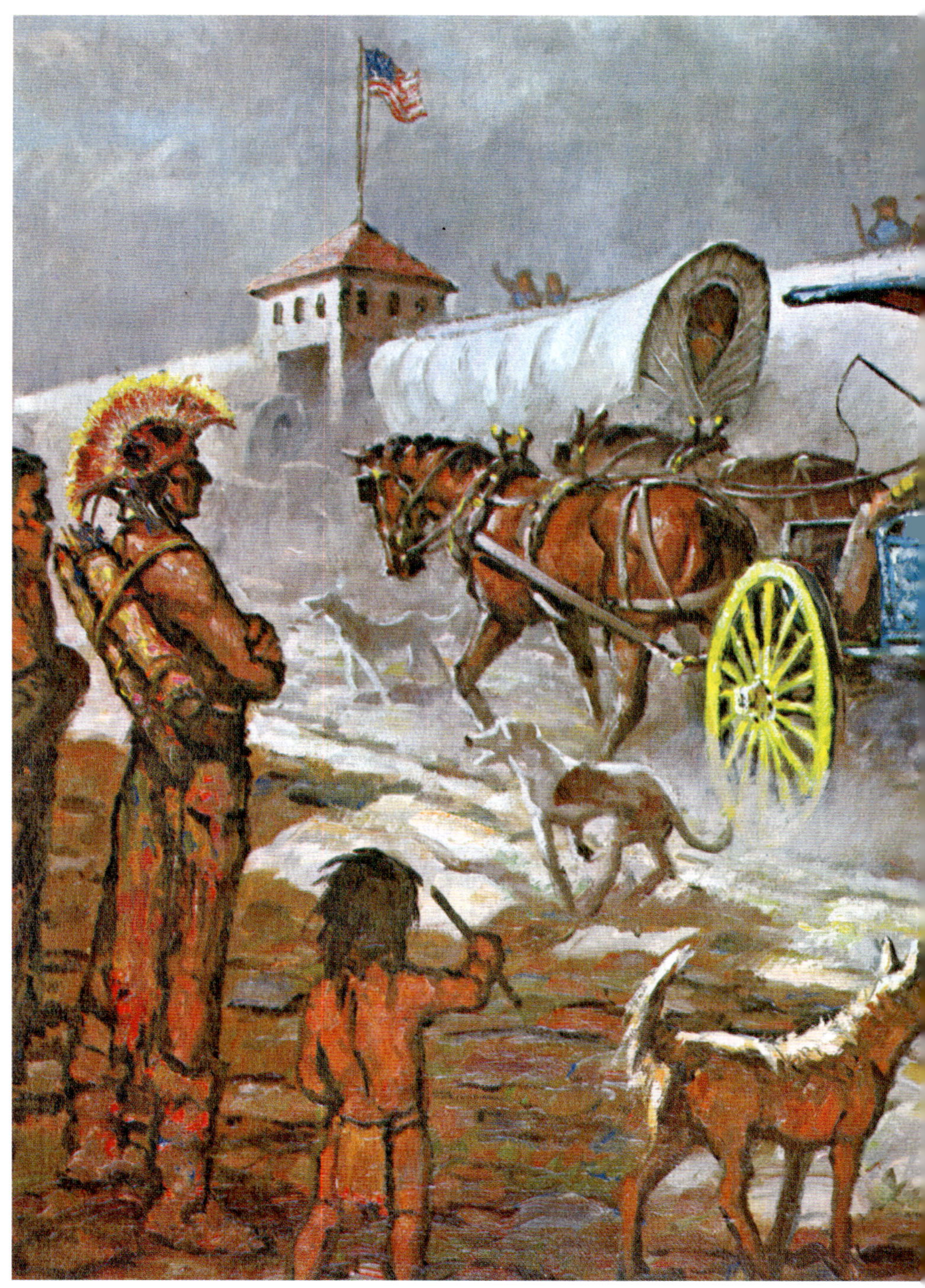

Lord Gore Arriving at Fort Laramie. Travis Anderson Collection. Courtesy of Hope Kapsner.

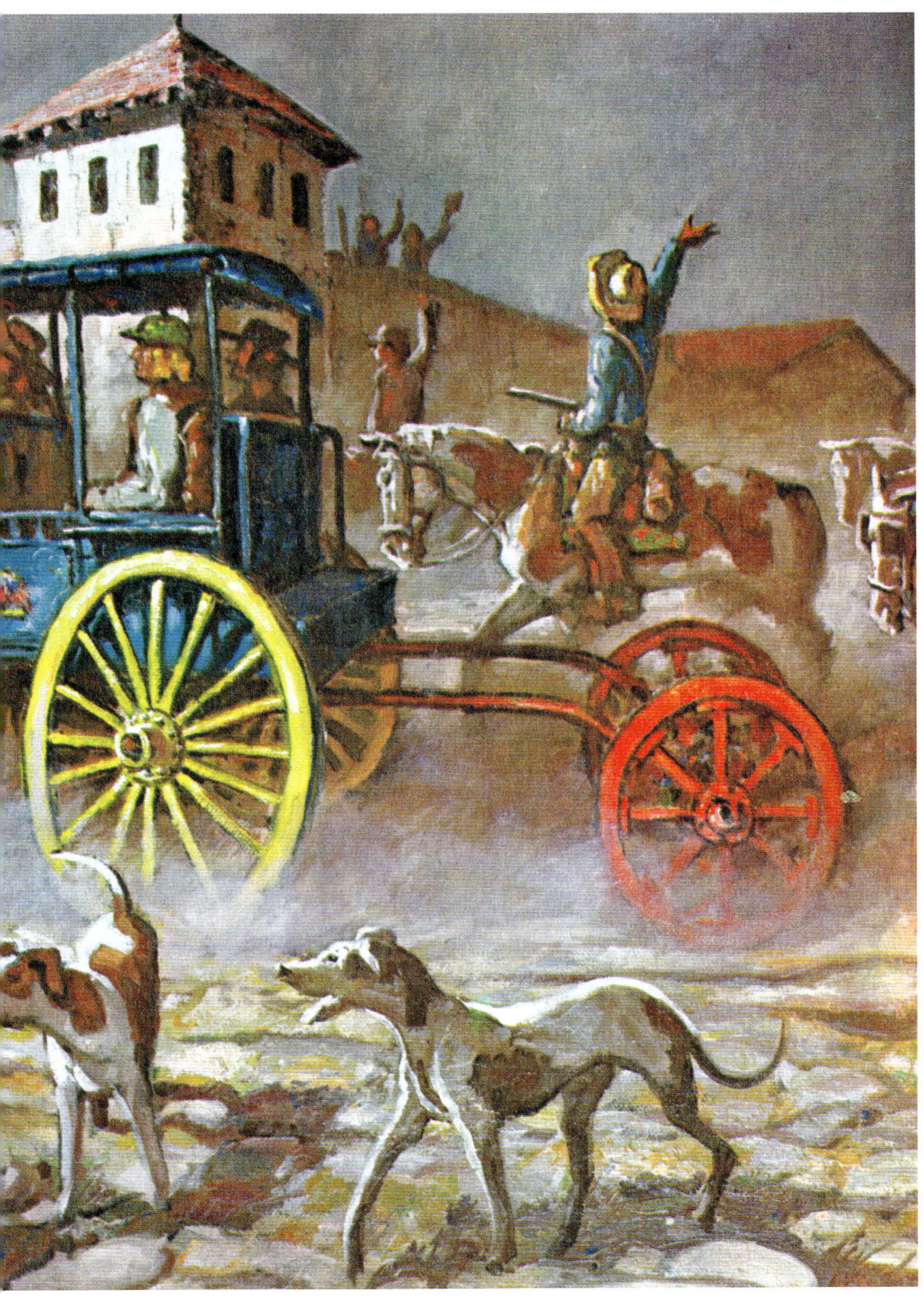

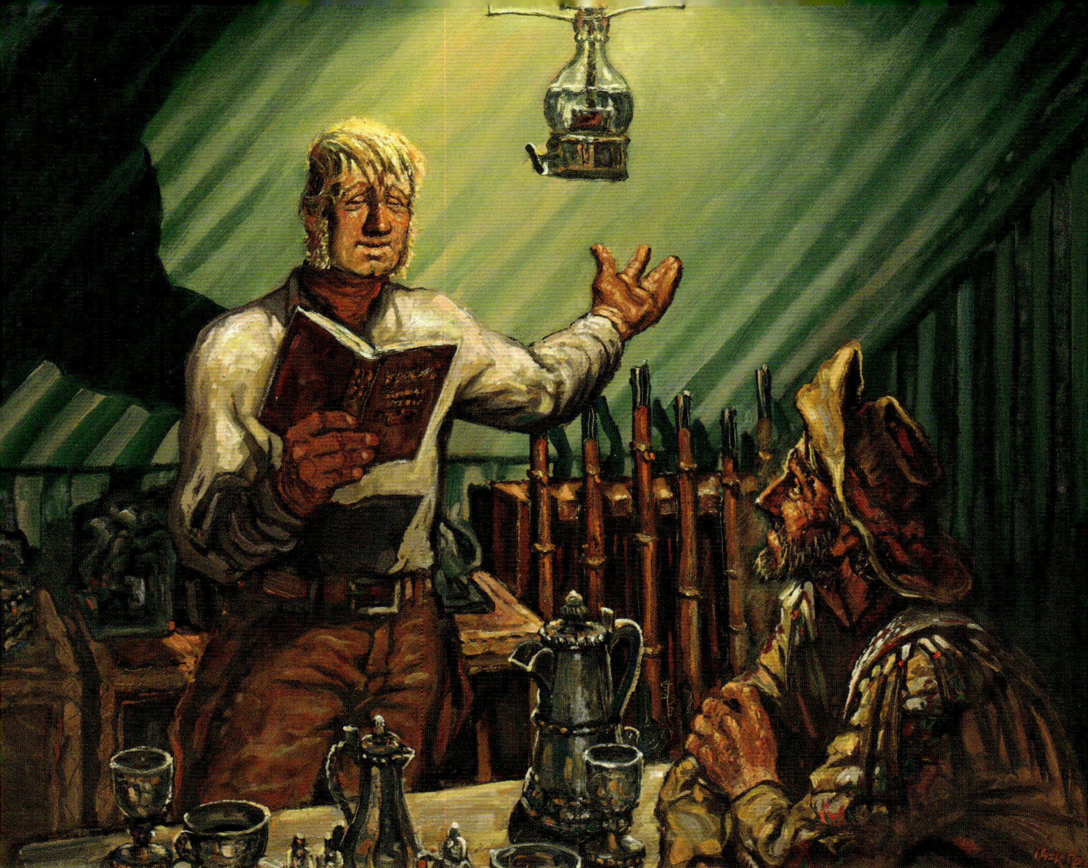

Lord Gore Reading Shakespeare to Jim Bridger. Photo Credit: William J. O'Connor. Courtesy of American Museum of Western Art, the Anschutz Collection.

Eventually, Anschutz agreed to purchase the entire set of twelve paintings. Delighted, Jack proclaimed: "I am ready to paint…These proposed six, along with the six that hang in your office now, will tell the story of Lord Gore's hunting expedition." By late 1968, however, Jack indicated that he intended to expand the scope of the project to include a book that would require additional paintings and scores of pen illustrations. Another six paintings, he suggested to Anschutz, were needed to illustrate Lord Gore's vanity and luxurious accommodations, his friendly meeting with the Indians, his skill in hunting, his relations with the forty-man retinue that accompanied him and his crossing over Gore Pass under the guidance of Jim Bridger.[42]

Jack explained that the additional paintings were on subjects that he had in mind for the Denver Public Library and the Lord Gore Club. However, characteristic of his optimistic nature, Jack counted on a commission that was not to be. After he had completed four of the six additional scenes, the Denver Public Library informed him that its budget would not allow it to purchase the paintings. Jack was devastated and desperate. He immediately turned to his friend. "This turn of events has placed me in an embarrassing situation," he wrote to Anschutz.

> *I had planned to begin construction on my new studio in Redstone with money received for these paintings. I desperately need the money and I need it very soon, otherwise I will not be solvent enough to borrow the balance of the estimated construction cost ($28,000) from the bank. Therefore I am offering these paintings to you for the same price that had been verbally agreed upon with the Denver Public Library—$1,000 per painting.*[43]

The paintings, Jack added, would fit very well with the Lord Gore collection he already had.

Anschutz's rejection of the offer was only a temporary setback for Jack. He sold the six pictures to Travis Anderson, a prominent rancher near Gypsum, Colorado. Additionally, Charles Gersbach purchased three more paintings for the Lord Gore Club, including the scene of Gore and Bridger dining in the baronet's large green tent. In all, Jack completed twenty-three paintings depicting the Lord Gore hunting expedition. They, as well as scores of pen-and-ink drawings, illustrated his detailed written account of the expedition titled *The Amazing Adventures of Lord Gore: A True Saga from the Old West.* The book demonstrated that Jack was both an accomplished artist and historian.

Jack felt a sense of destiny in undertaking this monumental task, as he noted in a letter to his son, Gary:

> *I think Lord Gore is a project worthy of everything I can give, in fact, the project has been waiting more than a century for me and only me! Who else but me would devote the amount of time that is necessary to research and develop such a mysterious legend? Who else but me would be qualified to paint pictures of this legendary character? Who else but me would pursue this ideal in the face of overwhelming odds? You know, it takes a certain measure of blind ignorance to stay with something this long.*[44]

Jack was deeply affected by the Lord Gore adventure. It was, he believed, a story of transformation and redemption. After he destroyed the vehicles and "unexampled camp luxuries" he had used and enjoyed during the hunting expedition in a great sacrificial fire, Gore and twelve other men, including Bridger, attempted to pass through the unexplored

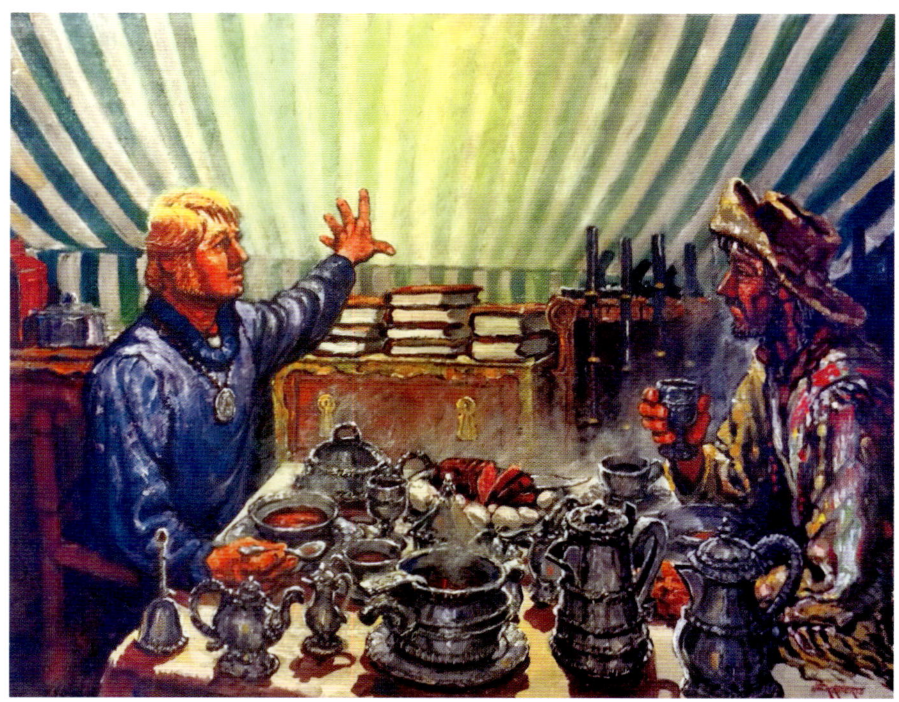

Lord Gore and Jim Bridger Dining. Charles Gersbach Collection. Courtesy of Robert McCleary, Manor Vail Lodge, Vail, Colorado.

Black Hills territory on their return to St. Louis by way of Fort Pierre, only to be stopped and turned back by a war party of Sioux Indians. Bear's Rib, chief of the Uncpapa Sioux, severely punished the intruding party for entering the sacred Black Hills territory by confiscating all of their possessions, including horses, oxen, weapons and clothes, and forced them to retreat naked out of the territory. Gore accepted Bear's Rib's punishment as just for the offenses he had committed against the Indians. He felt guilt for his reckless slaughter of their precious game. The ordeal transformed him from an Irish baronet to a common man who enjoyed life among the Indians. Instead of continuing their trip to St. Louis after being rescued by a hunting band of Hidatsa Indians, he and six other men from his original retinue decided to stay and live with their Indian friends for over six months as guests of Crow's Breast, a Hidatsa chief. The Hidatsa acceptance of Gore was his redemption.

Jack was transformed by the story of the Gore hunt as well. The adventure of the aristocratic gentleman turned Indian companion, he told

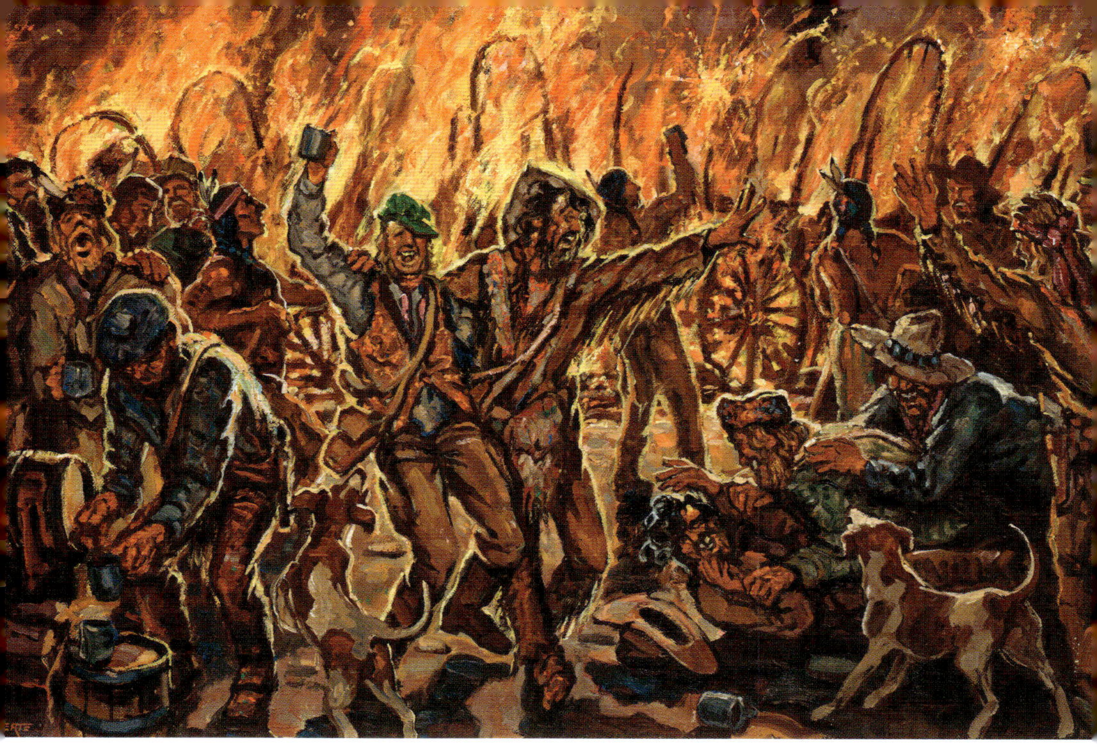

Above: The Sacrificial Fire at Fort Union. *Photo Credit: William J. O'Connor. Courtesy of American Museum of Western Art, the Anschutz Collection.*

Below: Bear Rib's War Party. Photo Credit: William J. O'Connor. Courtesy of American Museum of Western Art, the Anschutz Collection.

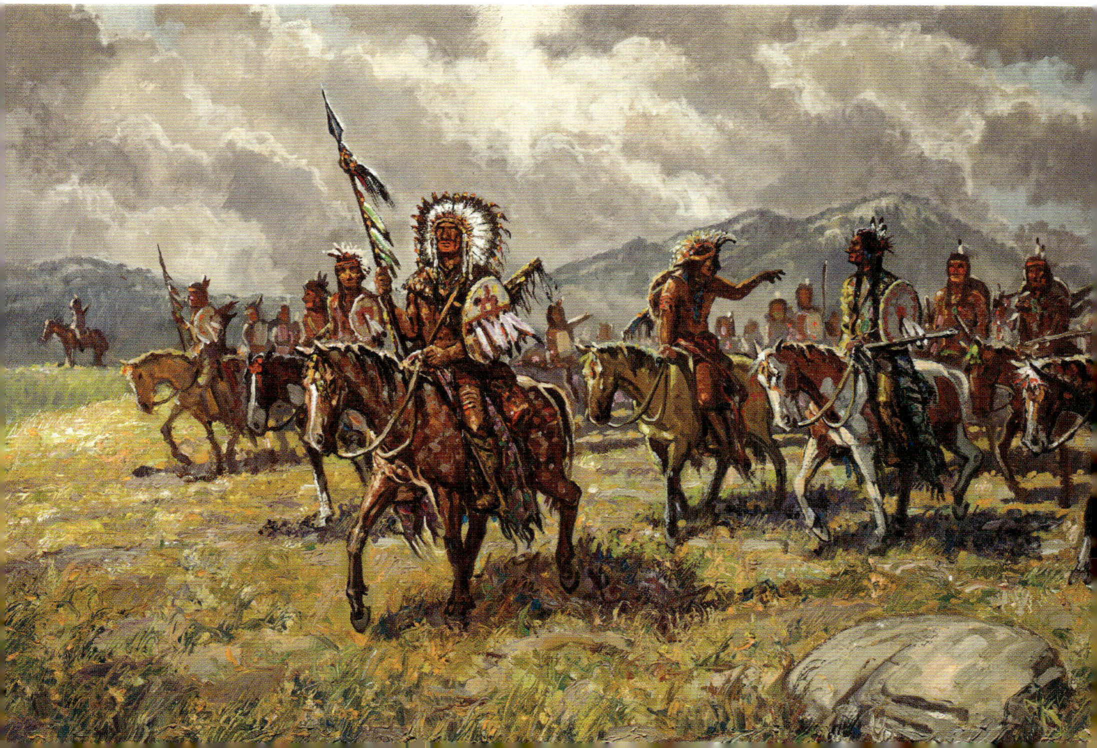

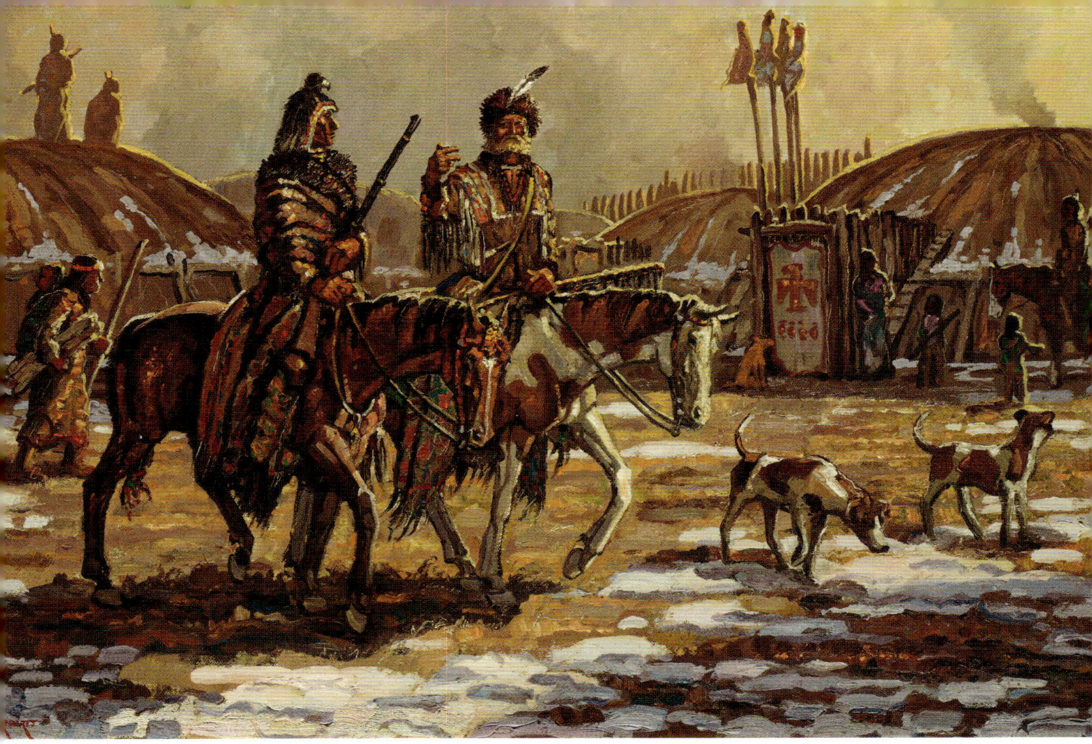

Lord Gore with Crow's Breast. Photo Credit: William J. O'Connor. Courtesy of American Museum of Western Art, the Anschutz Collection.

Lemon Saks, had "opened vistas into the richest subject matter that an artist could hope for. Lord Gore led me to the Gros Ventres and I am certain that I will remain on this subject for years to come." Through his study, he was introduced to the Indian way of life and the romance of the western frontier. Continuing in his letter to Saks, he said: "Years ago I took some pride in painting cowboys because I was depicting a way of life that was rapidly disappearing from the American scene, but today I have the higher satisfaction of reviving a flawless culture that has <u>totally</u> disappeared." White men, Jack lamented in a more personal letter to his son, destroyed this noble Indian culture and in so doing turned "the earth into a stinking cesspool beyond redemption," all in the name of progress. Learning about the Indian culture made him doubt that he could ever again respect white men enough to paint a picture of one. "At least for the forseeable [*sic*] future I will paint nothing but Indians."[45]

5

A LOST FATHER FOUND

By the mid-1960s, Jack's life had settled into an acceptable pattern. He was painting regularly, he had received local and national recognition and he was exploring new prospects and projects. But one more chapter was about to unfold that would bring him an expanded and positive outlook on life. He was about to meet his son.

Gary Miller wrote to his grandmother Myrtle early in August 1966 to let her know that he was interested in meeting with her and learning about the Roberts family. Though he had reached young adulthood, he knew little about his heritage. He also expressed a desire to meet his biological father, Jack Roberts. When asked why, Gary's answer, based on information he had pieced together as a child, was simple. Out of curiosity, he wanted to meet this "drunk," this "man who lived in a cave," this "failure as a human being."[46]

Now remarried and living in New Mexico, Myrtle Roberts Rose was more than willing to arrange a meeting between her son, Jack, and her grandson Gary. In fact, she insisted that both of them come to Albuquerque, New Mexico, in early September 1966, when the Roberts family was in attendance for her grandson Charles Hopkins's wedding. Most of the family would be there, including Jack's sisters Cosette Evelyn Roberts Hopkins, Charles's mother, and Mary Elizabeth Roberts Dey and her daughter, Mary Catherine. Jack already planned to attend, and Gary accepted the invitation as well.

Gary traveled to Albuquerque hoping that he would have a day or two with his grandmother before meeting his father. He wanted this time to learn more about Jack, but the timing was not right. Jack was there when Gary arrived at Myrtle's house. Without a "hello" or even a "how are you," Jack greeted his son with startling words: "Do you drink?" Surprised, Gary answered, "Yes." Then Jack asked, "Do you get sick?" "Yes," Gary responded. With a sigh of relief, Jack exclaimed, "Oh thank God, I didn't."[47] The brief exchange convinced Jack that he had not inflicted the disease of alcoholism upon his son. Having passed the critical test, the rest of the short visit proved to be a glorious occasion for Gary, who became acquainted with not only his father and grandmother but also other members of the Roberts family.

The visit could not have been better for both Jack and Gary. Although she had been opposed to the reunion, Phyllis Miller, Gary's mother and Jack's former wife, was delighted to learn that the meeting went so well, as she expressed in a letter to Myrtle:

> *You will never know how elated and pleased we are that Gary was so well received and had such a great time being with you and meeting all of you. As far as we are concerned, he is a mature young man and able to understand and manage his own life.*
>
> *Isn't he a "great guy"? He has been a joy to us all those years and grows more wonderful with each maturing year.*
>
> *Again, we are most pleased you have established this marvelous relationship and thank you again for showing him such a wonderful time. He was a most happy boy telling us all about it.[48]*

Jack was ecstatic when Gary arrived in Glenwood Springs in May 1967 to take a job at the Hot Springs Lodge and Pool. He was also delighted when he learned that Gary was engaged to Monica Anderson and that they planned to make their home in Monica's hometown of Glenwood Springs after their marriage. After he and Monica were settled, Gary wrote to his grandmother that he was excited to be close to his father. He added:

> *Jack sent me a beautiful ink sketch for my birthday. I now have a very nice collection of his work and I'm very proud of it.*
>
> *Grandmother, I think that Jack is the most interesting person I have EVER met…and I'm so proud to say he is my father. I think the world of him, and through the past couple of years I've grown to love him as a father. He is great and I'm sure you share my feelings.[49]*

As important as it was for Gary to reunite with his father, it was equally important for Jack, who always believed his son eventually would seek him out. But Jack was surprised to learn that Gary did so without seeing any of his paintings or knowing anything about his career. It was simply a case of a son's need to find his biological father that brought the two together. For Jack, it provided a family companionship that he desperately needed and could not make elsewhere. To have his son nearby was a gratifying experience for a man who had lived so many years without this type of relationship. The mutual dependence made the bond between them stronger.

For years, Jack remained apologetic to Gary about abandoning him and not being a father to him when he was growing up. Gary finally put the matter to rest by telling his father there was no reason to be apologetic or to have feelings of guilt:

> *Jack, you and I both know that my mother and step dad did a much better job of raising me than you could have done. It was a blessing. You didn't have the ability to do it. You made up for it since then. The first summer we spent together, you took care of me—jeep trips, target practice. I didn't lift a finger. We did everything I wanted to do. You waited on me hand and foot. You should not have any regrets. This was your life. This is how you led it. I don't have any regrets about it. Jack, I'm sorry, but I didn't care to have you raise me.*[50]

Jack never raised the matter again.

It was not easy for Jack to fit into this new family relationship. As an artist, he considered himself a "misfit" incapable of adjusting to a "normal" lifestyle. He still had frequent mood swings—though they were less prevalent than during his drinking days—when he was either gregarious and friendly or irascible and arrogant. In his better moods, he was funny and entertaining but sometimes very insensitive. He craved attention and loved drama. Frequently, he purposely made loud, provocative statements in bars and restaurants or other public places to draw attention to himself. At times, his outbursts were disdainful. This appeared to be the case when he made his last mortgage payment at the First National Bank in Glenwood Springs with a shout for everyone to hear: "I'll never pay another goddamn dime to you!" It was, in fact, a prideful rather than a contemptuous exclamation that expressed Jack's triumphant joy at overcoming a great financial burden. It took time for him to change, but change he did, at least in certain ways.

Becoming sober and finding his son were the two most important factors in Jack's personal transformation. Gary and Monica quickly enfolded him into their family structure. He adored his grandson, Wade, who symbolically became the young son he did not have with Gary. His new family also included Monica's sister, Angela (Angie), and her husband, Don Parkison; Angie and Don's daughters, Amanda and Jessica; and Monica and Angie's parents, Phil and Joan Anderson of Glenwood Springs. A conservative and traditional family, the Andersons were at first a little uncertain about Jack. With his reputation of being a flamboyant nonconformist, Angie admitted that she was not thrilled at the prospect of his becoming a part of the family circle. She was uncertain how he would fit in or how they would react. Nevertheless, the Andersons always invited him to their family holiday celebrations. Jack wanted what a family offered, but according to the Parkisons, he at first did not know how to go about obtaining it. At family gatherings, he commanded the center of attention while mainly talking about himself and what he was doing. Those around him were resigned to listening as he described his life as a lonely artist whose career was greatly underappreciated.

After years of observation, Jack finally figured it out. "We were his 'labrats,'" Angie explained. "He was trying to find a window into the world." Gradually, he became comfortable with people in normal conversations and took more interest in what others were doing. "He finally felt accepted and knew we didn't need to be entertained and he didn't need to be entertaining." On occasion, however, Angie added, "he got in an entertaining mood and regaled us with his knowledge and opinions of Teddy Roosevelt or on art, but those times were just as much for his pleasure as for ours."

The Anderson family found him to be quite intellectual and well versed on a wide range of subjects. They also found him to be a much more enjoyable and generous man than the one they had first met. In some respects, Monica and Angie reminded Jack of his sisters, Cosette and Mary, whom he worshiped. He admired their intelligence and the way they made the family structure work. With this transformation in Jack's personality and attitude, the family learned to love and accept him as "Grandpa Jack." Together they helped him obtain a life that was centered on more than himself. He needed someone to build up his confidence. They did that. Even though his mood swings moderated, he still had moments of doubt. As Don Parkison recounts: "One day he would be down on himself—that he had been a drunk, had thrown away much of his life, had almost lost Gary. The next day he would be proud of himself—that the future was bright and that he was a great artist." His new family played a major role in leveling out his temperament. Now his gusto for life was made much more enjoyable. Without this change, Angie believed he would have died much sooner.[51]

Gary, Monica and Wade were the perfect family for Jack. They provided companionship, support and encouragement. On one occasion, accompanied by Phil and Joan Anderson, they took him to his old camp in the Derby Ridge area to rekindle his interest in painting from his cowboy experience. Gary often accompanied his father on research trips to find documentation or to set the stage for the historical accounts that Jack depicted on his canvases. By becoming Jack's agent, Gary assumed some of the aspects of business, an area in which Jack was quite deficient. In this capacity, Gary negotiated with potential patrons to secure commissions, contacted buyers for paintings and organized shows to display Jack's paintings. Although Gary was unable to change Jack's routine, which he admitted was a good thing, he at least persuaded him to take the hours and hours of research that he had conducted into account when pricing his paintings. "He would have made a lot more money if he [hadn't done] so much research," Gary explained shortly after his father's death. "But he wanted his paintings to be historically accurate and stand the test of time."[52] Still, some of Jack's paintings sold for $8,000 or more by the late part of his career.

Jack's new family became increasingly important to him as his old one slipped away. He had maintained contact with his mother and sisters and their families after his move to Colorado, and they visited him several times at his studio at Hanging Lake. He also spent an extended time with his mother in Albuquerque during the winter months of the mid-1950s. He made the trip from Hanging Lake to Albuquerque in his 1947 Willys Jeep, packed with his easel and painting supplies. He did handyman jobs around the house when he was not painting. His niece, Mary Catherine, the daughter of his sister Mary, watched him paint for hours in the front bedroom. Once she asked him if he would teach her how to paint. Laughing, he teased, "I'd rather teach you how to smoke a marijuana cigarette than how to paint!"[53]

Jack's trips to New Mexico were also pilgrimages to places that exhibited Ben Turner's paintings. His trip to his nephew's wedding in September 1966, at which time he met Gary, was particularly poignant, as it came only a few months after Ben's death. A visit to La Placita, the oldest structure in Old Town Albuquerque, was still mandatory. It was there that Ben had a studio from 1946 to 1951, and it was there—in the La Placita Restaurant, where several Turner paintings hung on the walls—that Jack enjoyed a reunification dinner with his son and members of his Roberts family. There could not have been a more appropriate venue to mark the passing of an old friendship to the beginning of a new one. It was a propitious moment in the lives of both father and son.

Myrtle's death in 1973 followed by that of his sister Cosette in 1981 drew Jack closer to Mary, his eldest sister. But the years were not kind to Mary, as dementia gradually captured her mind. Jack visited her for the last time in 1987, but the occasion was too much for him. He could not bear to see his sister in the condition she was in. In 1992, Jack and Gary traveled to Albuquerque to help scatter Mary's ashes. That was the last time she saw Jack, Mary Catherine noted. Of his Oklahoma relatives, only "shirttail" cousin Bartlett, who had moved to Aspen, Colorado, remained in regular contact with Jack. They became close companions during his Redstone years.

THE REMBRANDT OF REDSTONE

Jack's Hanging Lake days came to an end with the construction of Interstate 70 through Glenwood Canyon. The path of the highway and access roads required the removal of the buildings, including Jack's studio, at the Hanging Lake Resort. Familiar with the Redstone area, he purchased a building lot in 1968 from his friend and fellow artist Tony Antonides on the site of John Cleveland Osgood's original Crystal Farm about two miles south of the village. Inspired by the natural beauty of the area, he eagerly drew up plans for the cabin/studio that would become his final workplace and residence.

The picturesque village of Redstone was a thriving community of antique and gift shops, art galleries and historic cottages and buildings when Jack arrived as a new resident artist in November 1969. Founded during the early years of the twentieth century by the millionaire John C. Osgood as his model industrial village, the small mountain community was a popular tourist spot. Jack's late friend Ben Turner had introduced him to the village, which years earlier had been the residence of the renowned artist Frank Mechau. Jack fit nicely into this community that, according to an old-time resident, contained few "ordinary" people. By and large, they were creative, innovative individuals who had figured out how to make a living in a place they wanted to live. With Jack's personality and lifestyle, it was not surprising that he was enthusiastically welcomed into this community of an enterprising and somewhat iconoclastic cast of characters.

When he was not totally engrossed in his painting, Jack frequently visited the shops on Redstone Boulevard, the main and only paved street in the village. Although he liked looking at the merchandise and artwork on display, he was much more interested in catching up with local gossip and romancing some of the female shopkeepers. On occasion, he was good at timing his visits. Sylvia Morrison, known for her culinary skills, knew that he expected an invitation for dinner when he showed up at her shop late in the afternoon just before closing. She and her husband, Bob, were happy to extend that invitation because they enjoyed his company. For many years, they remained close friends with Jack, even though they were on opposite sides on some major issues concerning Redstone and the Crystal River Valley.[54]

Jack's favorite stop in Redstone was the General Store, where he bought cigars and talked for hours with his good friend Jill Briggs, the owner. Jack, the creative storyteller, delighted in having a co-conspirator. Sometimes they played the "Apple sisters prank" if there were "turkeys" (tourists) in the store. As Jack entered the store, Jill would ask, "Hey Goober! How's everything at the Feather Factory?" Beaming, Jack would mention that he had just come from the factory in his tumblebug and that he had recently talked to boss Kil Frickens and the Apple sisters. Once in a while, a tourist would bite: "Where's this factory? Can I visit it?" Jack obligingly told them it wasn't far and gave them whatever directions popped into his mind that day. By the time they left, Jill recounted, "Jack was dying laughing and couldn't stand it."[55] Such occasions made his day.

Jack often needed these midmorning trips for motivation. Without them, he confessed, he could not shake off a debilitating sense of loneliness. He needed people to talk to and listen to his stories, perhaps even to express interest in what he was doing. Although he sometimes described himself or was described by others as a recluse, he was seldom that. An hour or two of conversation with Jill or Joyce Illian or whoever else was in Jill's store at any given time rejuvenated him and put him in the mood to paint or pursue his other interests in the afternoon, leaving time later for long walks.

His studio was his shelter. As a reformed alcoholic, he realized the need to have a controlled environment to resist the temptation to drink. "This is my world," he said of his residence. "I control it, and when I step out into the world, I'm at risk. So I come back here to my little briar patch."[56] And there in the evening, he painted or, more likely, read from sources that prepared him to tell the story on canvas of Indians, fur traders, trading posts or bear hunts—whatever sparked his interest.

Jack dubbed himself the "Rembrandt of Redstone." When he telephoned his fellow artist and friend Lanny Grant in Silt, Colorado, the routine was always the same. Jack: "Is this the Picasso of Silt?" Lanny: "Yup. Is this the

Rembrandt of Redstone?" Lanny often dropped by Jack's studio, where they enjoyed sharing ideas about art or exploring the local area. Over the years, they became close friends. Lanny considered Jack a mentor whose brutally honest criticism of his work helped to make him an accomplished artist. He admired him for his ability, knowledge and sincerity. "I was lucky to have known him," he said. "We all need a hero, someone to set a standard we can look up to. It is a legacy of one artist to another." He ranked Jack among the unique, talented and incredible artists who set a very high standard for others to follow.[57]

Among Jack's friends in Redstone were his neighbors, Joan and Steve Benson, whom he met in a most unorthodox way. Shortly after the Bensons moved into their Crystal Farm home near his studio, an excited Jack confronted Joan in the drive between their houses. Even before introducing himself, he launched into an explanation of what he was painting. As Joan recalls, it had something to do with Indians and wolves. He became so excited that he jumped up and down and waved his arms in front of her in what appeared to be an angry and intimidating way. Seeing this, Steve rushed out of his shop to protect his wife but quickly realized that Jack was only being himself: a man passionate about what he was doing and animate in explaining it.

Eventually, the Bensons accepted Jack as a virtual family member. He relied on them for many things. Frequently, he used the entire family, including son Brad, Kona the dog and Flaco the burro, as models for his paintings. Steve once posed in red underwear darning socks at a table. When completed, the painting portrayed a weathered cowboy darning socks in his red underwear in a rustic cabin setting. Steve also was the model for the courier delivering a mail pouch in the Theodore Roosevelt series, and Joan was the lady wearing a sunbonnet in a field of flowers. For a scene Jack was painting depicting the laying of rails for a railroad, Brad posed with his shirt off swinging a sledgehammer like he was driving spikes. He had to swing the hammer many times before Jack captured the right motion or position with his Polaroid. Kona, Brad's husky, played the role of a wolf quite convincingly, and Flaco, of whom Jack was very fond, appeared in at least one painting.[58]

Jack's obsession with capturing the right pose for the characters in his paintings was prompted by his dedication to accuracy. Sketching was equally important. Harvey Dunn had taught him the importance of sketching to develop an idea and establish the pictorial concept of a scene, and Jack applied that lesson with diligence. He made thousands of sketches for his projected paintings over the years, many of them ending on his studio floor or in his fireplace because they did not capture the idea he had in mind or the details he believed to be essential. Sometimes the details could be as small as the position of hands or the posture of bodies to reflect a particular action. He never completed a picture until he had worked out the total concept.

For the most part, Jack did his best to be a good neighbor. On one occasion, however, he stubbornly refused the Bensons' request to repaint his deck railings, which he had painted a bright orange. The railings were distasteful, Steve told Jack, and were a distraction to the whole neighborhood. Orange was his favorite color, Jack responded defiantly. To no avail, Steve and Joan tried everything they could think of to get Jack to redo the railings, including hanging a large banner on his house that they had obtained from the co-op in Carbondale and altered from "FALL IS THE TIME FOR PLANTING" to "FALL IS THE TIME FOR PAINTING." Finally, after everything else had failed, they confronted Jack with a letter from the "committee" ordering him to paint his railings a different color. There was no "committee" and no "order," but Jack fell for the trick. He went ballistic, shouting and demanding, "What committee? Who were the members?" Receiving no answers, he finally calmed down and started painting his railings brown the next day.[59]

Jack became more animated than ever when politics or the environment became the topic of conversation. He had a disdain for most politicians and detested Presidents Richard Nixon and Ronald Reagan. More than likely, he turned against Nixon because of the Watergate scandal. What really griped him the most, he noted in a letter to Lemon Saks, was that he had actually voted for him! He flew into a rage at the mere mention of Reagan's name. His cousin Bartlett warned people not to mention Reagan when talking with Jack. When they did, she noted, his tirade was quite a scene.[60]

Jerry Falwell was another victim of Jack's derision. If not the man, he hated what Falwell stood for. Countless times, he made his views about him clear to his son, Gary. He would always start the discussion the same way, Gary noted. As he leaned forward and put his finger in Gary's face, he would shout, "Have I told you?" After a pause he would ask again, "Have I told you?" Having experienced this many times, Gary knew what was coming next. It was either Jack's vow to dynamite the first bulldozer that came to the Crystal River Valley to build a dam or an expression of his opinion of Falwell. "Oh, here it comes again," Gary would mutter under his breath. If it was Falwell, Jack pointed to the ground and exclaimed in a loud and agitated manner, "I want to go to the exact, the exact opposite place where Jerry Falwell is going. Are you clear on that?" With fire in his eyes, Jack again pointed downward. "That's where he's going. He's a bad person and he's going to Hell."[61]

When Jack admired someone, however, he was noticeably more tolerant. One politician he liked and with whom he formed a close friendship was Scott McInnis. Scott grew up in Glenwood Springs and became acquainted with Jack through his father and later through Gary, when he worked as a lifeguard at the Hot Springs Pool. Although friends who spent countless hours exchanging stories, the two political opposites—Scott the conservative Republican and Jack the liberal Democrat and radical environmentalist—seldom talked politics. Yet there was enough in common between them that they got along very well. Jack was very patriotic and loved Washington, D.C., and the election of McInnis to the U.S. House of Representatives in 1992 provided him additional opportunities as a guest of the congressman to visit the city, where he spent many hours at the National Gallery of Art and other museums. The museums were awe inspiring, he exclaimed to his cousin Bartlett: "It is refreshing to my spirit to go to the National Gallery and stand in the presence of Greatness and feel the message from great artists that have taken their genius to the very highest level."[62]

Another chance to visit the museums and galleries in the nation's capital occurred when McInnis invited Jack to attend President Bill Clinton's State of the Union Address in 1995. Jack's excitement to be able to witness a political event at the center of power, as well as visit centers of national culture, is revealed in his letter to Gary on January 30, 1995:

> *I really enjoyed the State of the Union Address. It was an American ceremony I will <u>never</u> forget.*
>
> *My seat was in Gallery 4, which was to the President's right. Newt Gingrich's wife was on one side of me and* [Colorado congressman] *David Skaggs' secretary was on the other side. Mrs. Gingrich never applauded unless her husband did…*
>
> *It was altogether a fascinating experience. Of course I enjoyed the National Art Gallery and the American History Museum, along with the Museum of Art.*

"It wasn't easy being on my good behavior," he remarked when asked about sitting next to Mrs. Gingrich, the Republican Speaker's wife.[63]

As much as he enjoyed occasional travel, Jack's true spirit of adventure thrived closer to home. He loved the outdoors and seldom missed an opportunity to take people on jeep rides in the rugged high country near

Redstone. Everyone recognized his open-topped Willys Jeep. Covered with orange and yellow splotches and sprouting deer antlers from the grill, it was hard to overlook. With poor steering and brakes that worked only when pumped several times, it was about as dangerous as one could imagine. But Jack dared to go anywhere with it, even on roads that were closed and posted. Lanny Grant recalls one trip with Jack on a road that was abundantly decorated with No Trespassing signs and a cable across it that was too high to block their passage. As they wound their way up the steep grade of the narrow road toward the Little Darling Mine, Lanny spotted two men brandishing rifles peering down at them. "Aw, don't worry!" Jack shouted. "I've been up here before. Those guys up there won't shoot us. They know who we are. Everyone knows this jeep." Fearing that he would either be shot or thrown overboard into the abyss below, Lanny hung on as Jack swung around the sharp hairpin turns at breakneck speed until they reached the mine. Sure enough, Jack knew the two guys, one of whom was Kirk Blue, an employee of the Little Darling Mining Company. They and Jack had a good laugh at Lanny's expense. It was not the first time Jack had pulled this stunt on unsuspecting passengers.[64]

According to Lanny, Jack drove his jeep like he did everything in life—boisterously and vigorously. On a trip over Huntsman Ridge west of Redstone, Jack was at his wildest. The road was deeply rutted and

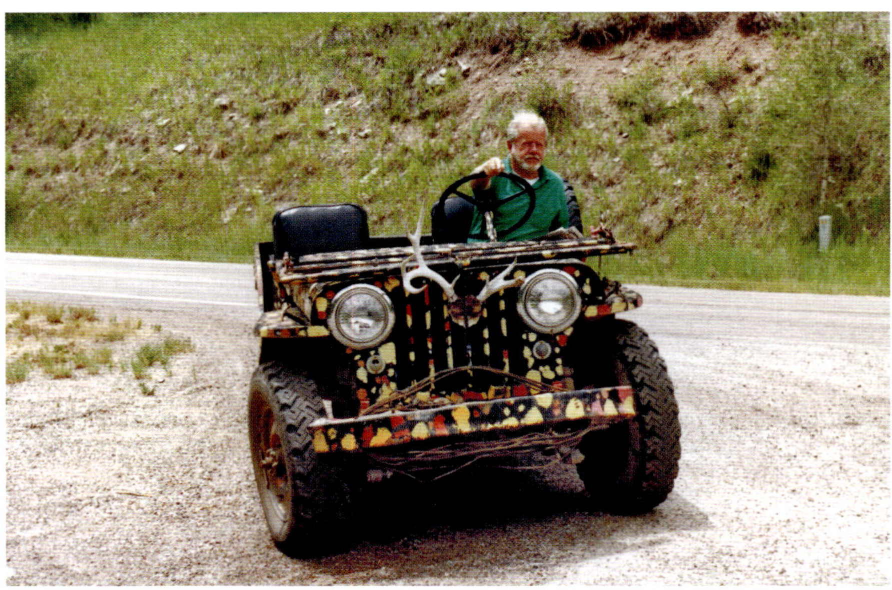

Jack Roberts in his 1947 Willys Jeep. *Courtesy of Gary Miller.*

extremely rocky. As the jeep bounced over the ruts and rocks and veered from side to side, with Lanny clinging to his seat, Jack, puffing on a cigar, yelled, "Yahoo!" "Yahoo, yahoo!" he bellowed again and again as the brakeless jeep picked up speed going down the slope. It was as if he were riding a wild bronco at a rodeo, competing for the top prize.[65]

Fortunately, not all trips were so harrowing. Jack loved Marble, particularly the defunct marble quarry, and the nearby attractions of Crystal and Lead King Basin. When in Lead King Basin, he usually visited his friend "Lead King" Paul Harris, a truly modern mountain man, whom he used as a model for several of his paintings. With Jack serving both as tour guide and local historian, these trips were great fun according to those who took them. He knew the area well, and he delighted in relating the history of Marble, Crystal, Schofield and other long-forgotten settlements or cabin ruins. He seldom sketched on these excursions. Instead, he formed a mental image of what he believed the scene had looked like one hundred or more years ago. Being outdoors in the mountains he loved and entertaining his guests with stories about the history of the area were pleasurable experiences.

But there were other pleasures as well. Looking at the orange- and yellow-spotted jeep one day, Lanny suggested to Jack that he name it "Speckles." "No," Jack said laughing. "It's the 'Whores' Dream.' That's the name of it. It's my gal catcher."[66] Indeed, Jack had many "gal" friends. From time to time, one of them would appear, decked out in a fancy dress and hat and ready to go on a picnic. "We're going up to Lead King Basin," Jack would announce. "We'll be back later. If we don't, come look for us." Off they would go in the "Whores' Dream" with a blanket and a lunch basket packed with sandwiches.[67] It was obvious Jack expected more than just having lunch. According to local gossip and his own reports, his lunches were very successful.

On the day the "Whores' Dream" died in 1996, Jack asked Steve Benson to bury it. Recounting the story, Steve described Jack as a wild man running over to his shop, yelling and demanding, "Stevie, get your backhoe! I want you to dig a hole beside the highway near the mail boxes and bury that jeep." Surprised, Steve asked, "Why do you want to do that, Jack?" "It died and it's never going to run again," Jack bellowed. "I'm so tired of it I just want you to bury it out by the mail boxes." "I can't and won't do that," Steve replied, adding that Jack's designated grave site was in the highway right of way. "I'll get it running for you." But Jack doubted that claim. "You'll never do that," he adamantly insisted. "Bury it! I don't ever want to see it again."[68]

Steve moved the lifeless jeep to the front of his shop. It took him a couple of weeks to get to it, but he got it running again, like a sewing machine as

Jack used to say. Meanwhile, Jack purchased another jeep and was more determined than ever to have nothing to do with his old "Whores' Dream." "Jack, I got your jeep running," Steve duly announced, but Jack refused to listen. "That piece of junk should have been buried," he countered. "If you're not going to bury it, why don't you keep it?" Steve insisted he did not want it, but Jack would have it no other way. "Get it off my property. I'll never drive it again."

Steve finally relented. "I'll need a title," he told Jack. "Do you have a title?" "Title? What's a title?" Jack asked. Astonished, Steve answered, "You know what that is. You need that to register a vehicle and get license plates for it." "Oh, I don't need that," Jack declared. "I just pick up plates and put them on. If one falls off, I just replace it with another." After thinking about it further, he exclaimed, "Wait a second" and pulled out his wallet and rifled through it. He finally found a slip of paper among the scores he searched and asked, "Here, what's this?" He handed Steve a registration receipt that had been in his wallet since the 1953 purchase date. "That'll do," Steve responded. Through a lost title search, the jeep was made legal again. Steve still has the jeep, he mentioned with a broad grin on his face, and it still runs like a sewing machine.

CARPETBAGGERS AND BULLDOZERS

Jack loved the outdoor environment and was passionate about preserving it. He proclaimed himself a radical environmentalist. Moving to the Redstone area at the time he did provided an opportunity to become involved in two major issues that threatened the Crystal River Valley, the valley he now called home. With characteristic vigor and determination, he attacked the planned development of a large ski resort in the upper valley near Marble, Colorado, and the project to dam the river at Placita between Marble and Redstone. To Jack, the first represented the evils of corporate America and the second the stupidity of the bureaucratic political world. Both projects, he rigidly believed, proved how far some individuals would go in destroying the sacred environment in pursuit of greed.

Jack's hostile view of corporate America included an animosity toward ski corporations. He did not have far to look to find one. Just a few miles up valley from his studio, Marble Ski Area Inc. (MSA) built a chair lift in 1971 and opened new ski slopes on the south-facing side of Mount Daly just north of the town of Marble. Although the first year's operation was limited, mainly to attract investors, the corporation's future plans alarmed many of the valley's residents. The plans included opening more slopes, adding twelve ski lifts and two gondolas and developing a ski resort village. The proposed Marble Village would consist of condominiums, a lodge/hotel, retail shops, taverns, restaurants, nightclubs, a theater and a convention center. There also would be tennis courts and a golf course.

Most alarming of all for those who opposed the development was the corporation's proposed Planned Unit Development (PUD) plat, which envisaged subdividing nearly 2,000 of the corporation's 2,700 acres in the narrow valley to accommodate 8,833 dwelling units for an estimated population of twenty-six thousand residents at its peak. If approved, critics claimed, the PUD would create the largest urban area in the Roaring Fork River watershed. It would be a city the size of Grand Junction, Colorado.

In 1972, residents from Marble and Redstone formed the Crystal Valley Environmental Protection Association (CVEPA) to fight the development of the ski resort. Although not a charter member, Jack joined CVEPA soon after its inception. He immersed himself in the details of the environmental issues of the valley and became ardently involved in the controversies that ensued. In presenting his arguments, he did what he did best: he created an editorial cartoon series entitled the *Carpetbaggers of Marble*. Thirteen cartoons illustrating his interpretation of CVEPA's campaign against the MSA were published in the *Glenwood Springs Sage-Reminder* between April 18 and July 18, 1973. They drew both praise and condemnation.

With his belief that money in the hands of corporate evil was the root of the problem, Jack drew the first illustration to reflect CVEPA's anger in failing to prevent the United States Forest Service from approving a preliminary special use permit for 624 acres of public land to MSA for ski development. One month later, Jack also vented his feelings on the matter in a letter to Thomas Evans, White River National Forest supervisor:

> *The developers of the Marble Ski Area are carpetbaggers of the very lowest stamp. A Forest Service permit would be an excellent selling point for their condominiums and home sites and if you think they have any other interest in this country you are simply out of your mind. How many mudslides does it take to wake you up? For heinous offenses, there is no case of bloody rape in criminal history that can match the mudslide of May 14 [1973] on Mount Daly. That mudslide started on a road the Marble Ski Area cut into the mountain but of course it wasn't their fault. Shit.*
>
> *It will forever be a mystery to me how you can seriously consider allowing such an unscrupulous pack of opportunists to plunder 624 acres of our National Forest Land. Is there nothing sacred on this earth anymore? Why don't you ask them how much of their own money is invested in their*

THE CARPETBAGGERS OF MARBLE
by Jack Roberts

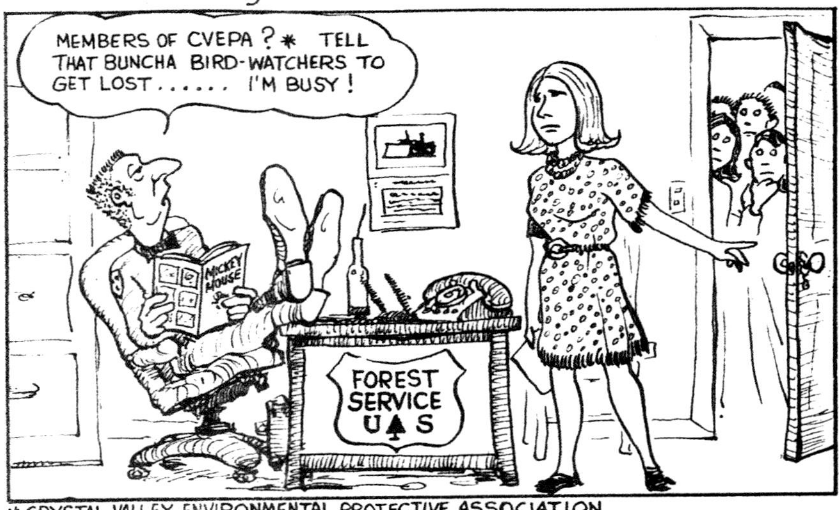

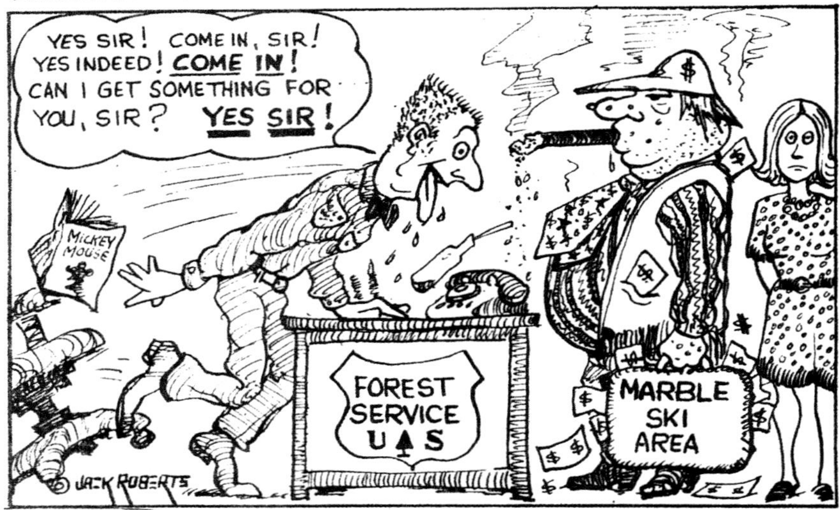

"The Carpetbaggers of Marble." *Courtesy of Gary Miller.*

venture? *Every penny comes from gullible investors that actually believe those glowing reports of Forest Service cooperation.*

The Marble Ski Area is an obscene act. It is like phlegm on beautiful velvet, snot on a Victorian doorknob.[69]

Opinion was divided among Crystal Valley residents on the MSA development. CVEPA's opposition was countered by FOR Inc.'s support. The latter organization was formed largely by an assortment of realtors, builders, landowners and individuals associated with MSA. At their organizational meeting in March 1973, members blasted CVEPA for its opposition to the development. With Pitkin County officials joining the opposition, FOR also vowed to fight the commissioners' antidevelopment policies.

Jack, who portrayed FOR as a mangy mutt in his cartoons, did not escape its scorn, especially that of the vice-president of the organization. Blue Stroud of Marble expressed outrage over his cartoon to the editors of the *Sage-Reminder*:

> *Regarding the Jack Roberts cartoon, Carpet Baggers of Marble, I'm not surprised by Jack's Bigotry. What shocks me is that you had the incredibly bad taste to publish such unfounded, salacious garbage. You really hit a journalistic low!*
>
> *Jack should stick to his cowboys and Indians, where he can at least be respected for being knowledgeable about his subject matter.*[70]

Undeterred, Jack illustrated the next chapter in the saga, which unfolded in a Gunnison County courtroom. There, despite the vigorous opposition of the CVEPA representatives and Pitkin County officials, the Gunnison County commissioners approved MSA's PUD. The approval hearing was, according to Jack's interpretation, an orchestrated affair with MSA president John Zakovich (Zak) leading the commissioners' chorus of Charles Ruland, Kenneth Watters and George Means, with FOR howling approval in the background.

MSA vice-president Don Weixelman promised that the corporation would take every environmental issue into account and stressed that the corporation would "make this the most beautiful valley on the North American continent." If that were not enough, President Zakovich boasted, "We will develop this valley as well as God would have, if He'd had the money."[71] Ah, yes. Jack imagined Zak swooping down with FOR in his arms to give life to the valley.

Although unsuccessful in halting the MSA development, CVEPA's protests caused enough delay in the proceedings to allow other groups to become involved, such as the Environmental Task Force and the Colorado Land Use Commission. Mother Nature also added to the muddy mix. Mudslides in May 1973 dealt devastating blows to the ski development. The

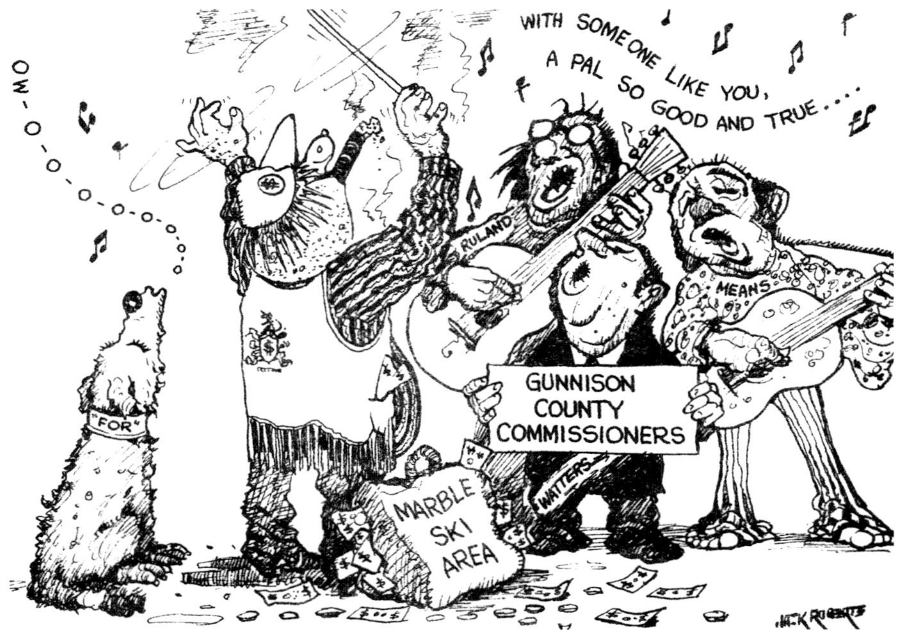

"The Gunnison County Commissioners." *Courtesy of Gary Miller.*

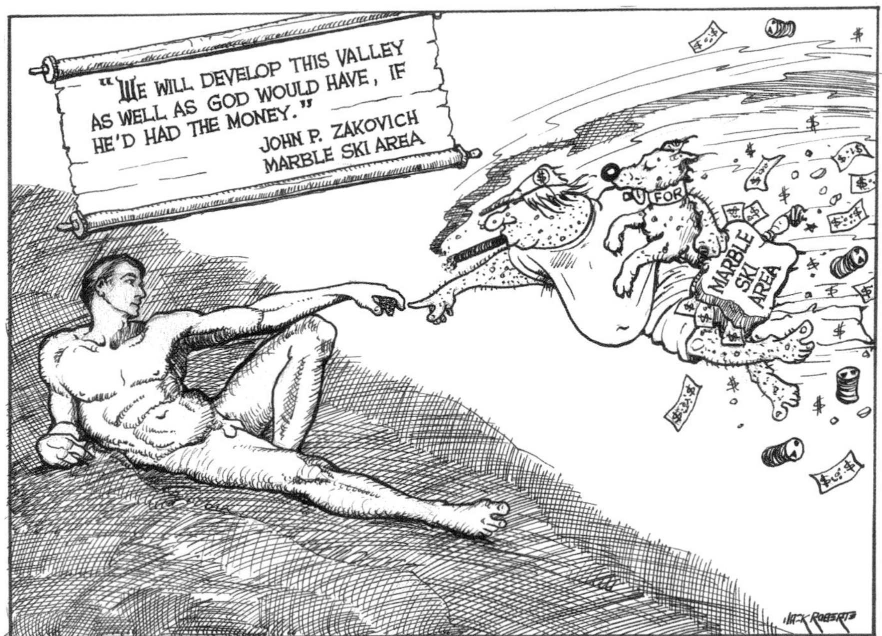

"We Will Develop This Valley." *Courtesy of Gary Miller.*

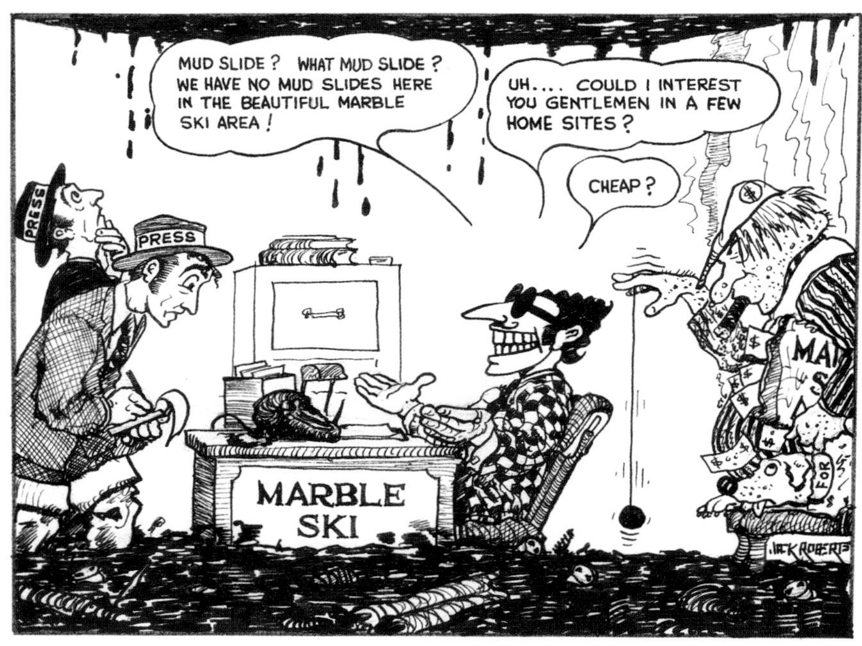

"Mud Slide? What Mud Slide?" *Courtesy of Gary Miller.*

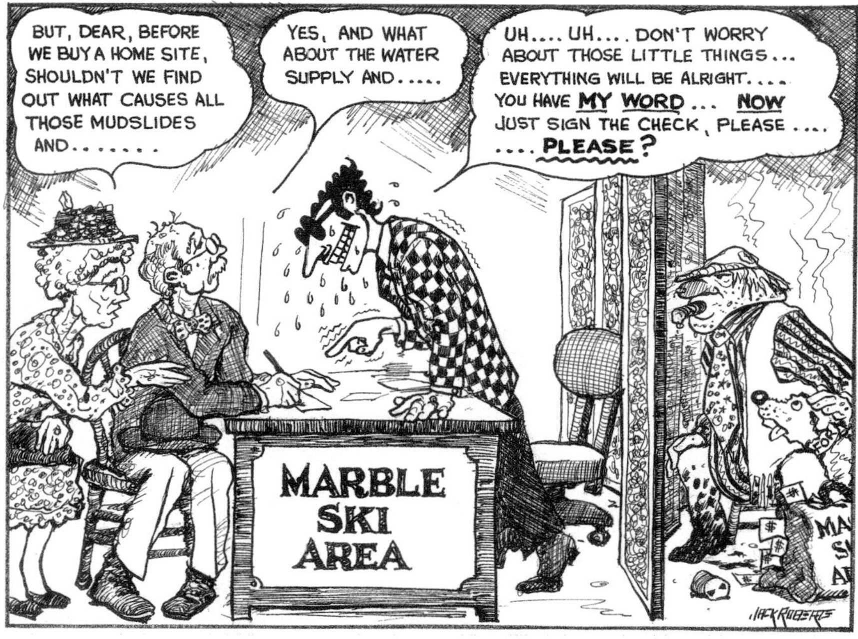

"Please Just Sign the Check." *Courtesy of Gary Miller.*

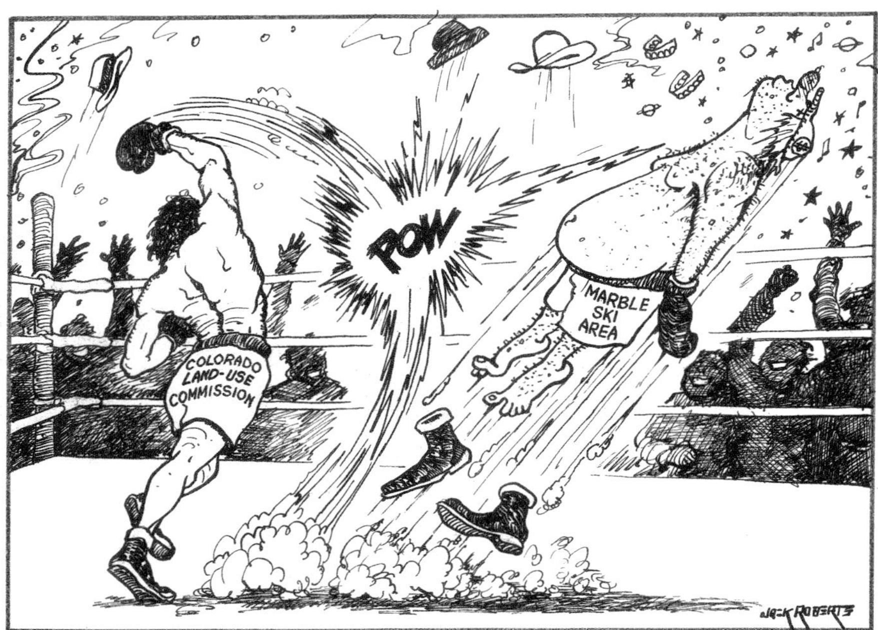

"The Knockout Blow." *Courtesy of Gary Miller.*

slides brought considerable press attention and confirmed state geologist John Rold's opinion that the ski corporation planned to build on land that was too hazardous. Nonetheless, President Zakovich and Vice-President Weixelman vowed to carry on, particularly in their effort to sell lots to maximize their profits and keep MSA from total financial disaster. Jack captured both their deceit and desperation in two of his cartoons.

Once again, Zak and Don pinned their hopes on obtaining a permanent special use permit from the National Forest Service that would allow them to expand the ski development. But the Colorado Land Use Commission delivered the knockout blow to their plans.

Faced with mounting adversity and legal problems, Zak and Don bailed out of their official positions in the corporation. With a carpetbag filled with money from land sales in hand, Zak led Don and FOR through the mud and environmentally degrading debris covering their dream development. Passing by the ski lift, Zak, Don and FOR reflected on what had gone wrong. Was it the Ute Indian curse on the Crystal River Valley?

Despite Jack's and CVEPA's dogged opposition, it was the corporation's own officials who drove the final stake into the heart of their enterprise.

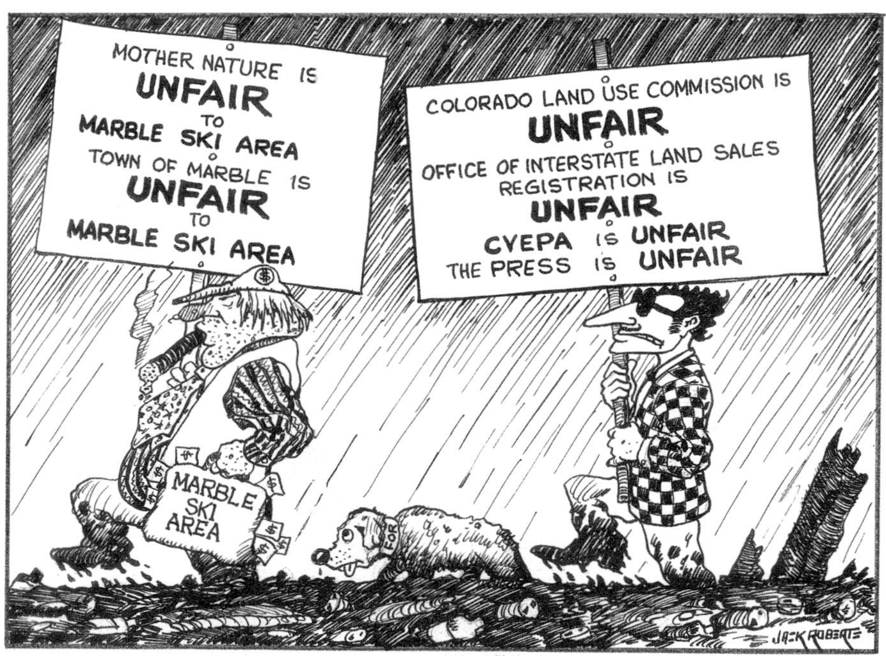

"Unfair." *Courtesy of Gary Miller.*

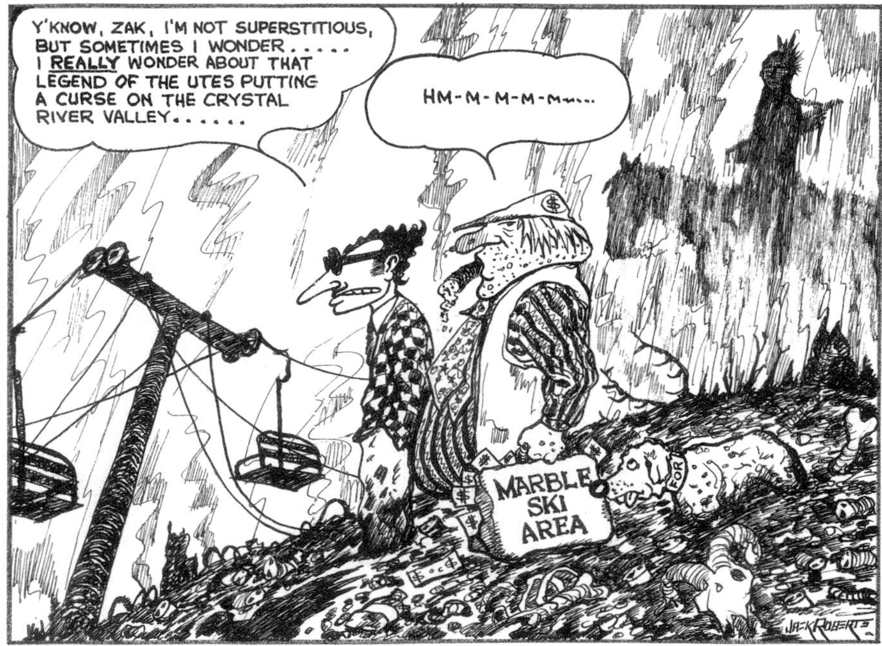

"The Ute Curse." *Courtesy of Gary Miller.*

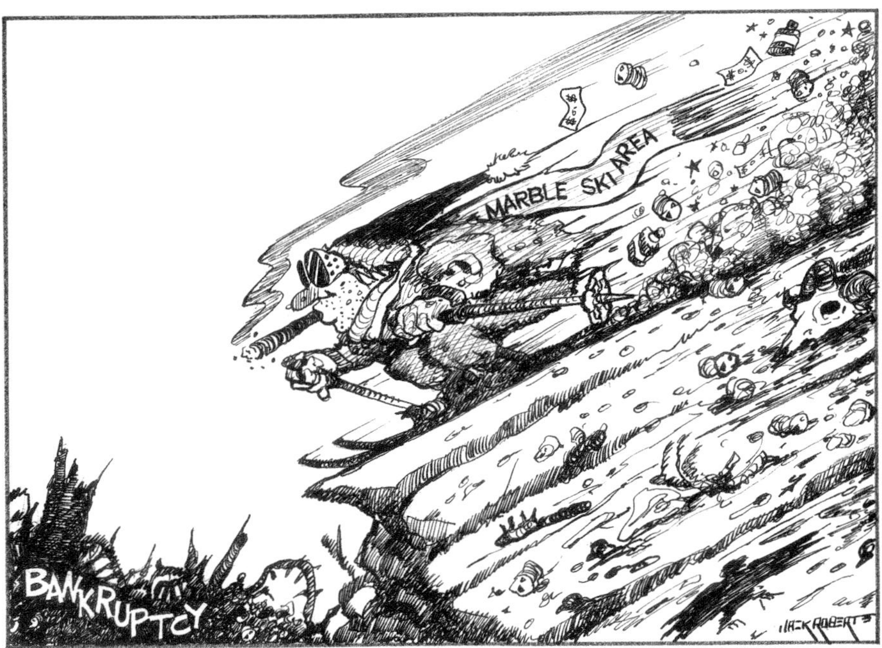

"Bankruptcy." *Courtesy of Gary Miller.*

Charges of illegal land sales and fraudulent representation of underlying mortgages by the corporation prompted the U.S. Department of Housing and Urban Development to launch an investigation into the corporation's activities. To head off the probe, the officials of MSA surrendered their license to sell property to the Colorado Real Estate Commission. Unable to sell lots, MSA skied off the cliff into bankruptcy.

With the end of the MSA controversy, Jack turned his attention to the other pending environmental issue of the valley: the Placita Dam affair.

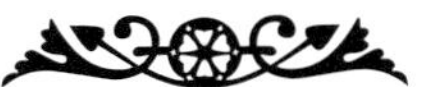

Jack drove up Highway 133 to a turnoff overlooking Placita a few miles south of Redstone in late January 1976. From this high vantage point, he saw the beautiful natural mountain park and the Crystal River below. With his binoculars, he saw the narrow part of the valley where the U.S. Bureau of Reclamation (BuRec) was poised to build a dam across the river. Looking around, he saw all the places that would be inundated by the huge reservoir the dam would create. His thoughts turned to what Placita, "Little Place" in Spanish, meant to him. Over the last two centuries, he recalled from his vast historical knowledge of the area, Placita "had nurtured and succored all men"—from Tabagauche Utes to trappers, prospectors, railroaders, miners and cowboys—who passed that way. As he expressed it in an impassioned article in the *Carbondale Valley Journal*: "Serenely beautiful at all times of the year, a visit to the 'Little Place' always makes you a better person. If the Bureau of Reclamation builds a dam here, we will have lost something as a people. There will be a little less depth to our souls."[72]

As he turned to leave, he took one more glance at the valley below. An imaginary scene of invading bulldozers churning up the ground flashed before his eyes. It was so vivid that he vowed to dynamite any bulldozer that appeared on the site. Later, when repeating his intention to startled listeners, he proclaimed, "I can paint just as well in prison as I can at home in my studio."[73]

No one doubted Jack's sincerity in vowing to do everything he could to stop the damming and diversion of water from the Crystal River that was included in a massive reclamation scheme known as the West Divide Project. Although he wrote letters to local newspapers protesting the BuRec proposal, his main line of attack was his *Jolly Rolly and Crafty Kenny* series of editorial cartoons published in the *Valley Journal*. As with his *Carpetbaggers of Marble* series, he wanted to show how ridiculous and catastrophic to the valley he believed the project was. In this case, his villains were Roland (Rollie) Fischer, secretary-engineer of the Colorado River Water Conservation District (CRWCD), and Kenneth Balcomb, counsel for both the CRWCD and the West Divide Water Conservancy District (WDWCD), the general administrative, fiscal and taxing authority for the West Divide Project. Balcomb, a brilliant water attorney, ran both the CRWCD and the WDWCD. He was the driving force behind the West Divide Project. Fischer was Balcomb's second at the River District—or, as one person put it, "Balcomb drove the fire engine and Fischer was the Dalmatian." In late December 1975, Jack introduced the two in his *Jolly Rolly and Crafty Kenny* series as "a comedic cabal bound and determined to stick the Placita Dam down the throats of a resisting Crystal Valley community."[74]

The lack of federal money for the West Divide Project and strong opposition by residents of the Crystal River Valley caused the WDWCD and the BuRec to reconsider the plan. The board appointed the West Divide Citizens Advisory Panel to study the feasibility of the original proposal or consider alternatives drafted by the BuRec. Carefully selected from West

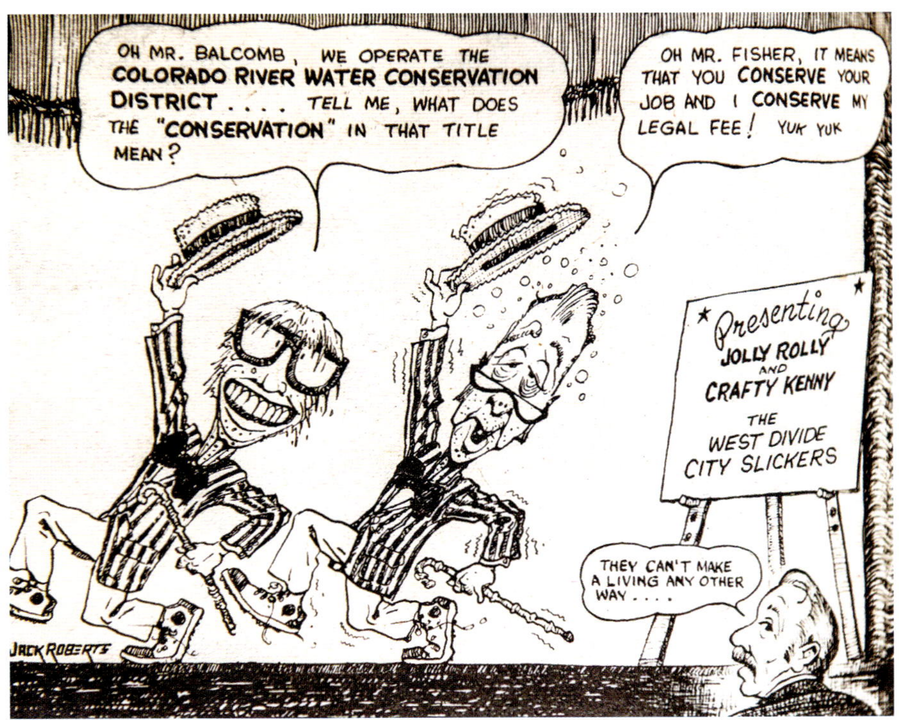

"The West Divide City Slickers." *Courtesy of Peggy DeVilbiss.*

Divide and Crystal River Valley residents, ranchers and landowners with vested interest in the project dominated the panel. As Jack noted in his cartoon of December 31, 1975, "Crafty Kenny" Balcomb directed the members of the panel to ensure a favorable outcome.

One argument both "Jolly Rolly" and "Crafty Kenny" used to defend the West Divide Project was the need to increase agricultural production in the area from East Divide Creek to Battlement Mesa south of the towns of Silt, Rifle and Parachute by irrigating the land with water diverted from the Crystal River. They also stressed that the Placita dam was essential to keep Western Slope water from being diverted to the Denver area. Jack thought these arguments were laughable.

The majority of the Citizens Advisory Panel recommended essentially what was proposed in the original plan with a dam at Placita and water diversion to the West Divide area from the reservoir. The dam would be 301 feet high. Could it be higher? "Jolly Rolly" and "Crafty Kenny" pondered. Nevermind, send in the bulldozers.

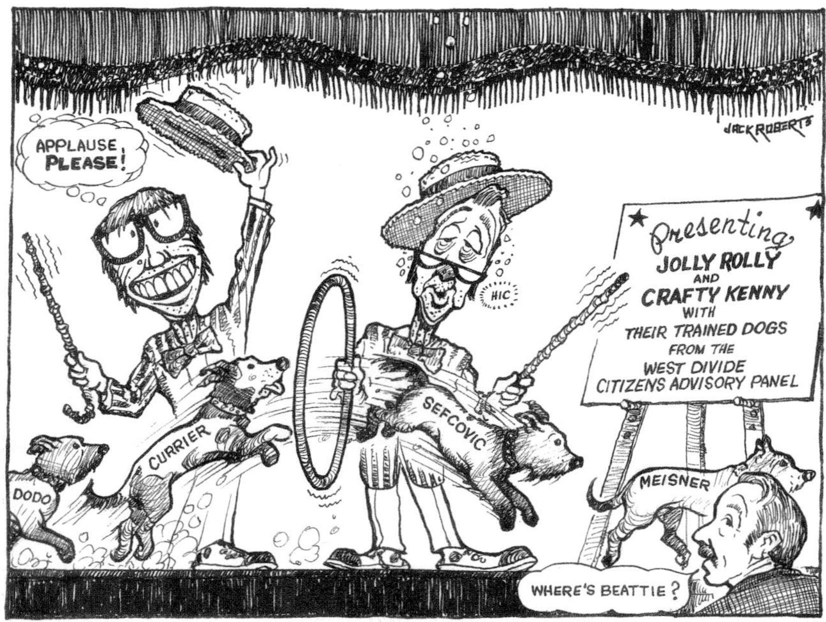

"The Trained Dogs from the West Divide Citizens Advisory Panel." *Courtesy of Gary Miller.*

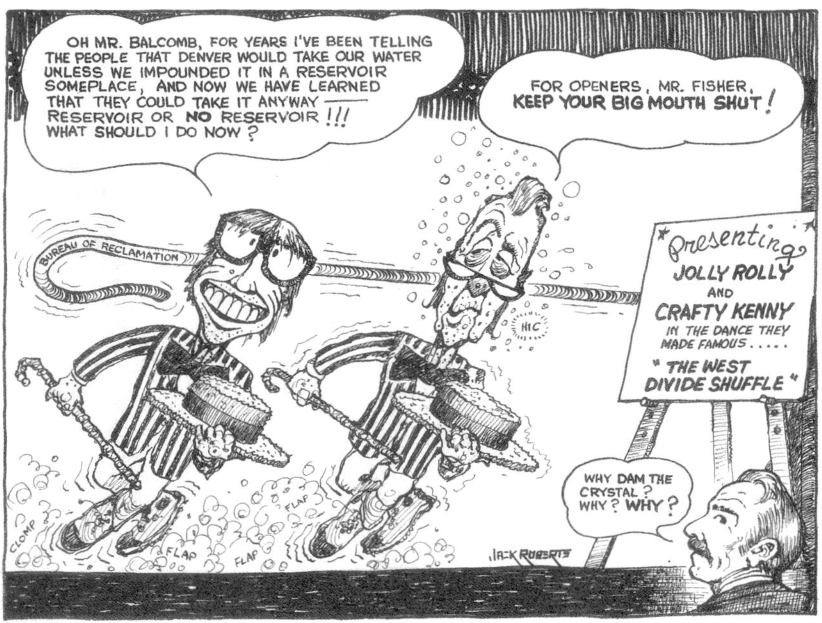

"The West Divide Shuffle." *Courtesy of Gary Miller.*

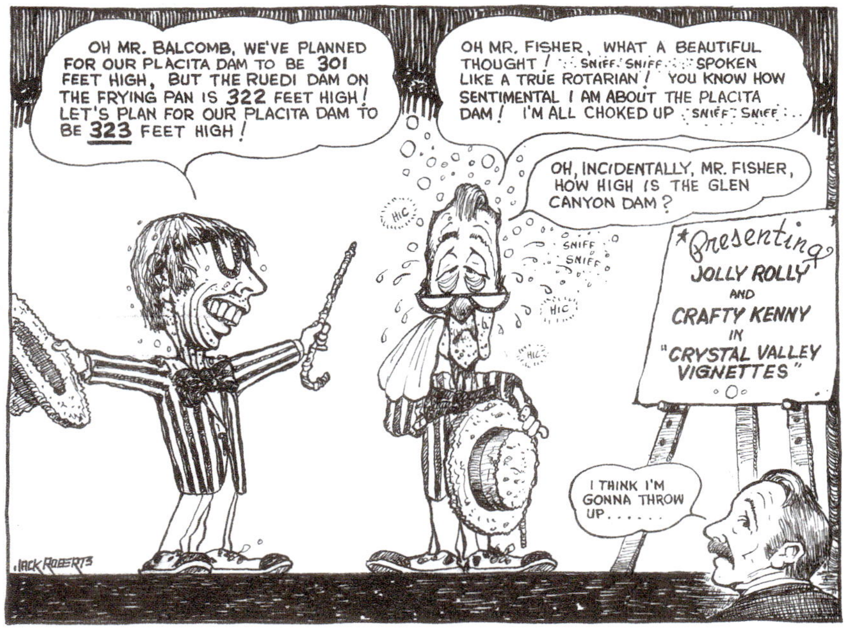

"Crystal Valley Vignettes." *Courtesy of Gary Miller.*

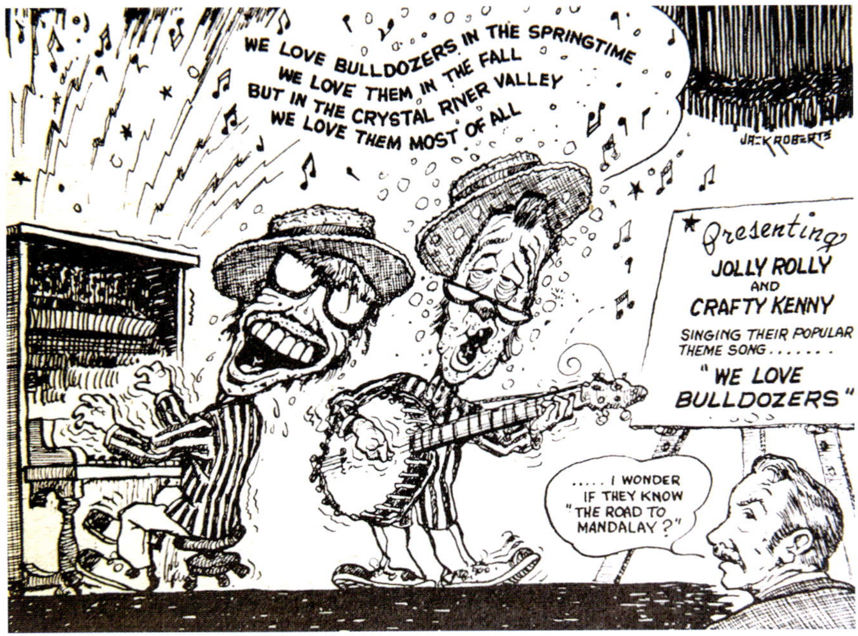

"We Love Bulldozers." *Courtesy of Gary Miller.*

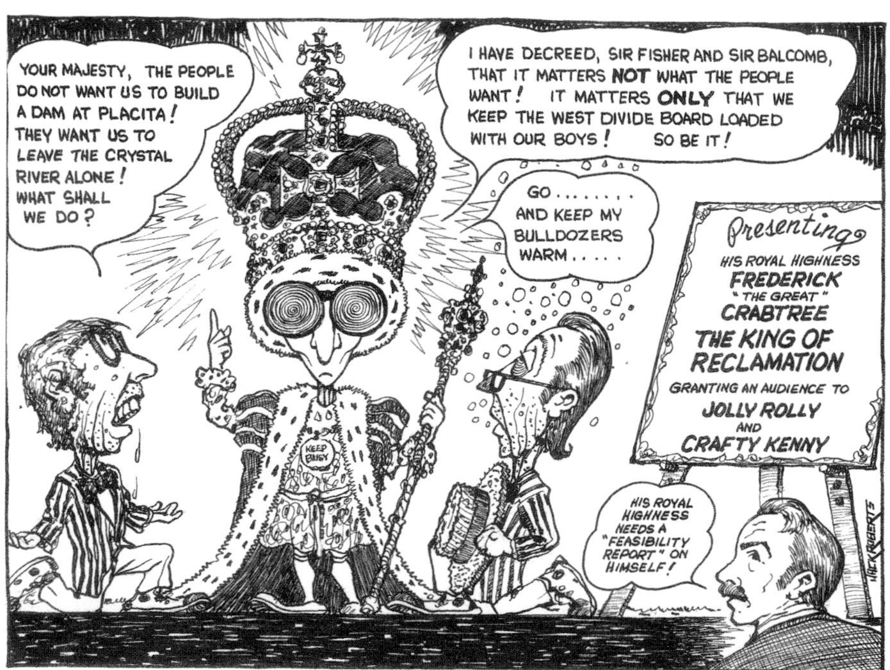

"His Royal Highness Frederick "the Great" Crabtree: King of Reclamation." *Courtesy of Gary Miller.*

But to Jack's delight, the bulldozers remained idle. Although the majority of the members of the Citizens Advisory Panel supported the original configuration of the West Divide Project with only minor modifications, the Crystal Valley Environmental Association's (CVEPA) opposition forced the proponents of the plan to admit there had been a change in public attitude that reflected negatively on the project. They also recognized that it would be impossible to move to the construction phase without municipal and industrial commitment to the project, which had waned over the years. Additionally, CVEPA filed a petition that asked for the election of WDWCD Board members in lieu of their appointment by the district judge, as was the prevailing practice. All these matters greatly concerned "Jolly Rolly" and "Crafty Kenny," who appealed to BuRec's Frederick Crabtree for support. Jack captured the scene at the king's court.

With opposition mounting from many quarters, the West Divide Board knew it faced an uphill battle to win approval for the high dam on the Crystal. Therefore, it was in a compromising mood by early February 1976. Scott Balcomb, Kenneth's son, proposed a meeting with CVEPA to see if there

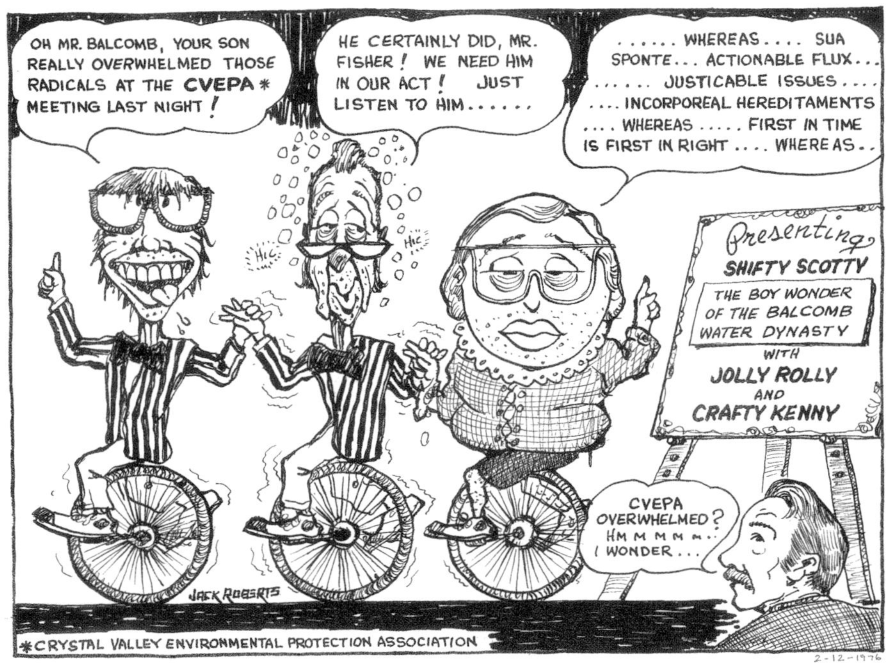

"Shifty Scotty with Jolly Rolly and Crafty Kenny." *Courtesy of Gary Miller.*

was any common ground between the two groups. Accepting the proposal, the environmentalists welcomed Scott to a special meeting on February 10. During the three-hour session, Scott strongly defended the need for diversion on the Crystal to keep the water on the Western Slope away from Front Range interests and to encourage agriculture in the West Divide area. Perhaps the high dam was not the way to go, he admitted. Instead, would CVEPA accept a gravity-diversion project near Marble with water storage on the West Divide as an alternative to the Placita dam? CVEPA's Michael Mechau dashed Balcomb's plan by stating that the organization would oppose any diversion of Crystal River water.

Although "Shifty Scotty" had failed in his mission, he signaled the West Divide Board's willingness to compromise. In early March, the board requested BuRec to study alternatives to the proposed dam at Placita. It was politically smart, Kenneth Balcomb suggested, "to give some serious thought to consideration of a plan that would obviate the need for Crystal River water." A few days earlier, at the CRWCD board meeting, both he and Fischer had conceded that they were losing the public relations war. "We have a particularly bad problem on the Crystal River," Fischer said.

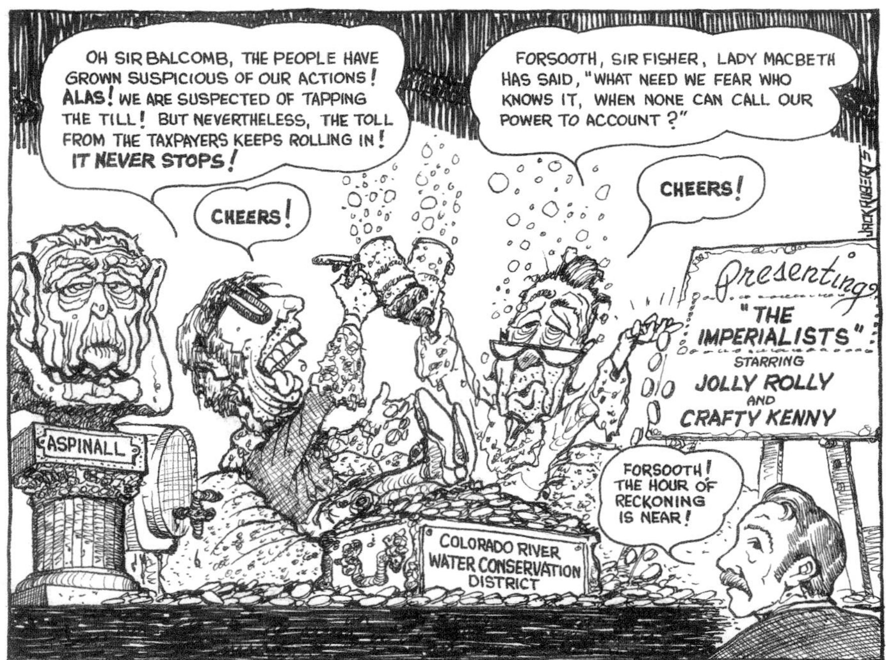

"The Imperialists." *Courtesy of Gary Miller.*

The reference was to editorials and Jack's cartoons in the *Valley Journal* that caricaturized Fischer and Balcomb as ringleaders of a board willing to use any means to achieve some form of the West Divide Project. Balcomb conceded that the *Valley Journal*'s attacks had convinced many people to regard the whole affair as a "big rip-off of the taxpayers."[75]

As a way to combat this problem, the board voted to create a public information program. Jack responded to the announcement of the new program in an open letter to Fischer that was published in the *Valley Journal* on March 11, 1976. The program, Jack argued, was a forlorn hope to win back the lost majority for dam building. Gone are the days, he wrote, when "[a]rm in arm with the Bureau of Reclamation and the happy [public] majority, the CRWCD marched bravely onward to the hormone-stirring roar of the bulldozers."[76] Sensing that his cartoons were drawing blood, Jack sharpened his attack by accusing "Jolly Rolly" and "Crafty Kenny" of malfeasance.

Angered by the cartoons, Fischer confronted Jack about them. Responding, Jack wrote, "I must admit that I have been giving you and Crafty Kenny some very rough treatment." But he had no intention of

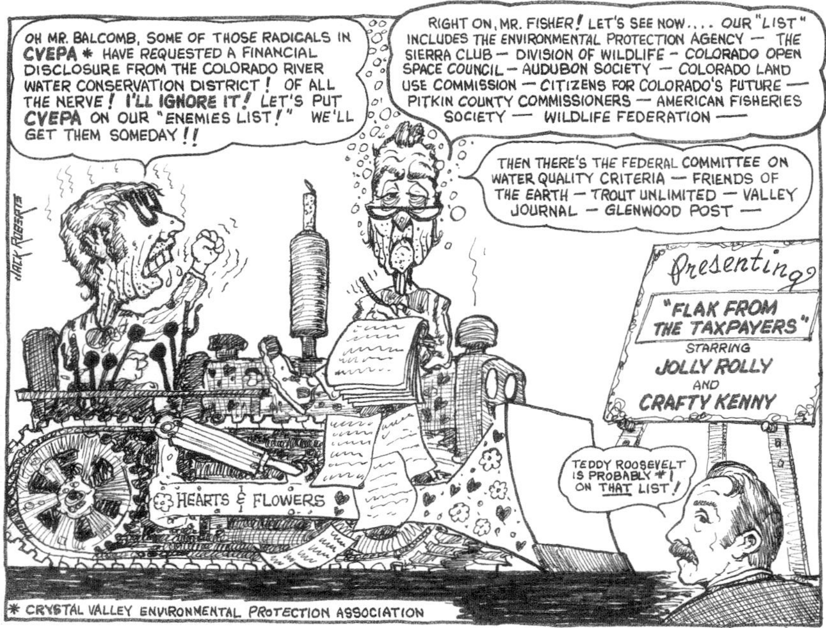

"Flak from the Taxpayers." *Courtesy of Gary Miller.*

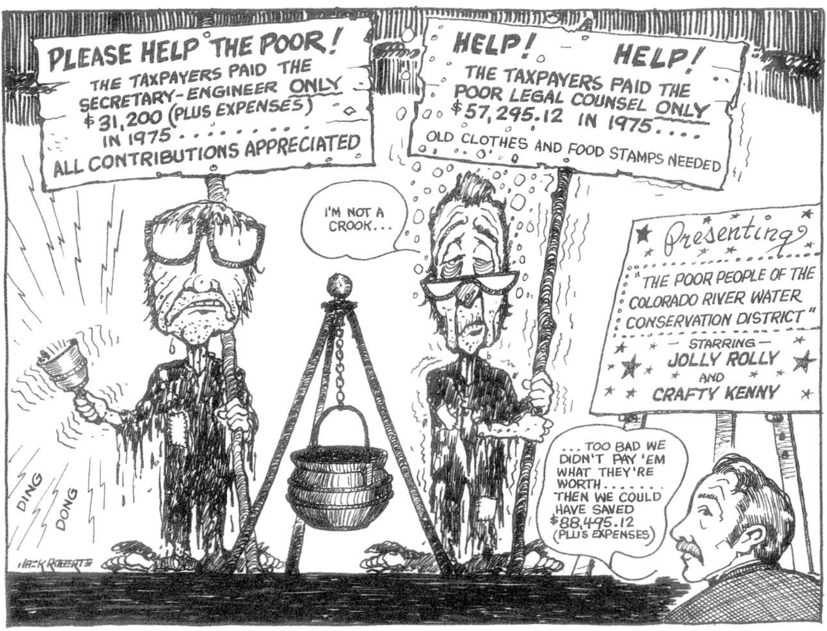

"The Poor People of the Colorado River Water Conservation District." *Courtesy of Gary Miller.*

letting up and would join CVEPA in requesting a financial disclosure from the CRWCD that would include salaries, legal fees and expenses for public relations and lobbying. "As an initial move in this direction," he continued, "I intend to make your salary the subject of a cartoon very soon…A phone call or a letter from you would be greatly appreciated so that we may explore this subject."[77] Jack's promised cartoon, which depicted "Jolly Rolly's" rejection of CVEPA's request for financial disclosure, appeared in the *Valley Journal* a few days later. When the river district relented and disclosed Fischer's and Balcomb's compensation, Jack immediately sent another cartoon to the paper.

CVEPA pressed the case for the election of the WDWCD Board of Directors. Although concerned about the matter, "Jolly Rolly" and "Crafty Kenny" were confident they would prevail in court. They were right, although CVEPA secured representation on the West Divide Board as a result of a compromise. Consequently, prospects for a dam on the Crystal River dimmed further.

Pursuing another line of attack, the members of the environmental group leveled a conflict of interest charge against Kenneth Balcomb. In an article in

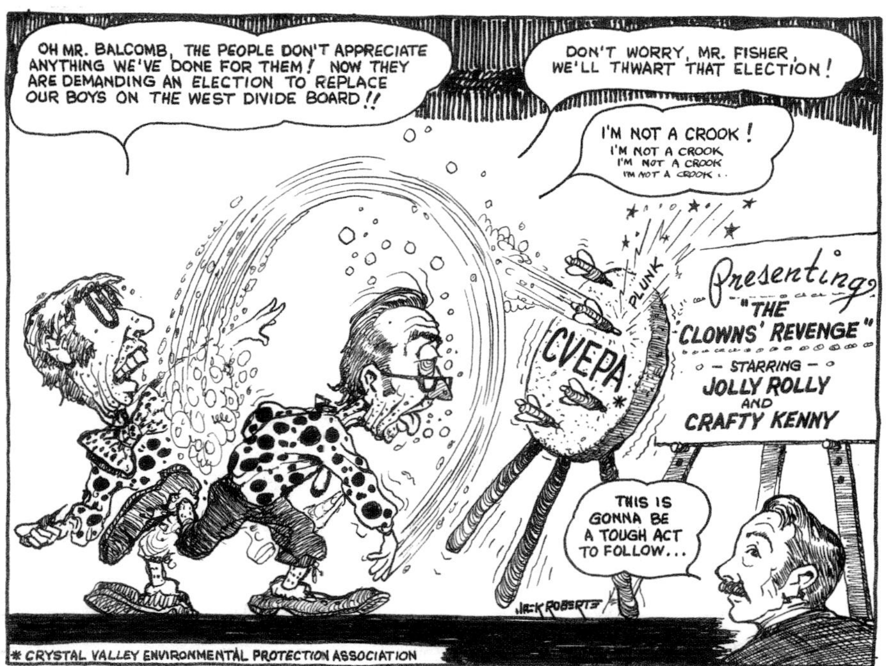

"The Clowns' Revenge." *Courtesy of Gary Miller.*

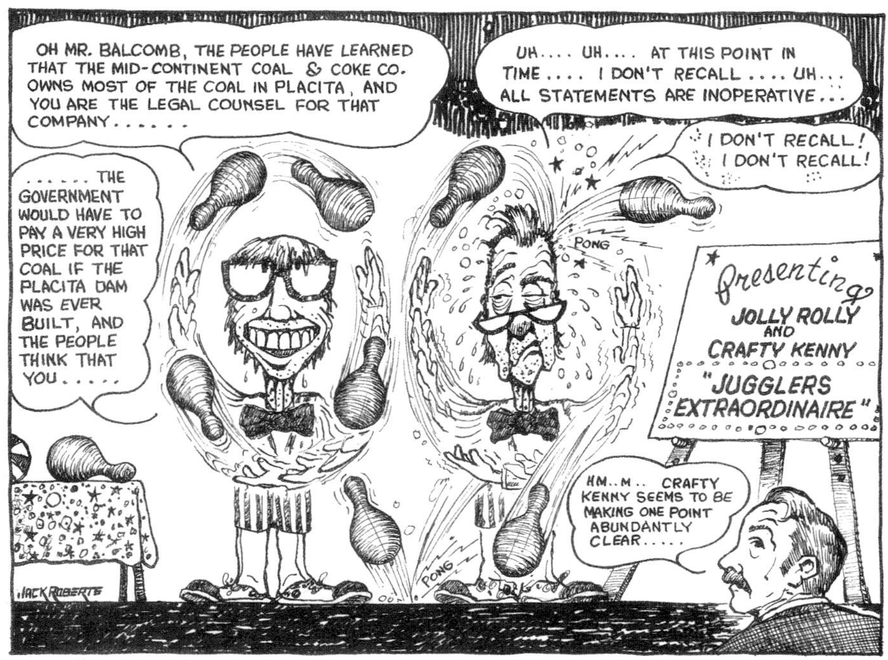

"Jugglers Extraordinaire." *Courtesy of Gary Miller.*

the March 11 issue of the *Valley Journal*, Michael Mechau, CVEPA president, noted that Balcomb was a partner in the Delaney and Balcomb law firm that represented the Mid-Continent Coal and Coke Company. Mid-Continent had substantial land and coal holdings at Placita, which, Mechau claimed, the government would have to purchase if the area was inundated by waters from the proposed reservoir. Mechau asserted that as attorney for both River Districts, "Mr. Balcomb's legal fees have been paid with public moneys, and while receiving that public money Mr. Balcomb has worked to get a reservoir built, again with public money, and the building of the reservoir would result in the necessity of spending yet more public money to acquire the mineral rights owned by another client of Mr. Balcomb's firm."[78] With this conflict of interest, Mechau stressed, Balcomb should resign. The issue was rich material for Jack.

Robert Delaney, vice-president of Mid-Continent Coal and Coke Company, fumed over CVEPA's charge. It was "sheer nonsense," he said, based on "unfounded insinuations." The *Valley Journal's* story on the matter "reflected very dubious journalism,"[79] he angrily added. Delaney and Kenneth Balcomb also defended Mid-Continent against the charge

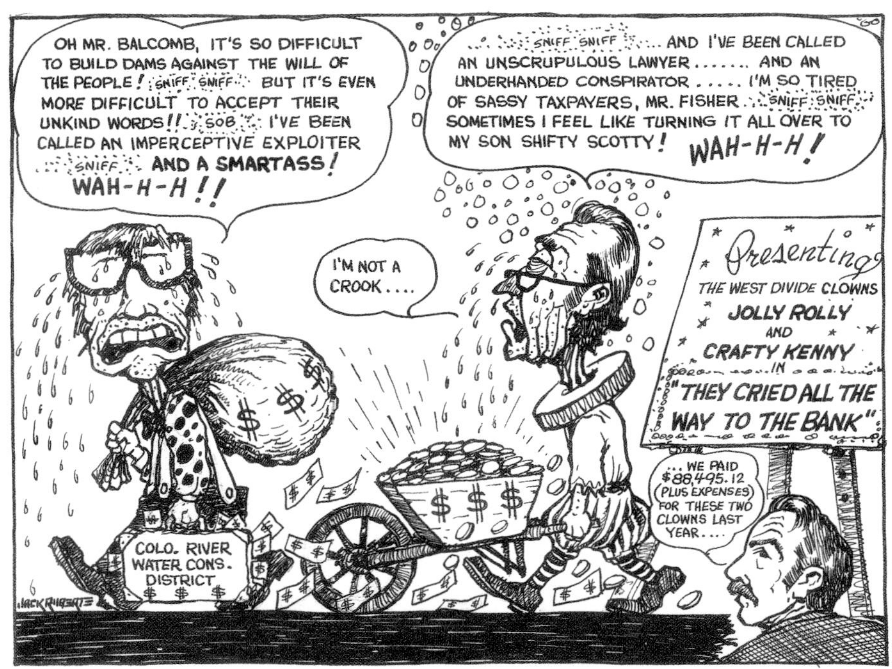

"They Cried All the Way to the Bank." *Courtesy of Gary Miller.*

that it had pulled strings to get the West Divide Board to exclude the company's coal-producing holdings at Coal Basin from the water district's tax assessment area.

Under attack, Dalaney and Balcomb gained some public support. To many people, the *Valley Journal*'s editorials and Jack's vitriolic cartoons were outside the pale of decency. To attack Rollie Fischer and Kenneth Balcomb was one thing, but to attack Wayne Aspinall, "the father of Colorado Reclamation," and the Delaneys—namely, Frank and his nephew Robert—was another.

Jack's description of former congressman Aspinall as "that insipid old curmudgeon" and his critical reference to Frank Delaney in his open letter to Rollie Fischer published in the *Valley Journal* of March 11 angered many of the defenders of old water politics in Colorado. One such defender wrote, "I…find your drawings and references, particularly to Frank Delaney (also my former employer) of questionable taste, lacking in 'class,' and, frankly, for an artist who is indisputably much admired for the gift of painting you have been given, you are making a fool of yourself, in my humble opinion."[80]

Patrick Noel, managing editor of the *Valley Journal*, admitted that there was a growing resentment from many who thought Jack's cartoons had been unfair. This was enough for him to consider discontinuing the publication of the cartoon series. But Robert Delaney's and Kenneth Balcomb's threat of legal action against both Jack and the *Valley Journal* forced the issue. The cartoons were scandalous and libelous, they told Noel, and they were prepared to go to court if the paper continued to publish them. Both Fischer and Balcomb were offended by the cartoons—Fischer by being lampooned as a buffoon and Balcomb by being depicted as a heavy drinker and man who would do anything to achieve his objective. Although Noel believed the cartoons and the paper's coverage had enlightened the public about the dam proposal, he reluctantly gave in to the pressure to discontinue the publication of Jack's cartoons. "Personally," he wrote in an editorial, "I'll miss Jack, Jolly Rolly and Crafty Kenny but, alas, all things must pass, and it would appear to be time to heal wounds and move on to some other areas. So long, fellas."[81]

To Jack, the whole thing was comical. It was a badge of honor, he told his friends, to be threatened with a lawsuit, particularly by "Crafty Kenny." Proudly, he announced that his cartoons had put Fischer and Balcomb "on the run" and that they did as much as anything to mobilize opposition to the Placita Dam Project. Silenced for a time, Jack eventually returned to his sketching easel to help illustrate the next chapter of the Placita dam saga.

The CRWCD's and WDWCD's challenge of the constitutionality of the Colorado Minimum Stream Flow Law gave Jack an opportunity to reengage in the fight against the West Divide Project. The law gave the state the authority to maintain minimum flows deemed necessary by the Colorado Division of Wildlife for the protection of the recreational, aesthetic and wildlife values of the state's streams and rivers. Using the Crystal River as a test case to challenge the constitutionality of the law, Kenneth and Scott Balcomb filed a suit for the water districts in District Water Court in August 1977. Rollie Fischer justified the lawsuit in a lengthy letter published in the *Valley Journal* on February 9, 1978. Upholding the law, he conceded, would almost certainly prevent any diversion from the river. Jack's cartoon published in the *Valley Journal* a week later was in response to Fischer's letter.

The Colorado Supreme Court upheld the law. The Crystal River minimum stream flow ruling was a landmark in the history of Colorado water law, and the Balcombs' fight against it with public money helped to undermine their positions as attorneys for the water districts. Both resigned

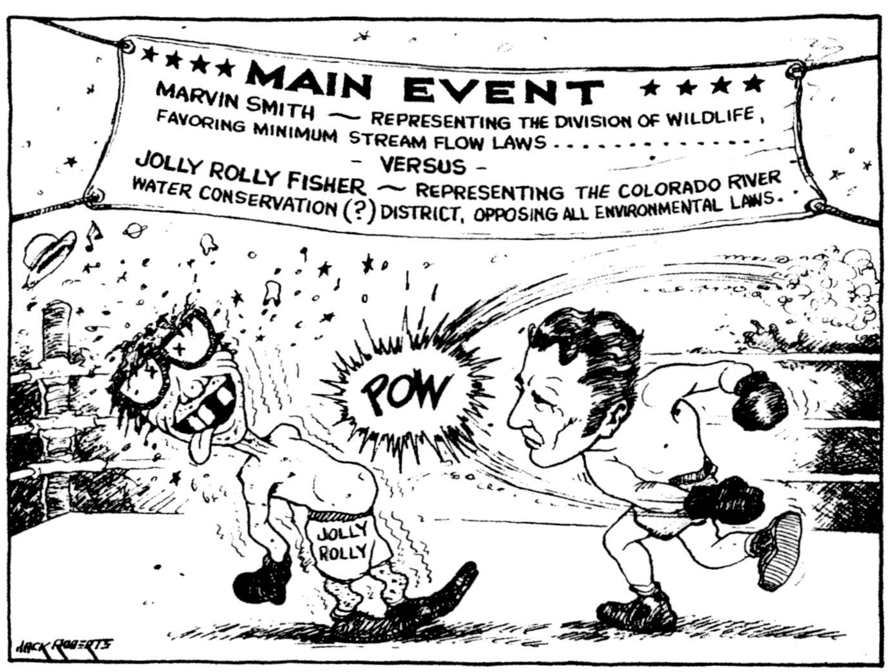

"Main Event." *Courtesy of Gary Miller.*

in October 1980 after they announced their association with the Exxon Corporation, a major supporter of water diversion for the development of the oil shale industry.

BuRec's determination in 1982 that the West Divide Project was economically infeasible removed the immediate threat of a dam at Placita. The bureau credited CVEPA and its environmental allies for organizing the opposition that shelved the project. With this development, Jack happily retired "Jolly Rolly" and "Crafty Kenney." There was never a doubt in his mind that he had played a major role in saving the Crystal River Valley from carpetbaggers and bulldozers.

8

GROS VENTRE ARAPAHOES AND TABAGAUCHE UTES

The first two paintings Jack completed in his new studio in Redstone were a part of his series on the Gros Ventre Arapahoes that he had started in the last months of his Hanging Lake days. On August 8, 1969, he told John M. King, who purchased the series, that he became interested in this band of Arapahoes after reading John Charles Frémont's 1844 journal. As his letter to King revealed, Jack was completely captivated by their way of life:

> *These are the Indians that Fremont encountered in June of 1844 on the upper Colorado, which was known as the Grand River then. It is regrettable that the explorer did not provide more detailed descriptions of these colorful people, but I have discovered other informative sources to augment his account. I have chosen the year 1844 as the time to best portray their culture since that was the time they were at the peak of their renown and affluence. It was a time when buffalo were plentiful and even the most visionary medicine man did not consider that the white men posed a threat to their way of life. It was a time when the Arapaho warriors were occasionally allied with the Cheyennes and Sioux and altogether they made a fighting force that bowed to no other force on the face of this earth. It was a time when the Arapaho way of life was truly magnificent.*

He also informed the oil and gas millionaire that all of his property near Granby, Colorado, including the John King Ranch, was a part of this

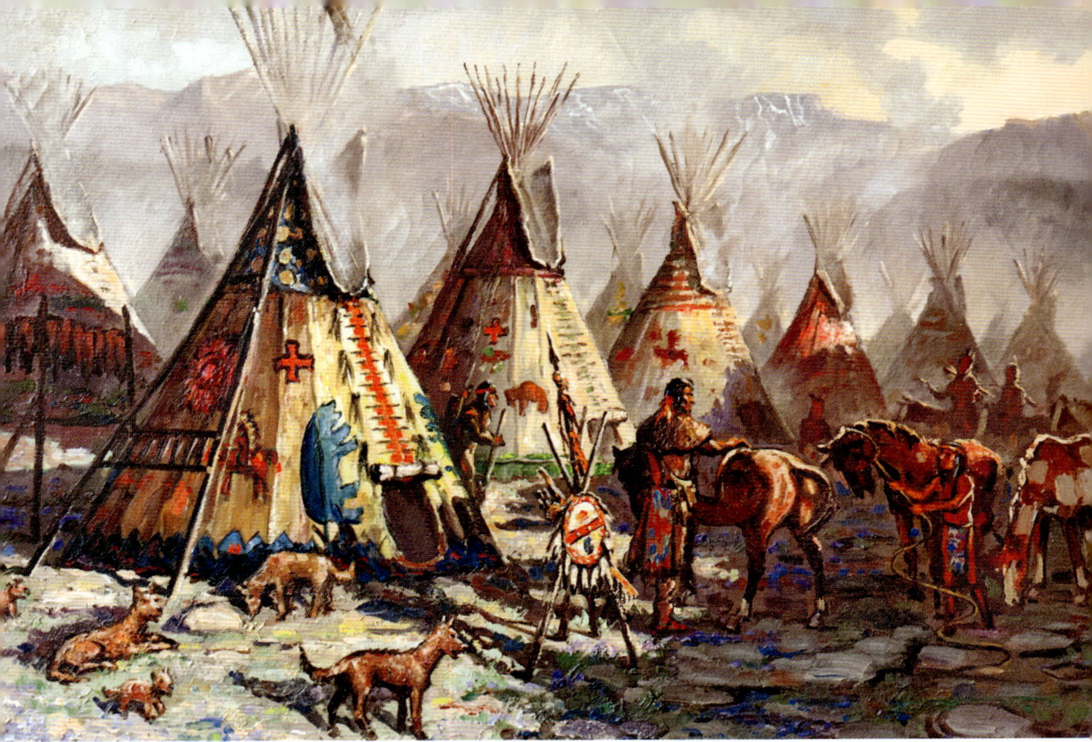

Arapaho Village. Gary and Monica Miller Collection. Courtesy of Gary Miller.

"Indian paradise" that existed until the Gros Ventres abandoned it to the Utes, their bitter enemy, in 1862 and rejoined their tribesmen on the plains.

In capturing these people on canvas, Jack selected scenes that in his estimation best exemplified Arapaho culture and way of life. He expressed to Lemon Saks that "[t]he Gros Ventres embodied everything that we think of when we think of the romance of the American Indian. They were fierce warriors, superb hunters, shrewd traders, dignified statesmen, skilled horse thieves, and they conducted their exploits in the most beautiful country on this continent—Western Colorado."[82] To document this in his series for John King, Jack painted scenes of Arapaho village life, hunting and war parties and religious ceremonies.

Jack continued to paint the Gros Ventre Arapahoes for the rest of 1970, stretching the King commission from six to twelve paintings and delivering several more to the Saks Gallery for sale. He hated to pay the commission Saks required, but he desperately needed to sell paintings. He admitted to Philip Anschutz that he was in the worst financial shape of his life. "I have simply over-extended myself on the construction of my studio and there is nobody to blame but Jack Roberts. Therefore, I intend to continue painting the Gros Ventre Arapahoes and most of these works will probably be sold through Saks."[83]

Lemon Saks, however, was not entirely satisfied with Jack's Indian paintings. With one or two exceptions, they were not selling. As a suggestion for his future work, he recommended that Jack adjust both his content and style. At first, Jack blamed a bad economy and was reluctant to accept advice, but he eventually realized that change was necessary. "As I reflect on the Gros Ventre paintings you have now," he answered Saks,

> *I realize that a few of them are not really "Indian," that is, they are not personal enough and seem almost like Indians placed in a cowboy setting, if you know what I mean. It takes an intimate identification with the subject matter in order for the message of the artist to come through with force and clarity. I have something to say about the Indians but am having some difficulty separating fact from fiction, history from tradition, idea from thought. Gradually I am coming into greater things but it is indeed very gradual. Just bear with me, Saks, and I will do some important work some day.*[84]

The greater things Jack mentioned in his letter pertained to his recent commission to paint a series on the Tabagauche Utes, a small band that migrated between the Uncompahgre and Roaring Fork Rivers in western Colorado during the period of their greatest glory. Early in 1971, Sheila and Aldo Bertozzi, the new owners of the Buffalo Valley Inn in Glenwood Springs, commissioned Jack to produce a series of five paintings entitled *Buffalo Culture* to complement his series of twelve cowboy paintings that were already there. With extensive research on the Utes already done, Jack immediately put brush to canvas and completed the assignment by late May.

To his delight, the paintings were featured in the *Denver Post Empire Magazine* on May 30, 1971, as he excitedly mentioned to Saks: "Perhaps you saw my spread in the *Empire* last Sunday. I have received several phone calls from prospective buyers in Denver and I referred them all to your galleries. The Publicity seemed to generate some interest."[85]

More publicity soon followed. Robert Campbell of the Grand Junction *Daily Sentinel* wrote a feature story about the Ute paintings on July 16, 1971, that was reprinted in other state papers, including the *Rocky Mountain News* and the *Boulder Daily Camera.* Jack, Campbell wrote, had a story to tell about the dignity and honor of the American Indian, and he was determined to tell it with complete historical accuracy and adherence to truth. Jack related that the paintings in the series depicted the life and culture of the Tabagauche Utes from about 1830 to 1842, the period of their greatest glory and affluence. "All the customs, all the romance, all the grandeur of those people stems from that period," he noted. The Utes were not savages. They had a highly advanced culture and a way of life that was "in tune with nature. Ours never has been."

In a printed pamphlet titled *The Tabagauche Utes*, Jack blamed the white pioneer settlers for destroying this culture and "truly magnificent society." Through this clash of cultures, he vehemently argued, the whites condemned the Utes to a life that was "pitifully poor, often sodden with illegal whiskey and reduced to beggary and petty thievery." In the article by Campbell, he passionately declared that he was "all the way on the American Indian" and that he would devote all of his time for the foreseeable future to telling their story. "I'm not planning my career on how I'd like to be remembered. Right now I'm working from day to day, painting the Utes and trying to do justice to them. I don't know what I'll be doing a few years from now, but today I doubt if I'll ever paint white people again."

Jack's passion in telling the Tabagauche Utes' story showed in his paintings, which became quite popular. They brought him some financial security as well. "I am…gradually coming out of the financial mess I got myself into, at least, I am not as desperate as I was a few months ago," he wrote to Lemon Saks on June 1, 1971. Eight months later, he wrote to Saks again:

> *Financially speaking, last year was the best year I ever had. Most of it came from people that came here to my studio and bought paintings off the wall. Every time I would sell one I would think it was probably the last one for awhile but the people haven't stopped coming yet. Several times I was about ready to bring five or six paintings to Denver to consign to you but each time somebody came by and bought them.*[86]

Jack was obviously buoyed by his success with the Indian paintings. He confessed, though, that the job of telling the story of the Tabagauche Utes was so big that he might not ever get it done. Nonetheless, he was determined to try, even though he feared the subject matter might be running dry. Evidently recalling Saks's earlier criticism of his Gros Ventre series, in which he suggested changes in method and theme, Jack added a guarded defense of his work in his February 1972 letter to Saks:

> *I wish I could report that I had made a revolutionary change in my work and was "knockin' them dead," so to speak, but such is not the case. I have made some improvement, to be sure, but my products are still basically*

about the same style and content. As you know, it is extremely difficult for an artist to effect even a slight change in a work style that has been thirty or more years in its development. I would dearly love to increase my production or advance the quality of my work but I just can't swing it overnight. I am changing, but awfully slow.

Although he was "working his way" into different subject matter, he emphatically stressed that he would not change until he had finished with the Tabagauche Utes. Until then, he wanted a show of his Ute paintings at Saks's Denver gallery. "I'm certain that I could sell my complete story of these fascinating people in thirty or more paintings," he explained to Saks. But he needed security of at least $200 per painting in advance for the thirty paintings proposed for the exhibit. "These works would be submitted eight or ten at a time and of course your choice from the lot would be retained in your storage until time for the showing. This plan would provide me with a bare subsistence during the interim and would presumably be a safe investment for you,"[87] he proffered.

Lemon Saks was lukewarm at best. "I will be very happy to look at some of your paintings," he responded, "but I will say now, as I have since I first saw your paintings, that your colors are too hard and the paintings are stiff." Continuing, he wrote:

You know I like you and I would like you to become known and successful as an artist. This would also be in my interest, so I hope you will appreciate my constructive criticism. I told you before and I will tell you again that if you could get Pawel Kontny to give you a few private lessons, you would certainly benefit greatly…

Don't compare the time now with 1965, when we had an exhibition and sold most of the paintings. First of all, your subject matter was totally different and secondly, but not least, the prices were a fraction of what they are today. In short, if we have an exhibition, I want to feel that the paintings are worth the price we are asking.[88]

Responding, Jack thanked Saks for his constructive criticism and told him that he was seriously considering his suggestion to contact Kontny. He had known several prominent artists in the past, including Harvey Dunn, who took "refresher courses" to improve their style and became greater artists for doing so. He admitted his figures had become too stiff and the colors too hard in his paintings. But he believed his problem was not technical errors

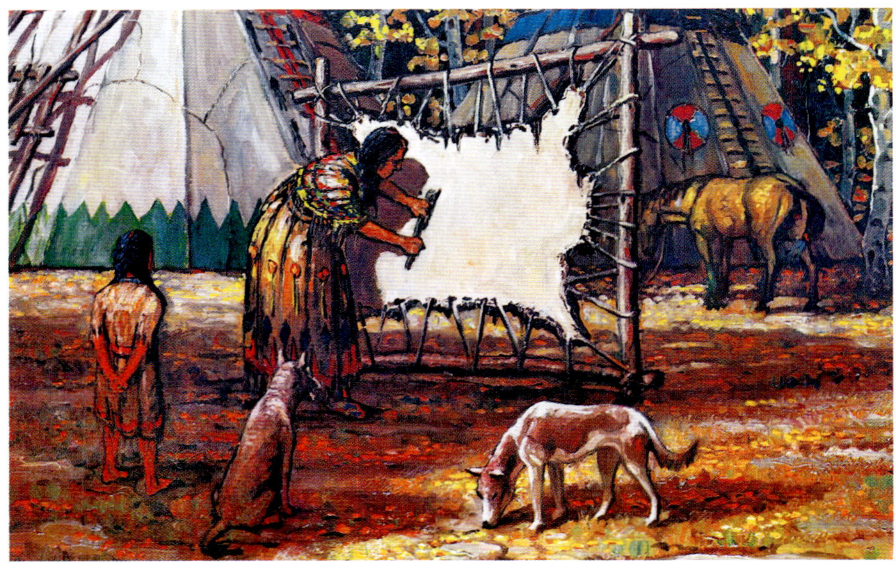

Buffalo Robe. Buffalo Valley Inn Ute Indian Collection. Courtesy of Sue Anschutz Rodgers.

but a matter of mental attitude. "I have found," he elaborated, "that I can paint an original, unprecedented idea with some facility and spontaneity, and the painting is appreciated and seems to sell fast. But then when I feel like I'm repeating myself on some old idea in a painting, that is when my interest lags and the painting becomes stiff and tense."[89] He was sure that adopting new subject matter would solve these difficulties.

Jack's plans for an exhibit of Indian paintings at the Saks Gallery changed after his sale of twelve paintings depicting various aspects of Tabagauche culture to the West Glenwood Springs Holiday Inn and eight more to the Buffalo Valley Inn. He was "in the chips" once again, he told Saks. "Confidentially," he added, "my interest in the Tabagauches is beginning to slacken a bit and I am thinking more and more about the early fur traders. It is difficult for me to plan a year ahead, but I hope to have about thirty paintings of the early fur trade within a year and then show them in your galleries. It would be a wonderful way to launch a new career."[90]

9

FUR TRADERS, TRADING POSTS AND MOUNTAIN MEN (AND MORE INDIANS)

By the summer of 1975, Jack had made the transition from his Indian phase into what he termed "the mountain men type of pictures." The Indian way of life was still attractive to him, but he found it even more fascinating as it was integrated with the fur trade instead of being in "splendid isolation." "The early-day fur traders and trappers are exciting subjects to me," he wrote to Lemon Saks on July 29, 1975. "I hope to show you some of these works in the near future and see if you like them."

There was a sense of excitement and optimism in Jack's tone as he entered this new phase of his professional career. His improved financial situation and the upcoming publication of his Lord Gore book put him in a better state of mind. "I seem to be doing OK, at least I'm busy and happy," he told his friend "Saksie." Continuing in his letter of July 29, he wrote:

> *I'm not getting rich but at least I'm out of the financial bind I was in about four years ago with this house. I will be eternally grateful to you, Saks, for the kind and generous help you extended during that difficult period—You hustled customers for my paintings and even bought one painting for yourself to keep my head above water. I was in serious trouble with this expensive house and no income and no credit and you saved my hide. I'll never forget you.*

Jack intended to tell the history of the old trading posts in Colorado through both painting and historical narrative. Anticipating success with his

Lord Gore book, he excitedly announced plans for another "picture book" to be published for the Colorado bicentennial celebration in the summer of 1976. The book, he told Saks, "will simply be titled 'Fur Trading Posts in the Colorado Area, 1828–1854.'" Although the book deal never materialized, Jack received important commissions that allowed him to illustrate the old trading posts, mountain men (squaw men) and Indian-trapper relations. In a letter to Gary Aenchbacher on April 30, 1973, he predicted that these historical illustrations would be "the most distinctive collection of paintings in all the West."

Jack's paintings of trading posts began in 1972 with a depiction of the old trading post of Fort Laramie in southeastern Wyoming. He had done extensive research on the post, which became a military fort in 1849, for his Lord Gore study. "I have been fascinated by old Fort Laramie for years and I hope this feeling is apparent in the painting," he told Ed Trumble, to whom he had sent the painting for inclusion in the Leanin' Tree greeting card list. Continuing, he wrote:

> *I still plan to return to the historic site in early June, simply to walk around the area and chat with the Park Service men there. I want to listen for the voices and try to feel the spirit of the residents and visitors during that grand and glorious period from 1841 to 1845. These habitués include some of the greatest Americans of the nineteenth century: Bull Bear, Red Cloud, Man-Afraid-Of-His-Horses, Bear-That-Scatters, Friday, Smoke, Red Water, Black Bear, Tempest and many others that are lost in legend because the whites failed to mention them in writing history.*
>
> *Then of course there are many of the whites of that period that are also worthy of mention, mainly because they wholeheartedly adopted the Indian culture, taking Indian wives, learning the language and holding the laws of nature in a sacred manner. Most important of all, they did not look down their noses at the Indians like the missionaries and Government officials did. Such great men as Jim Bridger, Tom Fitzpatrick, Kit Carson, Lucian Fontenelle, Henry Chatillon, Joe Meek, and many others with less familiar names. They all trod upon that same ground at old Fort Laramie. Just the idea of old Jim Bridger leaning against the adobe wall near the gates of the fortress and chatting with the great Sioux head-chief, Bull Bear…what a thrill!![91]*

Even though the *Fort Laramie* card did not sell well, Ed Trumble liked the painting and bought it for his own collection.

Research on the Tabagauche Utes led Jack to Antoine Robidoux, an American fur trader of French Canadian descent. Robidoux reached an agreement with the Tabagauches to build a fortified trading post at the mouth of the Uncompahgre River, near the present town of Delta, Colorado. Constructed in 1828, Fort Robidoux became a thriving trading post, where the fine furs, hides and buffalo robes of the Tabagauches were bartered for English cooking ware, iron tools, coffee, sugar, jewelry and, most important of all, English-made flintlocks. In 1974, Jack portrayed the history of Robidoux and the thriving trade activities around Fort Robidoux during the period of 1828 to 1842 in paintings for Robert and Deanna Musgrave of Delta, Colorado. Jack included the Robidoux story in his short publication titled *The Tabagauche Utes*, one of several carefully researched and illustrated pamphlets that accompanied his major commissions.

At the same time, Jack completed twelve paintings that Gary Aenchbacher commissioned for the Holiday Inn of Greeley, Colorado, depicting the trade at old Fort Vasquez on the South Platte River during the peak year of 1839. Along with nearby Forts St. Vrain, Jackson and Lupton, Fort Vasquez was located in superb buffalo country and well situated for the Cheyenne-Arapaho trade. The paintings illustrated the full cycle of the trading year, beginning with the arrival of huge freight wagons drawn by oxen loaded with trade goods from St. Louis and ending with a Mackinaw boat with the proceeds of the trade—buffalo robes, buffalo tongues and furs—aboard and ready to sail down the South Platte River for St. Louis. Scenes in between included Arapahoes approaching Fort Vasquez with their travois loaded with buffalo robes; a trading session during which the Indians traded their goods for flintlock or percussion-cap rifles and ammunition, kettles, axes, jewelry and bolts of calico; and trappers with their squaws on their way to trade their furs at the South Platte posts.

The legend of the Cache La Poudre trappers and fur traders inspired Jack's *Mountain Men* series the following year. According to the legendary story, in November 1836, a large party of French trappers and fur traders employed by John Jacob Astor's American Fur Company on their way to Green River, Wyoming, were forced by a tremendous snowstorm to remain encamped for several days along a river near the present site of Bellvue near Fort Collins, Colorado. Because of the depth of the snow, hundreds of pounds of cargo had to be left behind before the wagon train could continue to its destination. Everything that could be spared was buried in a pit that was carefully prepared to preserve and hide the contents. Much that was buried was gunpowder. On their return trip several months later,

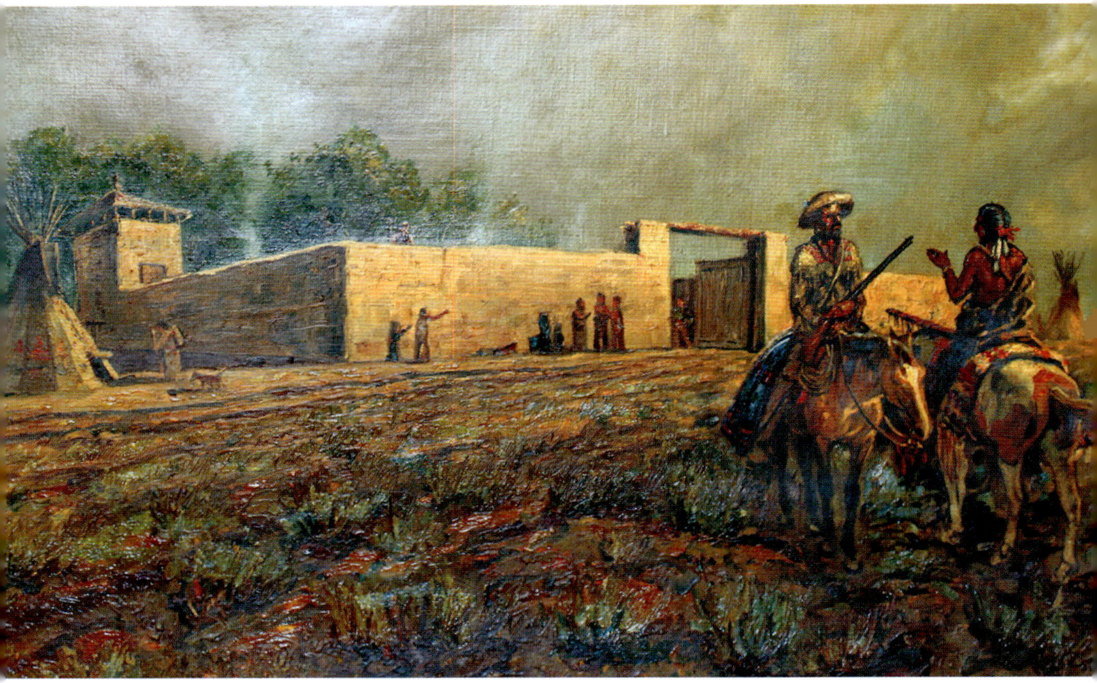

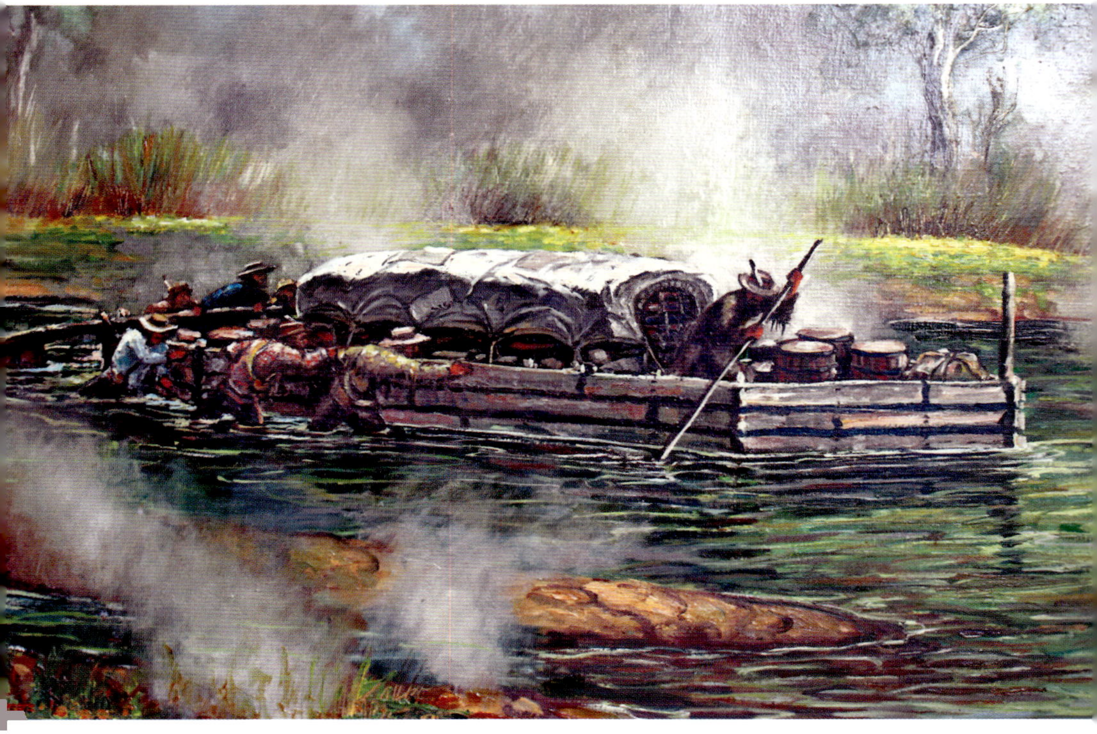

the men retrieved their buried goods from the place they called Cache La Poudre, "the hiding place of the powder." Eventually, the river nearby took on that name.

Jack's *Mountain Men* series consisted of fourteen paintings. Jack proposed the series for the new Sheraton Inn in Fort Collins; however, the commission fell through, leaving him no other choice than to sell the paintings individually. The Saks Denver Art Galleries eventually sold some of them. Angered by Saks's steep commission, Jack resolved never again to go through Saks or any other art gallery to sell his paintings. For a time, he was able to keep that resolution.

Several major commissions during the late 1970s and early 1980s enabled Jack to deal directly with patrons. One of the commissions was for Troy "Buck" Pollard and his wife, Gloria, from Rangely, Colorado. In keeping with his Indian-trapper theme, the ten paintings in the series portrayed life during the early 1840s around the old Fort Davy Crockett trading post in Brown's Park near Rangely. Gloria Pollard recounted how the commission came about:

> *We wanted paintings with a western motif for my husband's office, and he suggested something about a fort that was located in the Brown's Park area. I particularly liked the one he made for the…[Buffalo Valley Inn] of a Teepee with the horse tied outside in the moonlight. So we came to Trappers and Indians. He delivered each painting as they were finished and we got a history lesson with each of them. He titled them and would explain why he painted them doing something specific, like the trapper rode with his rifle pointed up so the ball wouldn't fall out.*[92]

The Pollard commission was typical of the way Jack matched his interests with those of his patrons. Instead of painting individual pictures with a western motif, he used the paintings to tell a story that was relevant to Rangely and had historical significance for Gloria and Buck. The Davy Crockett trading post also happened to be something he had long wanted to paint. In this case, as in others, he consciously tried to find relevance between subject matter and patron, and he rarely accepted a commission that did not allow him to tell a story.

Opposite, top: Fort Vasquez. *Bruce Carlson Collection. Courtesy of Joe Carlson.*

Opposite, bottom: Mackinaw Boat. *Bruce Carlson Collection. Courtesy of Joe Carlson.*

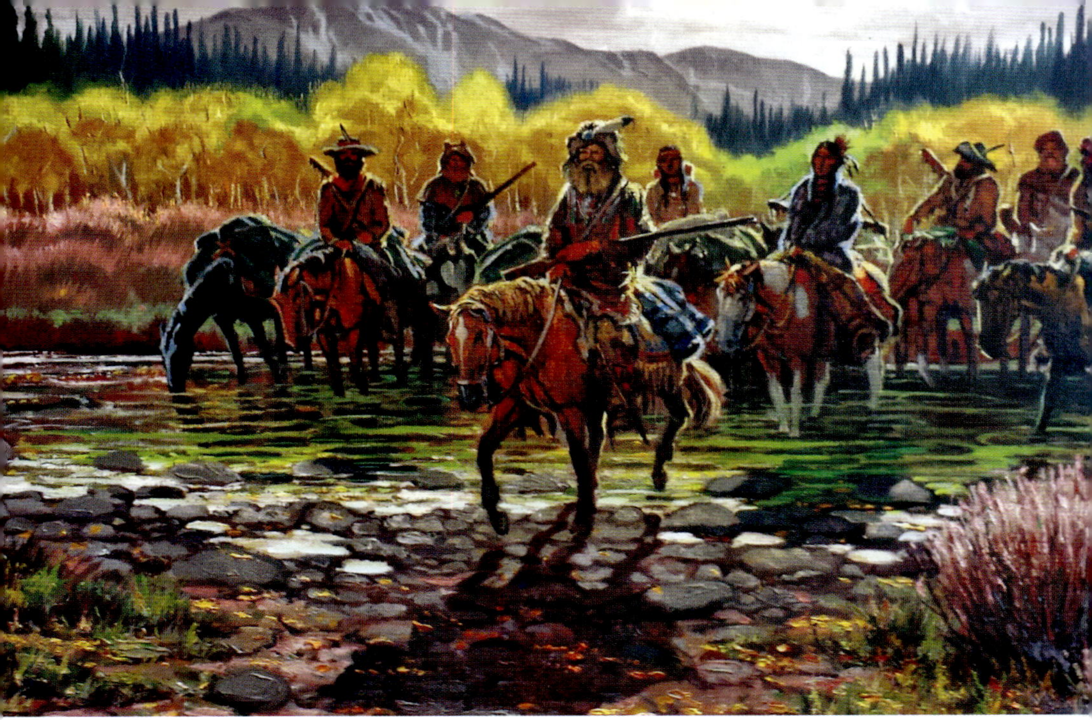

A Trapping Brigade. Pollard Collection. Courtesy of Troy and Gloria Pollard.

Of the trading posts Jack researched and painted, Bent's Old Fort was his favorite. He painted it in 1974 and subsequently made at least two trips to the reconstructed site. A visit there with his new wife, Mary Margaret, in June 1978 left a deep impression. "It was an unforgettable adventure into the Old West," Jack wrote the superintendent on January 24, 1980.

> *A visitor leaves with the unmistaken feeling that the National Park Service has spared nothing in its heartfelt pursuit of authenticity and historical accuracy. The trading room, the cistern, the blacksmith shop, the old well, even the old privy, have been reconstructed with such meticulous care that one can almost hear the voices of the trappers and Indians. We spent several hours on the rear bastion just absorbing the atmosphere and visualizing the Conestoga wagons approaching on the old Santa Fe Trail. We will never forget it. It was great, absolutely great.*

And then, Jack lamented, he watched an episode of *The Chisholms*. Although filmed at Bent's Old Fort, the story was about a family of pioneers bound for California who stopped at Fort Laramie in 1844 just before the fort was threatened by a band of Santee Sioux demanding five hundred sacks of grain. Eventually, the terrified people in the fort granted the demand, and the Indians went away happy.

What "an abomination!" he exclaimed to the superintendent.

> *I thought I had seen some trash on TV but "The Chisholms" sets a new low…In the first place, the only grain at Fort Laramie, or Bent's Fort, would have been oats for horse feed and even that is unlikely. And what would those Plains Indians have done with 500 sacks of grain anyway? Maybe they wanted to make apple turnovers for the tourists on the Oregon Trail. As dumb as I am, I know that Fort Laramie was in the Oglala Sioux country, but "Oglala" didn't sound savage enough for TV audiences so the scriptwriters lifted the name of a woodlands people that have never been west of the Mississippi River. The Santee Sioux wouldn't have known what to do with a buffalo.*
>
> *Perhaps the most flagrant abuse of western history was in the stereotyped Indians—Ugh! How! Givum grain! Heap Much! Haven't we had enough of that? Don't those TV writers ever refer to the works of David Lavender or Bernard DeVoto or Washington Irving or Wallace Stegner? Imagine, if you will, a band of Indians in 1844 making such a ridiculous demand at a trading post on the Great Plains. Actually, the post trader would probably be a brother-in-law to the chief. And also, being realistic, there weren't enough Indians on the North American continent to capture a formidable fortress like Fort Laramie or Bent's Fort.*
>
> *How can the American people accept such a travesty of history as that? In the name of some toothpaste, or hemorrhoid preparation, we permit those TV people to make a farce out of our most cherished history.*
>
> *Please, sir, I implore you to respect the romantic facts of Bent's Fort, and Fort Laramie, and insist that others respect it also.*

Although immersed in depicting trading posts and fur traders, Jack continued to get requests for Indian paintings. In 1977, he painted the *Medicine Man* series on the lives of Indian healers for a medical clinic in Ohio, and in 1990, he completed four paintings on the Oglala Souix for C.J. "Jack" Hire, also from Ohio. To review the history of the Oglala was a labor of love, he related to Hire, and it was his inspiration to paint a people who were the "prototype of the American Indian" and whose culture before the white man came represented "the adaptation of man to the environment." The white man destroyed this beautiful way of life, Jack lamented, and "[n]ow the earth is an environmental disaster."[93]

In 1979, Laurence F. Jonson, a consultant on art investment, became interested in a proposal Jack had made in 1975 for a series of twelve paintings illustrating the Indian calendar of the "Buffalo People" that would be the basis for a book similar to the one on Lord Gore. But the nearly four-year interval between proposal and response and his recent agony over the publication of *Lord Gore* caused Jack to have second thoughts about the project. "The LORD GORE book was my first and last experience as an author-illustrator," he wrote to Jonson on July 2, 1979. "The writing of historical non-fiction is not my forte. I am an artist and henceforth my time will be spent painting pictures. I cherish the experience of writing a book but I would not choose to do it again." He was eager to paint the pictures, and what Jonson did with them was up to him.

The project "died on the vine," but Jack brought it up again in a letter to Jonson two years later. "A couple of months ago, I took this idea out of my files for further research." After some thought, he added, "I prepared a new series of sketches that relate more specifically to the title of each month, or 'moon.' For instance, 'Moon of Birth of Calves' (April) is a moonlight scene with a cow buffalo sniffing her new-born calf that lies on the ground. A small herd of cows and young calves make up the background." He indicated that he had already painted six of the paintings and was working on the seventh. "A lot of new concepts have been brought into these works and I think I have something important to offer."[94]

Coincidentally, Jonson had already "stirred the embers up," and, as he told Jack, "the flame caught spark and interest was again raised for 'The Buffalo People' series." But Jack and Jonson were still not on the same wavelength. Jack simply wanted to sell the paintings. Jonson, on the other hand, was not interested in purchasing the paintings but in preparing a book proposal to present to an investor.[95] The flame for a book deal was soon extinguished, for Jack found a buyer for the paintings within days of his last correspondence with Jonson.

During a visit to Jack's studio in late June 1981, W.R. Hall of Grand Junction purchased five of the finished paintings and commissioned Jack to complete the rest of the series of twelve. Jack was elated that after developing in his mind for over fifteen years, the time for his "Calendar of the Buffalo People" had finally arrived.[96] He was equally pleased when Hall donated the series to the Museum of Western Colorado in Grand Junction.

In October 1985, the museum opened an exhibit of the paintings. At the opening reception, Jack detailed his intentions in depicting the scenes. "I have always been fascinated by the beautiful names Indians gave to

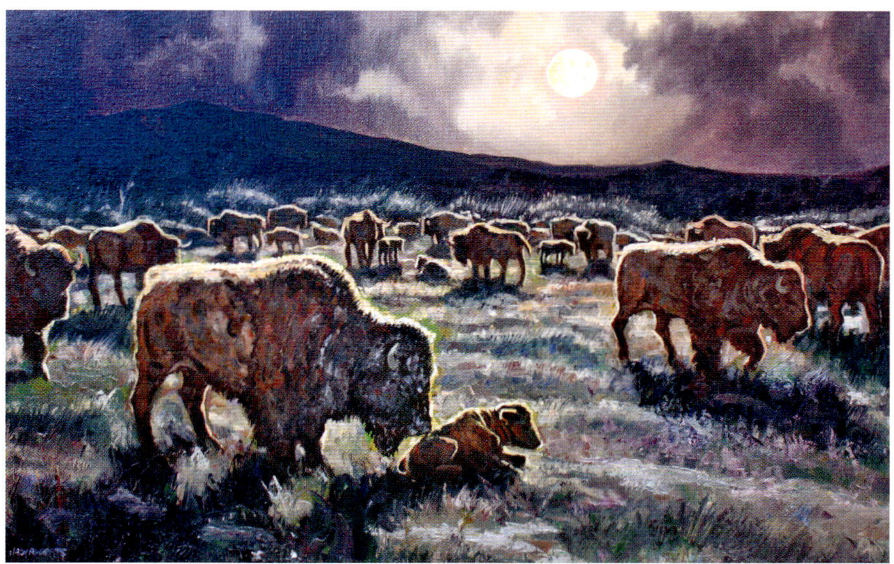

Moon of Birth of Calves. Jack Roberts's Indian Calendar Series. *W.R. Hall Collection. Courtesy of Museum of Western Colorado, Grand Junction, Colorado.*

the months," he explained. Each of the "moons" reflected aspects of the "Buffalo People's" way of life. The appearance of the new moon each month signaled the beginning of a period of time named after a recurring phenomenon. April, "Moon of Birth of Calves," was the beginning of the year for the buffalo-dependent Indians. "Moon of Yellow Leaves" described September; "Moon of Hairless Calf," November, when fetuses of butchered buffalo cows were found without hair; and "Moon of Sore Eyes," February, when Indians became snow blind while hunting from the reflection of the sun off the snow. Jack was proud that he had conceived and executed a concept that was, in his words, "the only totally original idea to enter the art market in years."[97]

Jack continued to extol the Indian way of life, and he never lost his enthusiasm for studying and illustrating Indian history and culture, even though some of his commissions during the late 1970s and through the decade of the 1980s began to draw him back to painting cowboys and saloon scenes. In addition, he received commissions to explore and illustrate the history of pioneer and frontier societies. He also found time to create scenes for the Leanin' Tree Publishing Company's line of greeting cards. It was the most productive and diverse period of his professional career.

10

GREETING CARDS

Ed Trumble, founder and president of the internationally known Leanin' Tree greeting card company, first saw a Jack Roberts painting in the Buffalo Valley Inn in the late 1960s. His discovery of Jack and his "wild and wooly" paintings of contemporary cowboys and saloon characters led to a lifelong friendship. Trumble found Jack fascinating and admired his "relentless struggle to improve" as an artist. He described his style as "bold, primitive impressionism" and his paintings as authentic depictions of realistic settings. He called Jack "a genuine Cowboy Artist," whose contribution to western art was significant. "Today as I look at his wide body of work," Ed wrote in 2008, "I believe that in the small world of western art he will ultimately become recognized as an authentic recorder of a West that now barely exists."[98]

It was Jack's "winsome, often humorous" paintings of cowboys working in cow camps that most impressed Trumble, and these scenes were among the most popular of his paintings reproduced by Leanin' Tree as greeting cards for over twenty-five years. "Although Jack never gained wide recognition outside western Colorado," Ed noted, "his annual Christmas card with Leanin' Tree became a tradition with many of our devoted customers."[99]

Jack worked closely with Trumble to find paintings with the right content and atmosphere for publication as greeting cards. At first, only *The Feast*, an Indian scene with the warm glow of a tepee fire, was a success while *Christmas in Auraria, 1858* was rejected as too "hairy" for Leanin' Tree customers. *Fort Laramie* failed because it was not cheerful and timely enough.

Jack quickly learned from this experience. After carefully studying Leanin' Tree's 1972 catalogue, he determined that "striking, harmonious color" was the main "stock in trade" for the company. To be successful, the card needed "a tremendous wallop of brilliant, arresting color." He also perceived that it needed the warm glow of a John Hilton sunset and the color impact of Melvin Warren and Doug Van Howd paintings.[100]

With these thoughts in mind, Jack sent Ed photos of three paintings from which he hoped one could be selected for the 1973 Christmas card line. All three were scenes he had painted in the 1960s: a cowboy wrapping a Christmas gift, two cowboys decorating a Christmas tree, and four cowboys singing at a bar. Of the three, he thought *The Quartet* offered the most promise for Ed's market, as he explained in a letter of November 11, 1972:

> *An old kerosene lamp could be placed on the table to provide the warm glow that is necessary to compete with the Hilton sunset in your catalog, and it [The Quartet] could be called "The Carolers." I would enjoy trying this [saloon] theme again after all these years. But, as an artist, I would have to retain certain inalienable rights and first and foremost would be my right to tell the truth. As an ex-cowboy myself, I know that cowboys are not particularly garrulous and very rarely are they moved to break into song. There is one thing and only one thing that can change this situation and that one thing is booze. Give 'em enough booze and they'll sing "O Little Town of Bethlehem" 'til hell freezes over.*
>
> *Of course I would consider the sensitivities of your customers, Ed, and would not dream of depicting a bunch of sloppy drunkards. But I'll be damned if I'll paint such a scene without plenty of evidence of booze in the picture. Such subjects can be handled with taste y'know.*

Responding a few days later, Ed wrote that he liked the picture of the beer drinkers but cautioned that Leanin' Tree's "few flirtations with barroom scenes" had been disastrous. On the other hand, he believed the intense emotionalism portrayed in the other two paintings would be well received. He especially liked the Christmas tree scene, which would fit Jack's "colorful palette" well and make "a very cheerful scene." There was nothing wrong with the bottle on the bench, he reassured Jack, for "the booze was incidental to and not the cause of what was happening."[101]

Jack was delighted to learn that the evidence of booze, if carefully handled, was not an issue. It had been with the Equitable Life Assurance Society. The society, Jack related to Ed, purchased the original Christmas

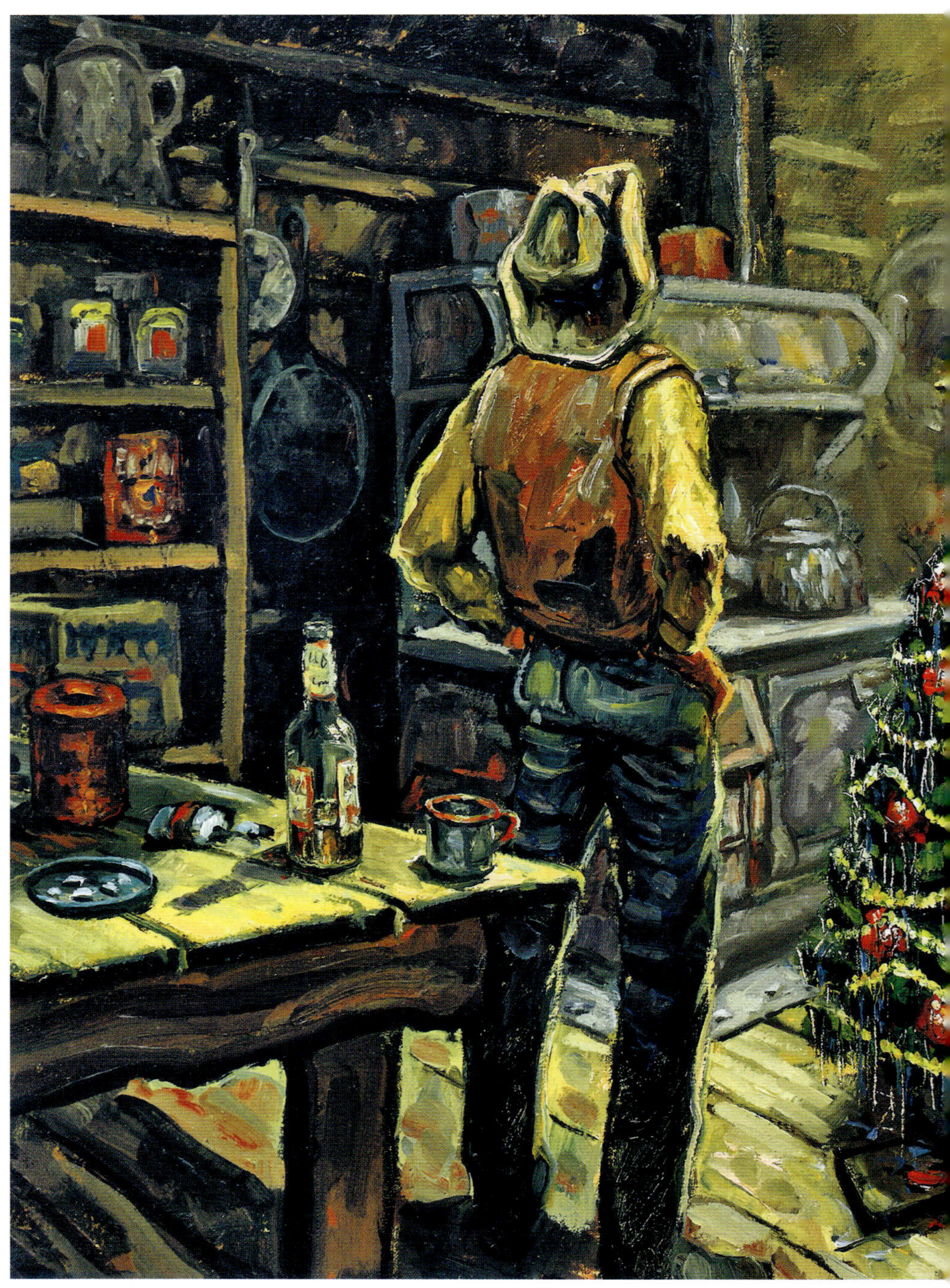

Looks 'Bout Right for Me Jim. Leanin' Tree Collection. Photo credit: Leanin' Tree Museum and Sculpture Garden of Western Art, Boulder, Colorado.

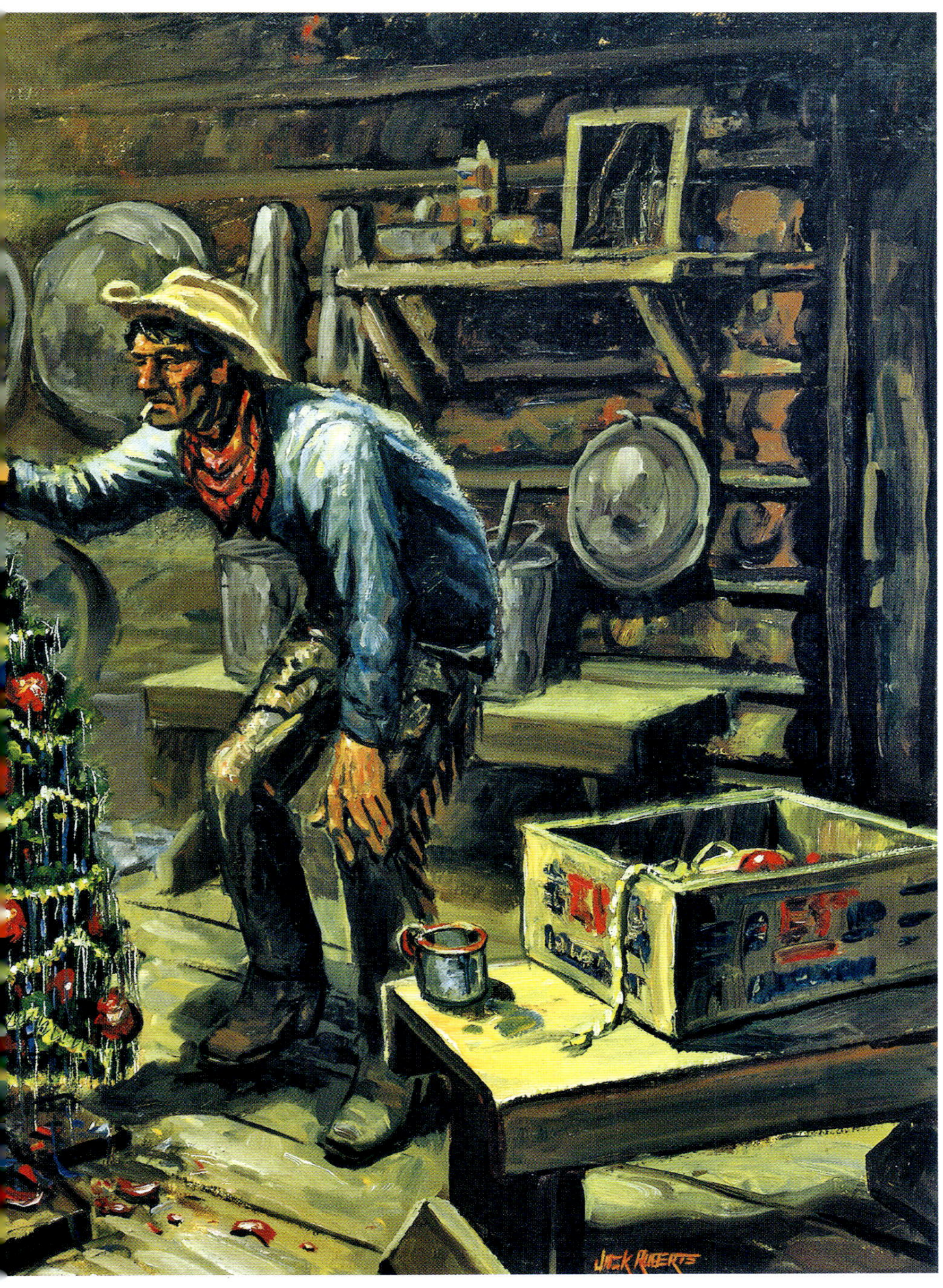

scene painting with the intention of using it for the December picture on its 1965 calendar. The society's staff, however, decided the booze bottle on the bench and the slightly tipsy behavior of the cowboys decorating the Christmas tree might offend some of their "bluenose policy holders." Therefore, the society commissioned Jack to do another painting on a safer theme—"Christmas Gifts"—which it published in place of the Christmas tree scene.[102]

Jack painted new versions of all three paintings, two of which, *Looks 'Bout Right for Me Jim* and *A Surgeon's Touch*, hang in the Leanin' Tree Museum of Western Art. All three were reproduced as greeting cards, but *The Quartet* did not sell well. "Perhaps it's a little crass, or harsh, for a Christmas card," Jack speculated. "The character in the middle was a bit too drunk, I think…Saloon scenes were always good sellers when I was painting cowboys, but apparently it's an altogether different market with Christmas cards. Live and learn, Jack Roberts."[103]

Fortunately for Jack, Leanin' Tree's market was not limited to Christmas cards. Birthday and anniversary cards gave him an opportunity to provide a variety of

A Surgeon's Touch. Leanin' Tree Collection. Photo credit: Leanin' Tree Museum and Sculpture Garden of Western Art, Boulder, Colorado.

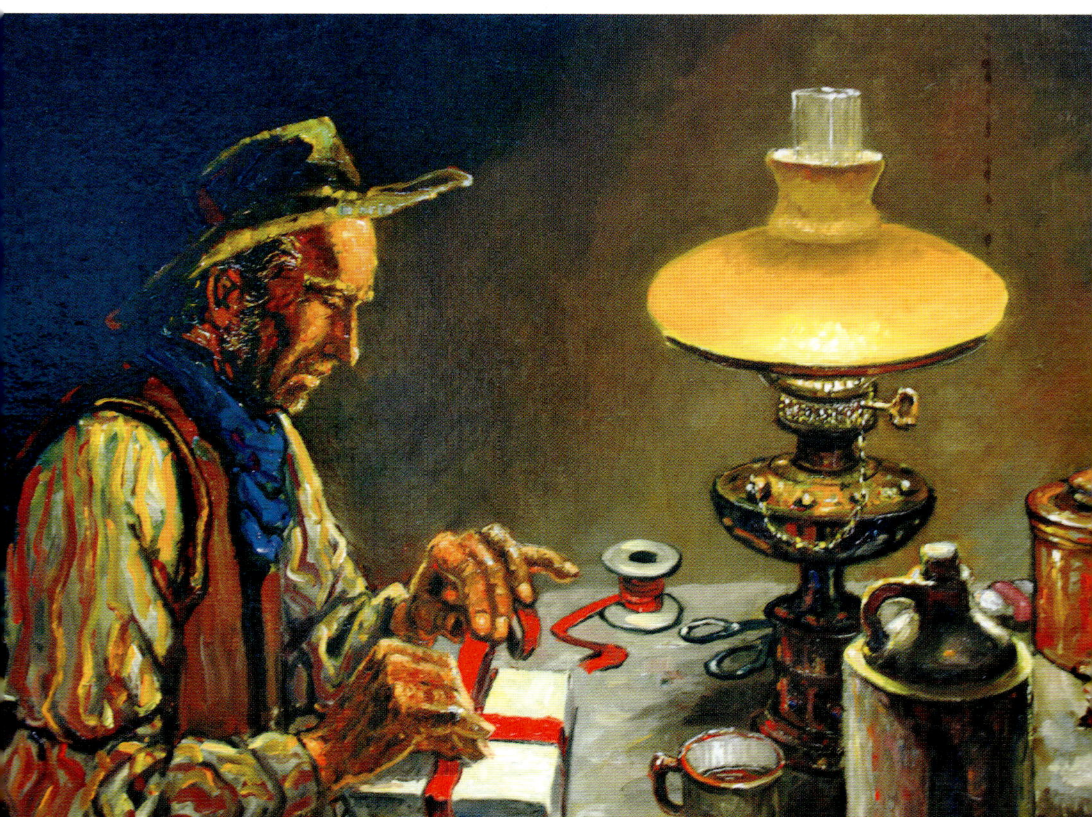

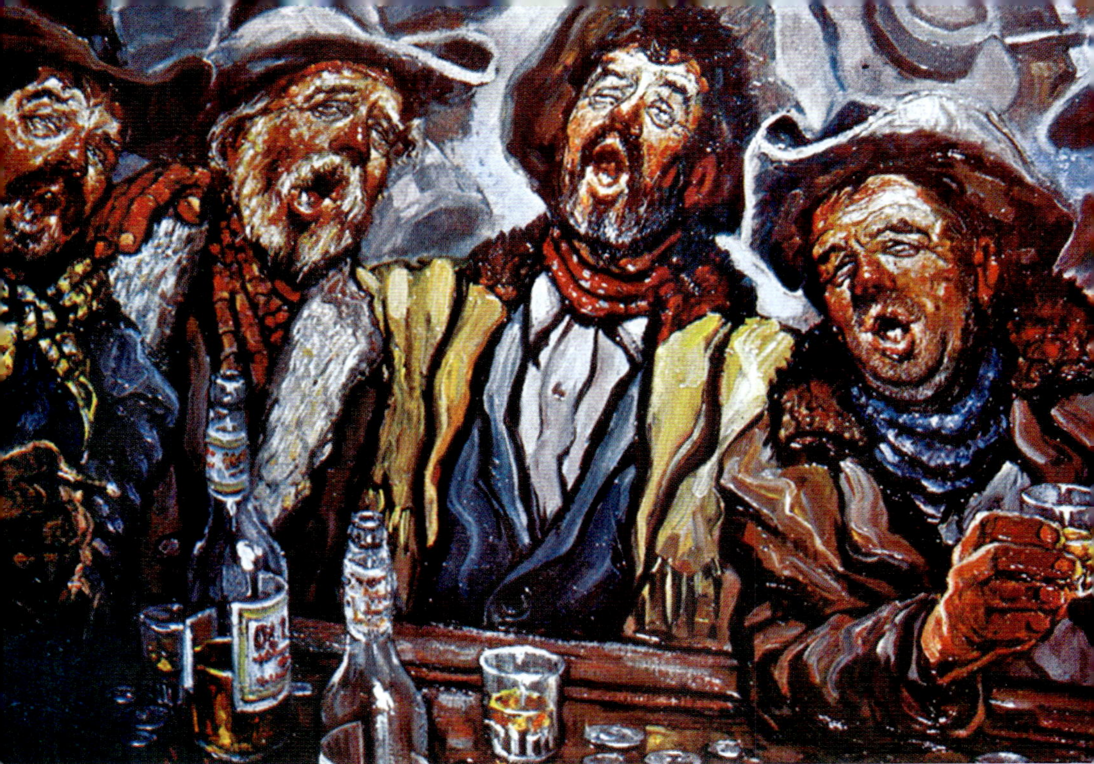

The Quartet. Photo credit: Leanin' Tree Museum and Sculpture Garden of Western Art, Boulder, Colorado.

subjects, including humorous barroom scenes. He appreciated any opportunity to have his paintings reproduced, for as he told Ed on January 20, 1975:

> *It is a matter of professional pride that I continue to be represented in The Leanin' Tree catalog. The prestige that an artist gains is beyond measure, therefore I can make almost any reasonable deal to get in the catalog. Actually I would prefer to loan you my works because I can sell them for much higher prices, particularly if I guarantee a buyer his painting will be in the Leanin' Tree catalog. It has undoubtedly become a status symbol for many western artists and I admit it.*

He was pleased that his colorful, robust and bawdy saloon paintings did well for cards in which humor was paramount, but he was even happier to return after several years to his cowboy roots to document life in the cow camps with warm emotion, nostalgia and authenticity. Annually from 1974 into the 1990s, Jack produced paintings with a cowboy theme for the Leanin' Tree's Christmas line. Intrigued by these paintings, Ed bought many of them for exhibit in the Jack Roberts room in the Leanin' Tree Museum of Western Art.

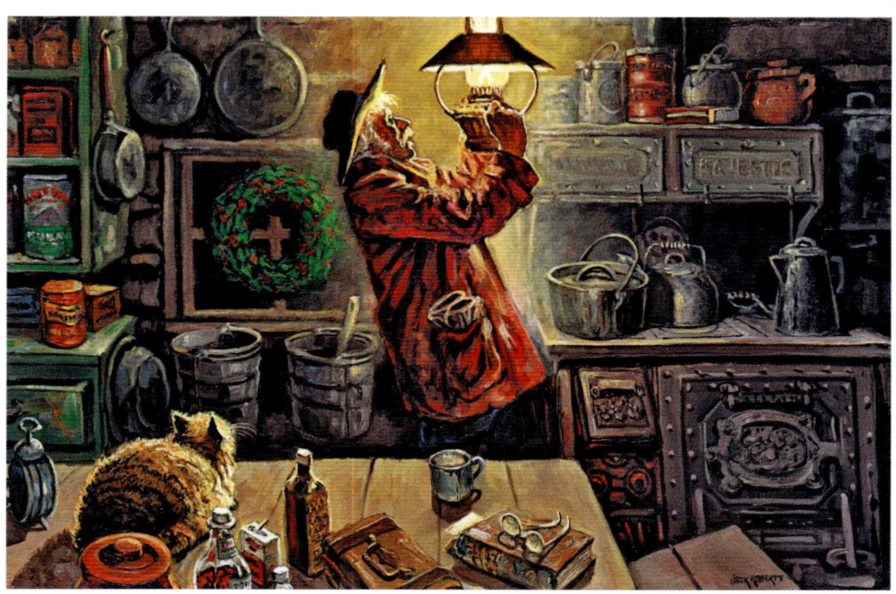

Inside for the Night. Leanin' Tree Collection. Photo credit: Leanin' Tree Museum and Sculpture Garden of Western Art, Boulder, Colorado

Opposite, top: Christmas Bottle. Leanin' Tree Collection. Photo credit: Leanin' Tree Museum and Sculpture Garden of Western Art, Boulder, Colorado.

Opposite, bottom: The Stereoscope. Photo credit: Leanin' Tree Museum and Sculpture Garden of Western Art, Boulder, Colorado. Courtesy of Scott and Lori McInnis..

Jack valued Ed's opinion, and submitted a sketch for each proposed painting to see what he thought of the general idea. Although Ed usually agreed with the concept, there were times when he offered suggestions that Jack incorporated into his paintings. Jack readily accepted Ed's idea to include Blubber Tub, Jack's favorite cat, in many of the paintings to show the gentle side of a tough cowboy and to make the old cow camp look a little more like home. "It was an excellent idea," Jack told Ed's daughter, Jane.[104]

The sentimental aspect of a cowboy's character was a theme Jack developed in many of his paintings for Leanin' Tree. Scenes of a cowboy addressing Christmas cards, wrapping a gift, reading a letter from his sister Nellie or feeding Blubber Tub showed this tender, human side of the otherwise weathered and burley cowboy. Some of the images were humorous, such as *The Christmas Bottle,* depicting two cowboys celebrating a fleeting moment of camaraderie and good humor. Others were nostalgic. *The Stereoscope,* for example, portrayed two cowboys sharing a

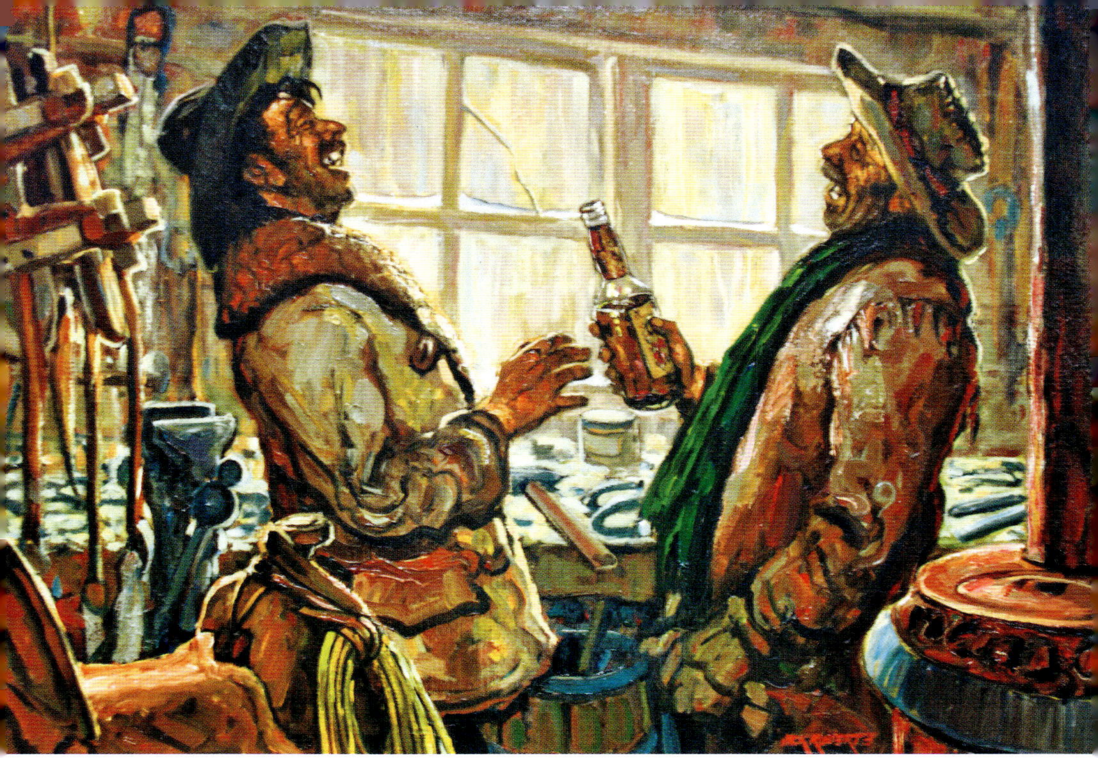

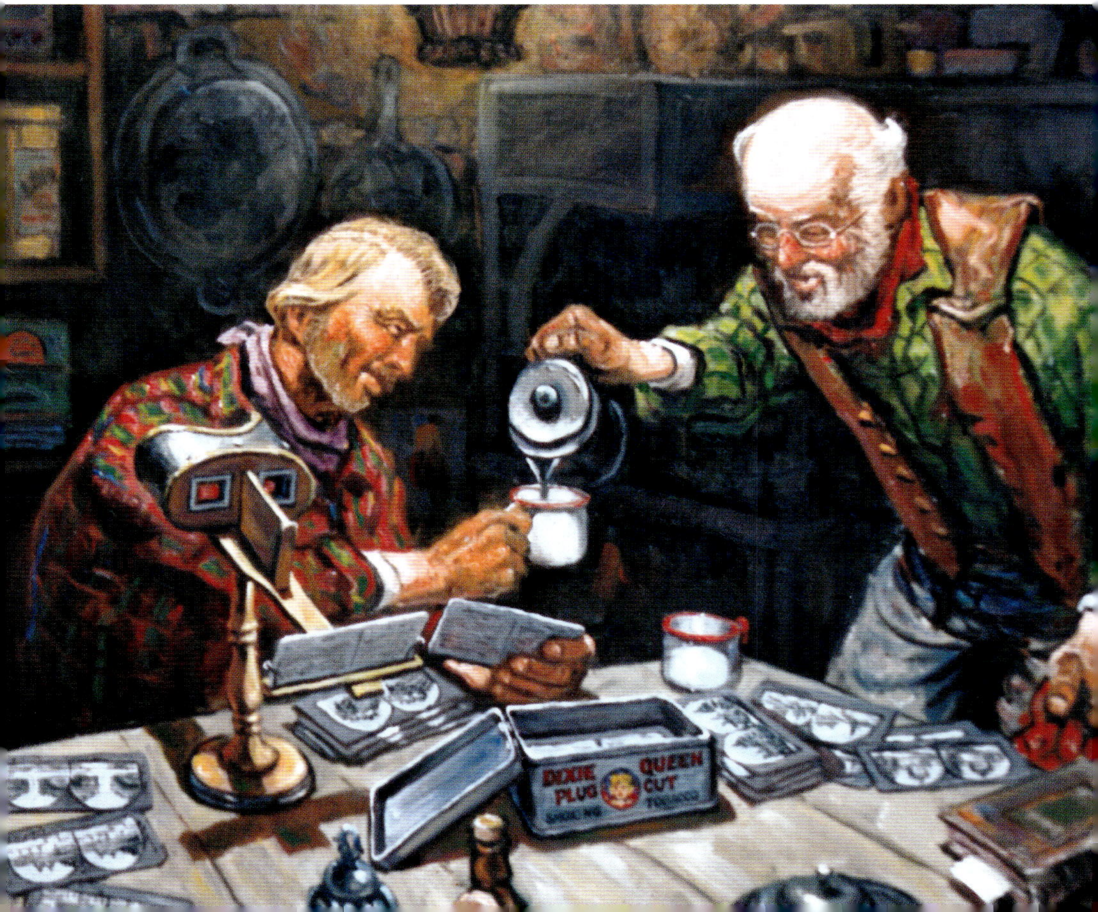

DIXIE QUEEN
PLUG CUT
TOBACCO

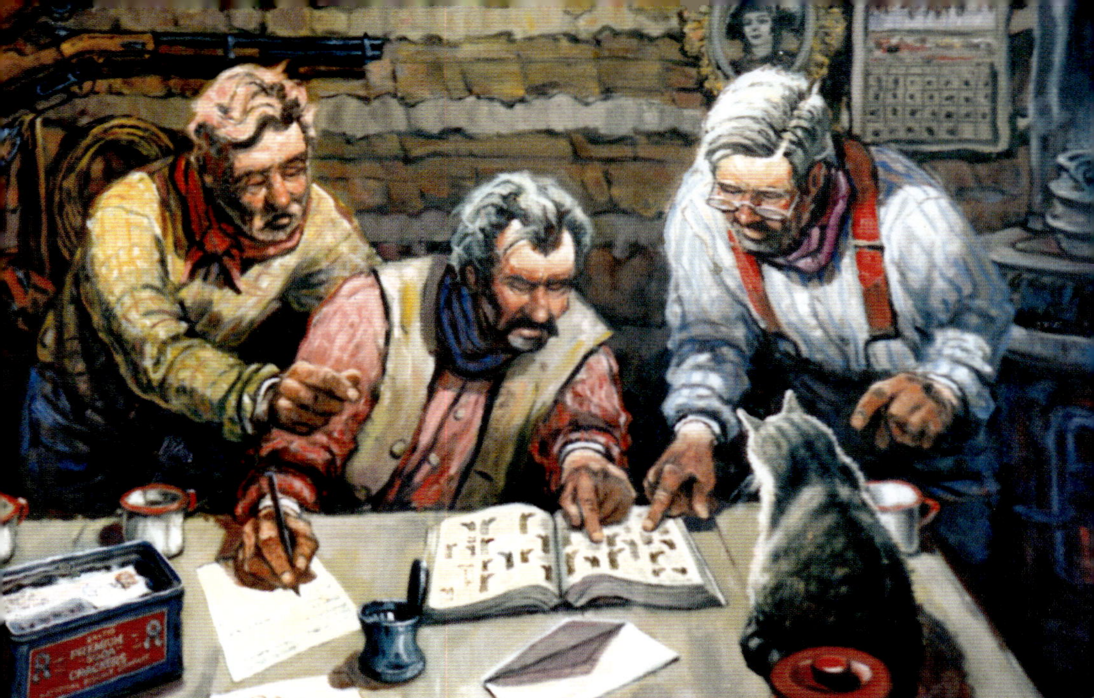

Christmas Catalog. Photo credit: Leanin' Tree Museum and Sculpture Garden of Western Art, Boulder, Colorado. Courtesy of Scott and Lori McInnis.

cup of coffee and enjoying an evening of viewing picturesque places in America through a stereoscope.

Authenticity of detail was crucial to Jack. He studied photographs of antique objects in books and magazines to copy, and he visited museums and antique shops to find period pieces to illustrate in his works. An antique music box, a Dixie Queen cut-plug tobacco tin, a stereoscope, kettles and pots and various kerosene lamps were examples of the historic artifacts Jack portrayed with precision and accuracy. He also drew illustrations within an illustration, as demonstrated in his nostalgic painting *The Christmas Catalog*, which depicts three cowboys putting together an order from an 1897 Sears and Roebuck catalogue. He wanted to show how extensively the catalogue was illustrated because of the large number of semi-illiterate people in rural America. To do so, he covered the open pages with tiny pictures, at which the men are intently pointing. To further the effect, the painting was "composed in such a way that all lines and angles point to the open pages," he explained. "Even the cat has focused his attention to the open pages."[105]

Jack also used illustrations of old photographs or color prints to add detail and fill open spaces on walls. In proposing *A Game of Hearts*, he explained to Jane:

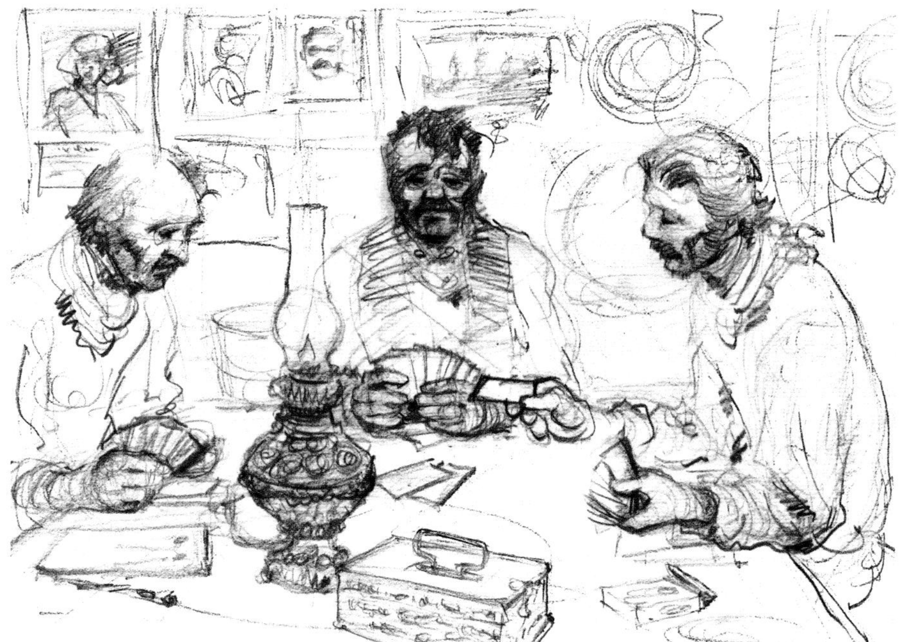

"Game of Hearts" sketch. *Courtesy of Gary Miller.*

The kerosene lamp on the table would make some strong lighting on the characters and the composition could be very dramatic. This is a bunkhouse scene and the log wall in the background would be decorated with Victorian style pictures and calendars, possibly a picture of Teddy Roosevelt. 1905 was a very good year in our history and they did have color reproductions of Charlie Russell's latest paintings. Perhaps such a color print could adorn this otherwise drab dwelling place.[106]

Early in 1981, Ed and Jack talked about a cow camp supper as the theme for that year's Christmas card. Jack immediately set the table for the painting, as described in his letter to Jan Graham, Ed's assistant, on February 9, 1981:

The table is of rough-cut lumber bleached almost white. The dishes are of porcelain, badly chipped, and the pots and pans are the same, with the exception of the baking pan, which is steel. I usually paint at least one old chipped porcelain dishpan hanging on the wall, so you know what I mean. In this painting, most of the food is served in the pans it was cooked in.

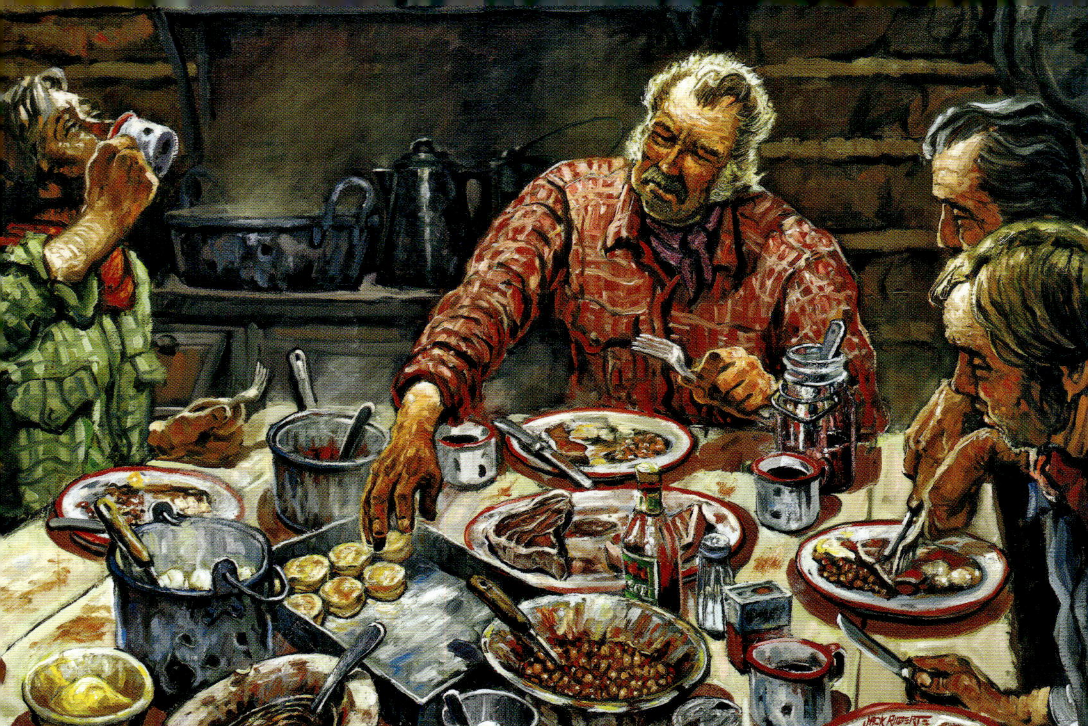

B'lieve I'll Have One More Biscuit. Leanin' Tree Collection. Photo credit: Leanin' Tree Museum and Sculpture Garden of Western Art, Boulder, Colorado.

He wrote again to Jan a month later to say that he had made a mistake in planning the painting: "Please advise Ed that I discovered a monumental oversight in my initial planning of the painting. In my description of the pan-fried steak, boiled potatoes, etc., I forgot that most important item of cowcamp fare—BEANS!" This oversight would be corrected, he assured Jan. "A big bowl of beans will be very clearly shown in the painting."[107]

Leanin' Tree began to include Jack's recipes in the cards that featured food as a central theme. *Sourdough Flapjacks* was the first of this kind. "As a bonus in this painting," he told Ed,

> *I will throw in my recipe for sourdough flapjacks, along with the "starter" formula. This comes from my old cowboy friend, [Andrew] "Mac" McCall…It's a basic recipe, not using any such high society things as eggs or fresh milk or baking powder or yeast. These are ingredients to be found in any cowcamp.*[108]

Jack also gave Ed the recipe for the beans in the painting *Sowbelly and Beans*, which, like the recipe for sourdough flapjacks, he got from Mac McCall. The ingredients were common in the cow camps of Mac's time, Jack explained to Ed:

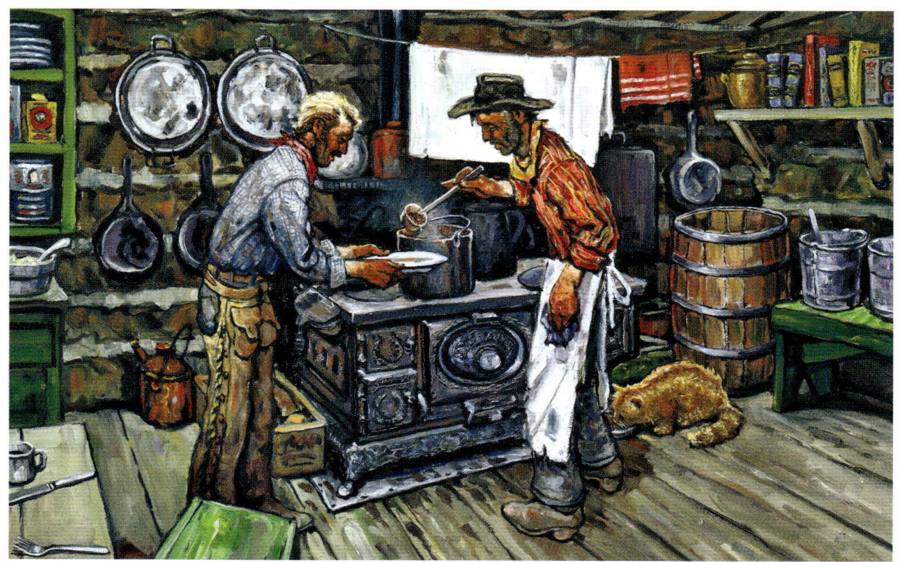

Sowbelly and Beans. Leanin' Tree Collection. Photo credit: Leanin' Tree Museum and Sculpture Garden of Western Art, Boulder, Colorado.

> *All of the trimmings from the salt pork were dumped into the pot and called "sowbelly" and that was never considered a vulgar term. Even today I think it is regarded as merely informal. With due respect to Mac, the recipe should be called "Sowbelly and Beans." Certainly nothing less than that.*[109]

All the reminiscences about Mac McCall and the ditch and cow camps made Jack nostalgic for former days, and he found renewed enjoyment in painting cowboys and illustrating their heritage in western Colorado history. Jack told Ed that he thought of Mac every time he painted a picture of a cowboy. They were, he said, a tribute to "dear old Mac, the quintessential cowboy."[110]

McCall was also the inspiration for Jack's series *Indoor Life of Outdoor Men* completed for Lori and Scott McInnis, who purchased *The Stereoscope* and *The Christmas Catalog* for their collection. After learning that some of the cowboys he knew had worked for Lori's father or grandfather at the David Smith Ranches near Meeker, Colorado, Jack decided to use images of his old cowboy friends for the series. Again, his memory focused on Mac, as he explained in his letter to Scott on December 7, 1993:

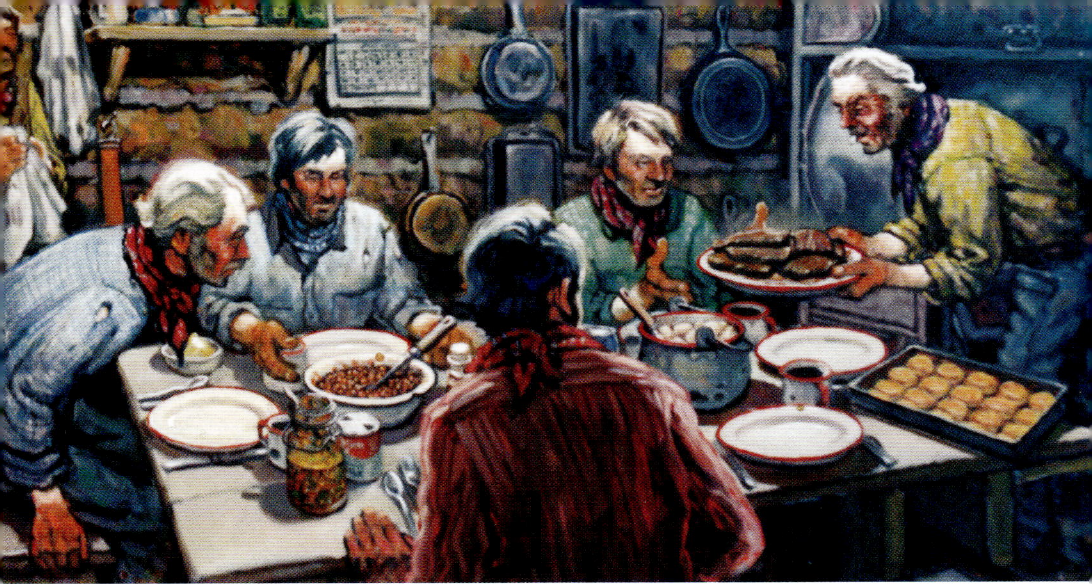

Ditch Camp Dinner. Courtesy of Scott and Lori McInnis.

> *Many years have passed and old Mac died long ago, but I still think of him when I paint a cowcamp, or ditchcamp, interior scene. He was on my mind when I painted the old ramrod seating himself at the left end of the table in the "Dinner at Ditchcamp" painting. The other men are stereotypes that I invented but old Mac is very special…Old Mac has been a strong influence in my career. But there have been other remarkable men I rode with and I think I paint composite images of them without realizing it.*

The passion Jack felt in telling the cowboy's colorful and romantic story is reflected in the Leanin' Tree paintings and those purchased by Scott and Lori McInnis. Reflecting on Jack's paintings and his career, Ed Trumble declared, "He was one helluva artist."[111]

OLD WEST SALOONS, OSGOOD'S REDSTONE AND THE FRONTIER PRESS

Several important commissions at the peak of Jack's career gave him the opportunity to illustrate a variety of topics. Three of them came from Ken Johnson, publisher of the *Grand Junction Daily Sentinel* and owner of Cleveholm Manor, better known as the Redstone Castle, located about a mile down the Crystal River Valley from Jack's studio.

The first commission was for a series of six saloon scenes for Peg Johnson, Ken's wife. The barroom scenes were typical of his early saloon paintings with, in Jack's own words, depictions of "rowdy, boisterous action," "lusty, bawdy moods" and "Rubensian girls." As for the latter, he told Ken, "I am in full agreement with America's frontiersmen, along with Peter Paul Rubens, on their ideas of feminine beauty. I don't like skinny women." Besides, Jack insisted, portraying women who resembled "Babe Ruth more than Farrah Fawcett-Majors" and men with ugly or missing teeth was in the interest of truth and authenticity. Ken agreed: "I like your Rubens women and as long as you and I are happy, who else counts."

Jack designed the fourth painting in the series, *The Dancers*, to depict "a rowdy, boisterous hoe-down" with music so good "that even the bartender joins the fun." Ken was delighted with it. "Once again your painting is terrific," he noted.[112]

Even before Jack finished the saloon paintings, Ken had another project in mind: a series of paintings depicting the opulence and industry of early Redstone and its founder, John Cleveland Osgood. "Before too long,"

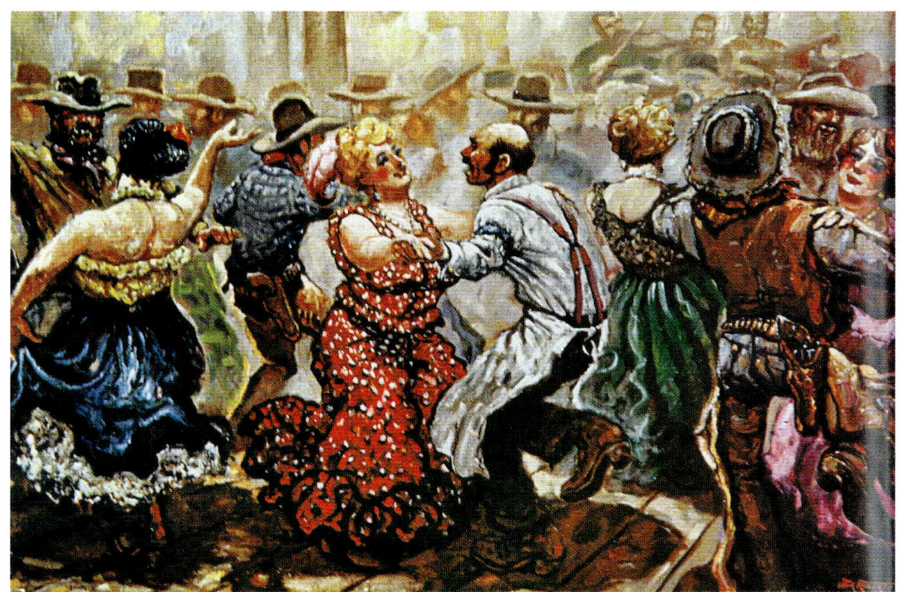

The Dancers. Courtesy of Ken Johnson.

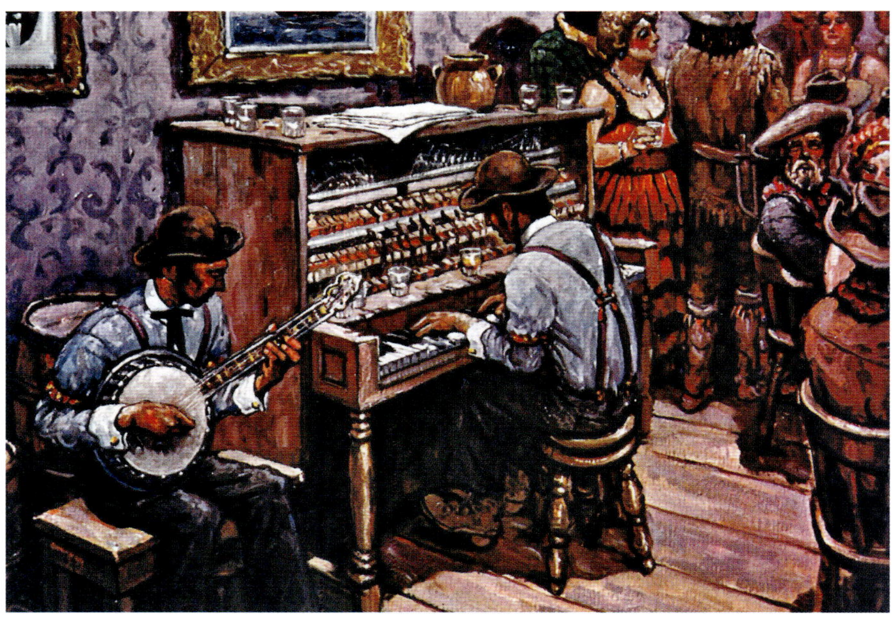

The Entertainers. Courtesy of Ken Johnson.

he wrote to Jack, "let's get together and talk about an 'Osgood' series for Redstone. Maybe you'd like to sketch out some thoughts and I will do the same—but mine will be with words!"[113] Jack immediately set to work, but preparations for a second venture in marriage briefly interrupted his progress. In early March, he traveled to Liberty, Missouri, to visit Mary Margaret Walker and her parents, Lyn and Haywood, to discuss wedding plans. Jack and the Walkers were longtime friends, dating back to the Hanging Lake days when Jack first took an interest in Mary Margaret. She was far too young for Jack then, the Walkers thought, but in 1978, she and they agreed to the marriage, which took place in June.

Between trips to Missouri to attend to some of Mary Margaret's business and to move her to Colorado, Jack researched John Osgood. He sorted through the Osgood files at the Denver Public Library and read the two main sources on him available at the time: *Pioneer Steelmaker in the West: The Colorado Fuel and Iron Company, 1872–1903* by H. Lee Scamehorn and George S. McGovern and Leonard F. Guttridge's *The Great Coalfield War.* On May 3, 1978, Jack wrote to Ken:

> *At this time I am reading George McGovern's book on the Great Coalfield War, which is essentially a history of the fight for control of Colorado's coal mines. Osgood is not treated as kindly in this book as he was in Scamehorn's "Pioneer Steelmaker of the West." There is a lot more documented evidence on Osgood than I previously thought. McGovern has some interesting opinions about Osgood. While he still considers him to be a "robber baron" he commends his experiments in "company paternalism" in Redstone.*

"I think," Ken responded, "I would be a little leery of either the C.F.&I. version or the McGovern version—each one has its own bias and I'm sure Osgood fits somewhere in between." Jack agreed with McGovern and Guttridge that Osgood was an "enigmatic entrepreneur" who was a product of his times and environment. "Osgood was a scoundrel, no doubt about it, but within that man somewhere was something as pure as the salt in the air." Even with his personal faults, Jack concluded, "he was still a pioneer in industrial paternalism and I admire him."[114]

With his opinion of Osgood set, Jack completed a series of nine paintings, which still hang in the Redstone Castle. Each scene captured the spirit and time of Redstone's glory at the beginning of the twentieth century. Of these, *The Host,* Jack's depiction of Osgood toasting guests at a dinner party, and *The*

Recital—featuring his wife, Alma, fondly known as Lady Bountiful, playing a gilded piano during a recital for guests—depicted the lavish lifestyle the Osgoods enjoyed in the elegant Cleveholm Manor. The paintings of Lady Bountiful riding into Redstone in her carriage to visit the villagers (*Lady Bountiful*) and the Christmas party at which children were gathered to receive gifts (*The Christmas Party*) represented the Osgoods' benevolence. *The Pagoda*, showing a group of villagers enjoying a concert on the lawn, added a romantic touch. "This is turn-of-the-century America," Jack explained, "with the ladies' big hats and parasols, and the gentlemen's straw hats and celluloid collars. And the children's bonnets, knickers and starched linen."[115]

Two paintings emphasized the industrial aspect of the Redstone story. *The Coke Ovens*, with its smoke and pollution, steam locomotives, rail cars and coal tipple, brought industrial Redstone to life while *Coal Basin* depicted the mine and camp that supplied the coal for the ovens. Of the paintings in this series, Jack liked that one the best. "I'm bragging," he confided to Ken, "but I believe it is something of value. Besides being historically accurate, it is a beautiful work of art. The sun is just setting in Coal Basin in late September of 1902, and the wives are building their fires to prepare dinner for their men. Was it really a better way of life then? You're damn right it was!" For Jack, having the paintings on display in the Redstone Castle was a matter of great pride, and he was delighted that the "pretty-girl guides" were using them during Castle tours as a part of their "oral culture."[116]

Ken soon had another assignment for Jack. He proposed a series of paintings on the pioneer newspapers of Colorado. Intrigued by the topic, Jack obtained several books and articles on the subject, and after further research in Denver, he concluded that the project had "exciting prospects." Sharing Jack's enthusiasm, Ken joined the effort by doing his own extensive research. Together they planned the scenes for the eight-piece series on the frontier press, with Ken offering acute suggestions. "I agree with your showing a Washington Hand Press either being unloaded or coming over a rough mountain road with canvas flapping," he wrote to Jack on March 21, 1979. "How about an editor at one of the old typesetters? And what about a typesetter sitting at an old steam-powered linotype machine?"

In late March, Jack sent Ken sketches of the proposed first three paintings. *The Washington Hand Press* depicted the press after it had been unloaded onto a boardwalk in front of a newspaper office. *The Editor* pictured the subject sitting at a small press in a log building with a six-shooter strapped to his

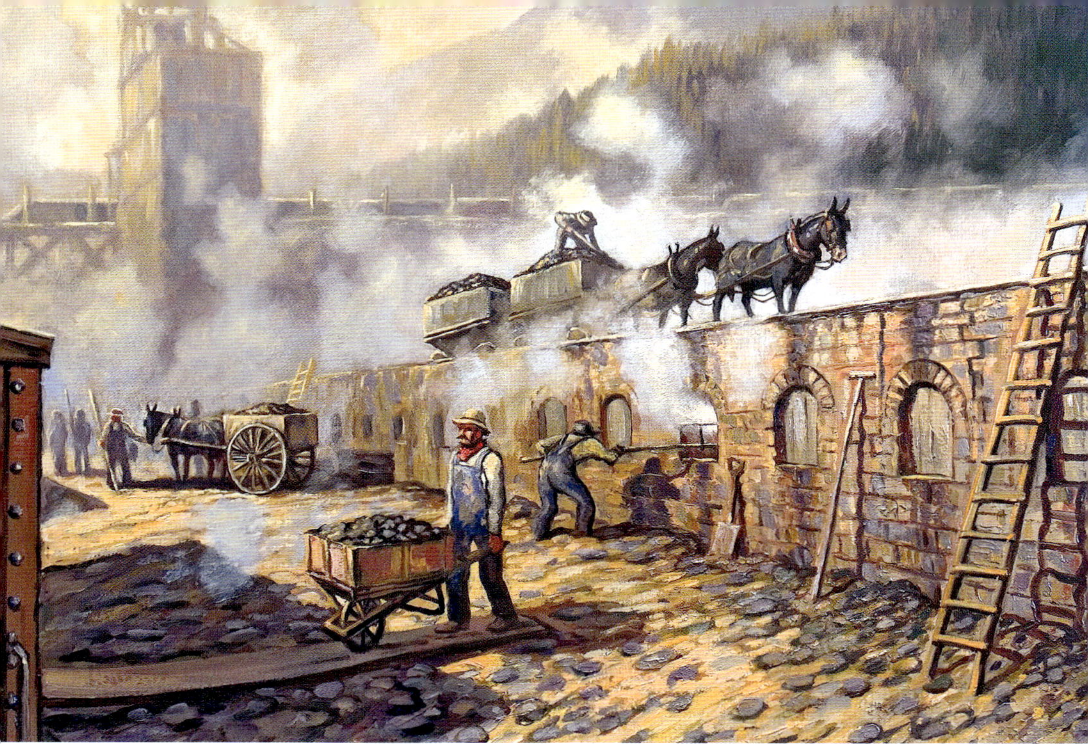

The Coke Ovens. Courtesy of Ken Johnson.

waist. *The Typesetter* featured a man with a green eyeshade and black printers' sleeves working at type cases under the light of a coal oil lamp.

Ken generally liked the scenes as presented but balked at a couple of details. "I really do not know of any early Colorado editors who wore a gun strapped around their waist," he stated. Nor did he know of any pistol-packing typesetters, and the idea of a log building was probably not the way to go. Along with historical accuracy, he stressed, it was just as important to set the right color and tone for the paintings. Therefore, he suggested:

> *As we go into this series, let's be sure that we capture the same sense of color that you established in your "Coke Ovens" of Redstone series—that's superb and the choice of colors establishes a mood the others in the series do not quite convey. I want to be sure our newspaper series has a special air about it that only your skill and choice of colors can impart.*[117]

"Gun-toting newsmen are out," Jack conceded as he organized his thoughts more clearly, and the editor would be typing notes on an 1874 Remington typewriter by light of a coal oil lamp in makeshift quarters rather than in a log structure. Jack finalized his sketches for the eight proposed paintings in June 1979. Writing to Ken on June 21, he noted:

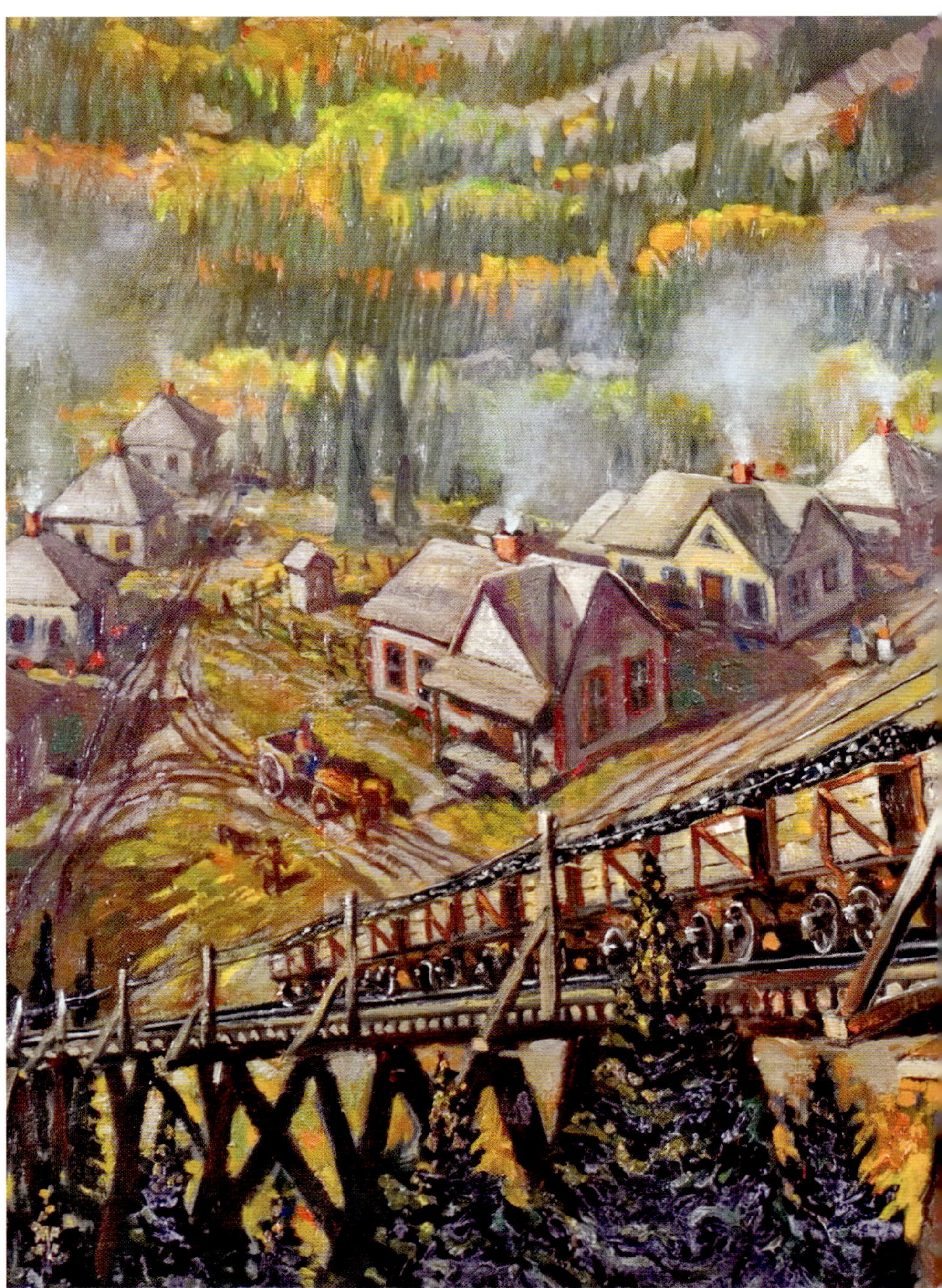

Coal Basin. Courtesy of Ken Johnson.

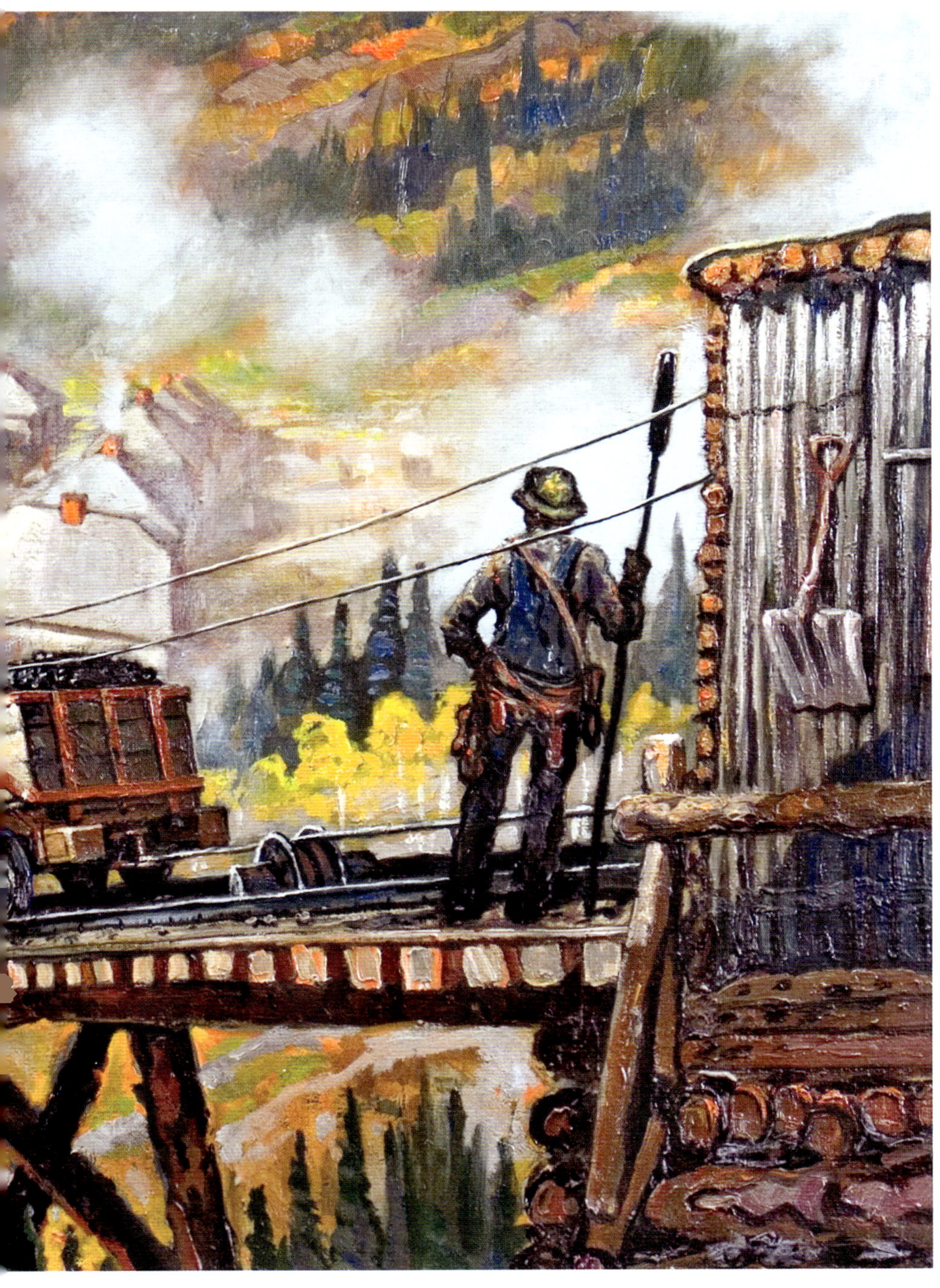

The sketches submitted here represent many hours of research. I'm convinced that the eight paintings will present a plausible, colorful and romantic portrayal of old-time journalism in Colorado. The paintings are composed with the purpose of depicting the most commonly known traditions and character-types of journalism and at the same time motivating the main theme of pioneer newspapering in Colorado. The characters and situations are instantly recognizable to most people and no explanations are really necessary.

The theme presents a wide variety of subject matter. An artifact or machine depicted in one painting is not repeated in another and there are different color schemes and light-dark compositions.

The collaboration between artist and editor guaranteed a series rich in nostalgia and historic detail. As a prominent newsman, Ken brought his vast knowledge of early newspaper publication to the project. Jack relied on his expertise to make sure the portrayals were accurate. Then he told the story through characterization, tone and setting. "Johnson would make suggestions and I'd put it in graphic form," Jack recalled in a 1993 interview published in the *Rocky Mountain News*. When finished, the series was a pictorial history of the boom time in Colorado between 1880 and 1900 when newspapers first

The Editor. Courtesy of Ken Johnson.

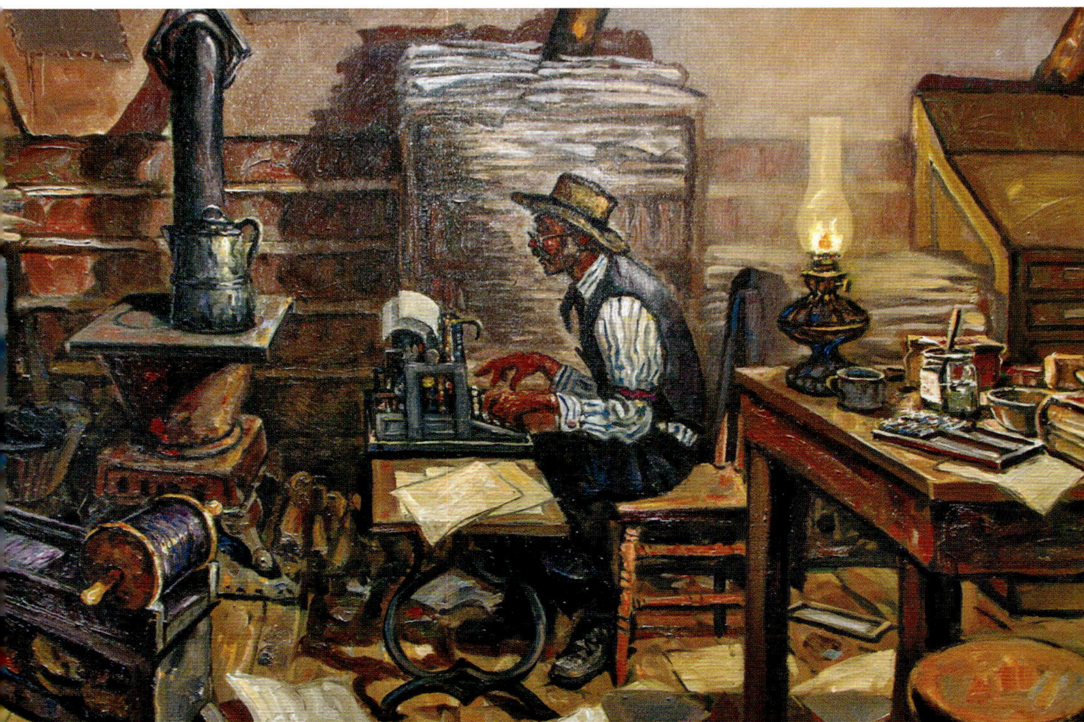

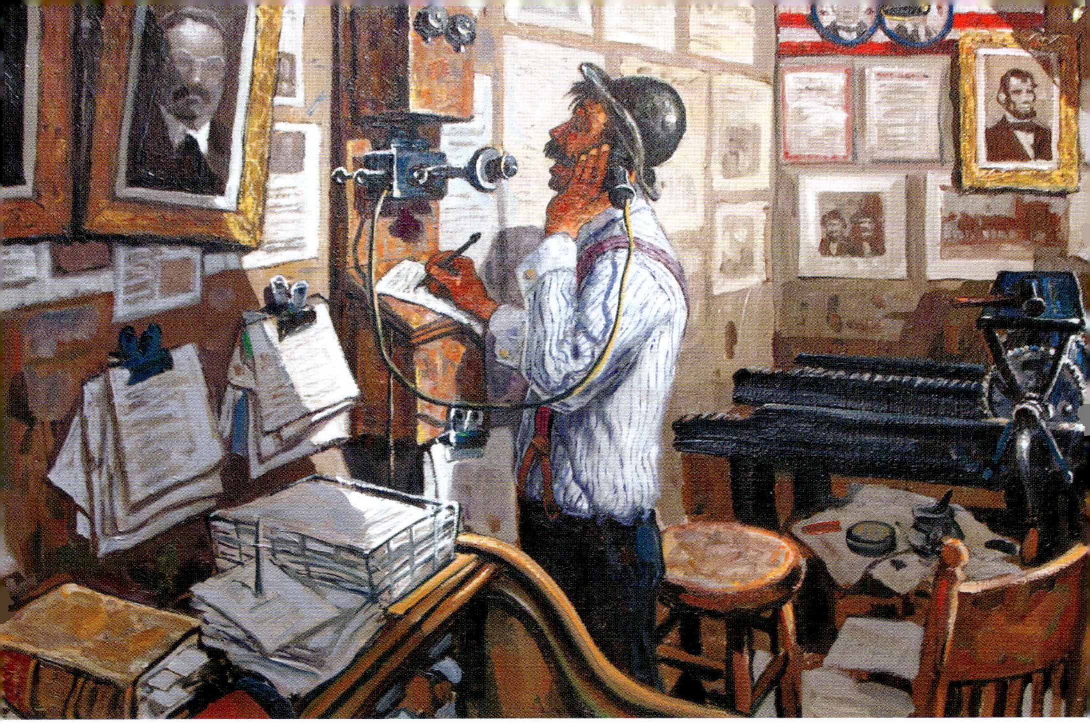

The Reporter. Courtesy of Ken Johnson.

appeared in mining camps. Beginning with *The Editor* in 1880 bent over his 1874 Remington typewriter in his tent and continuing to *The Reporter* in 1900 talking on a telephone, the paintings traced the evolution of the press in the American West. It was a story of a romantic era, Jack explained, during which the press strove through boosting community pride to eliminate the frontier. The early press disappeared with the closing of the mining camps, as Jack observed in *The Frontier Press*, an illustrated booklet he compiled to accompany the paintings:

> *Gone were the wild mining camps with editors living in leaky tents and publishing four-page weeklies on an old Washington Hand Press. The old treadle platen job press was in a museum. The Typesetter with his compositor's stick was gone. The Snowshoe Express was gone.*
>
> *The frontier press left a legacy. They held the torch that illuminated the path for the hundreds who would follow them.*

Ken Johnson donated the eight paintings to the Colorado Press Association in 1989. In 1993, the association featured the series during the annual Colorado Press Convention at the Brown Palace in Denver. In reviewing the collection, Alan Dumas of the *Rocky Mountain News* called Jack a "Pioneer Impressionist." "Each painting suggests a story, making the work reminiscent of Norman Rockwell's," he wrote. Of these eight paintings, *The Editor* was Jack's favorite, and he considered it the most important work he had ever done. It set the tone and atmosphere for the entire series through which he believed he had accomplished something significant and unique in western history. No other artist, he claimed, had even thought of painting newspapermen in a frontier setting. In an interview published in *Convention Daily*, he observed: "I'm lucky to have found a market for the type of thing I do. Regardless of my position in the western art world, I still think I'm very lucky to be a part of it." Without doubt, the series further established Jack's legacy as a western history illustrator.

A BEAR HUNT AND A TRAIN ROBBERY

From 1972 until 1984, Jack painted one major historical series a year. In 1983, the subject was President Theodore Roosevelt's 1905 hunting expedition in western Colorado. Commissioned by W.R. Hall of Grand Junction, the series of twelve oil paintings was entitled the *Colorado Bear Hunt, 1905*. To document the paintings, Jack used historic photographs and two major sources: Roosevelt's personal account of the hunt published as a chapter in his *Outdoor Pastimes of an American Hunter* and that of head guide John Goff in "The President's Bear Hunt" published in *Outdoor Life* in July 1905. The written words of these two men set the stage for Jack's illustrations of this interesting event. The series was one of his finest. With Teddy Roosevelt being his hero, it also was his favorite.

Jack presented the twelve paintings for possible publication as a calendar, with each month representing a distinct aspect of the hunt. *East Divide Creek* (January), set the scene as the hunting party neared its camp, which President Roosevelt described in the following way:

> *This first day we rode about twenty miles to where camp was pitched on the upper waters of East Divide Creek* [south of Silt, Colorado]. *It was a picturesque spot. At this altitude it was still late winter and the snow lay in drifts, even in the creek bottom, while the stream itself was not yet clear from ice.*[118]

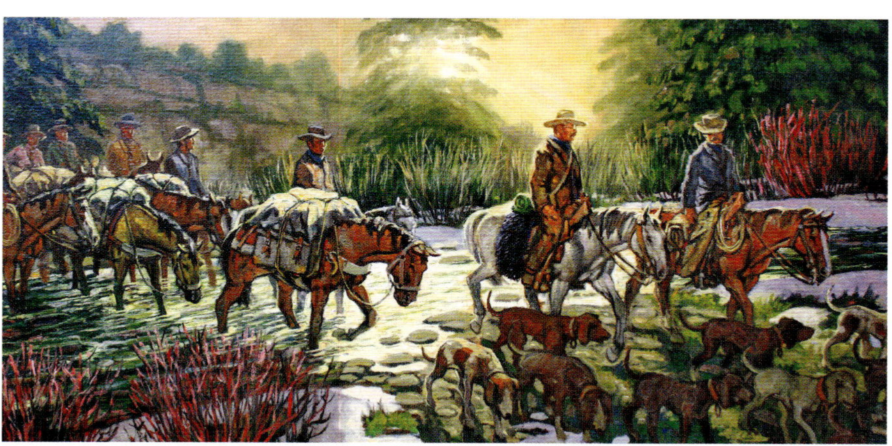

East Divide Creek. Jack Roberts's Roosevelt Series. *W.R. Hall Collection. Courtesy of the Museum of Western Colorado, Grand Junction, Colorado.*

Jack's depiction of the event shows the horses treading through the snow, the hunting hounds leading the way, while in the background a shimmer of light highlights this scene of tranquil passage.

Just beyond this point, the party welcomed the sight of the camp, which the president described as follows:

> *The tents were pitched in a grove of leafless aspens and great spruces, beside the rushing, ice-rimmed brook. The cook tent, with its stove, was an attractive place on the cool mornings and in stormy weather. [Jack] Fry, the cook, a most competent man, had rigged up a table, and we had folding camp-chairs—luxuries utterly unknown to my former camping trips.*[119]

The Dining Tent (February) is Jack's version, faithfully rendered from a historic photograph, of John Goff's account of the first evening meal:

> *We reached camp at 4:30 P.M., where Jack Fry had dinner ready. The party sat down to a bill of fare of chicken pot pie, stewed tomatoes, mashed potatoes, hot biscuits, corn cooked in cream, canned peaches, pumpkin pie and sauces. The President ate heartily, remarking as he finished: "This is better than we have at the White House; I feel that I ought not eat any more, but [redacted] Doctor [Alexander Lambert], please pass me another biscuit."*[120]

The next day the party turned their thoughts to the hunt. *The Hunting Party* (March) is based on President Roosevelt's observation that "[a]s guides and

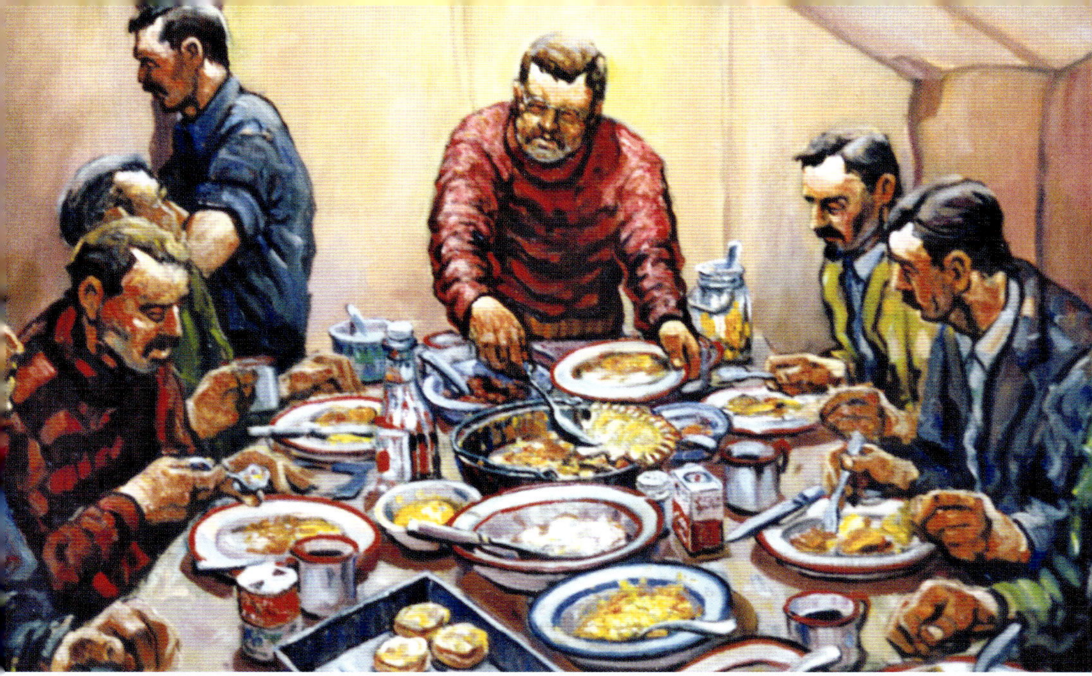

The Dining Tent. Jack Roberts's Roosevelt Series. *W.R. Hall Collection. Courtesy of the Museum of Western Colorado, Grand Junction, Colorado.*

hunters we had John Goff and Jake Borah, than whom there are no better men at their work of hunting bear in the mountains with hounds." The painting for April, *The Hounds*, shows the president riding through the spring snow with some of the twenty-six hounds and four half-blood terriers that were an essential element of the hunt, as the president noted: "The hounds were most interesting, and showed all the variations of character and temper to be expected in such a pack; a pack in which performance counted for everything and pedigree for nothing." Skip, a mongrel terrier, became so attached to Roosevelt that Goff gave him to the president to take back to the White House.[121]

The Chief Executive (May) depicts President Roosevelt in his tent working on official business late into the night, and *The Banjo Player* (June) features Joe Fosto of Glenwood Springs, who provided the only entertainment for the expedition. He played his banjo and sang pioneer songs. He also furnished a few packhorses for the hunt from his stables near Glenwood Springs.

Big Bear Country (July) captures a scene during the second day of the hunt, described here in the president's own words:

> [W]*e rode off early* [in the morning], *taking with us all twenty-six hounds and the four terriers. We…rode up a valley and then scrambled laboriously up the mountain-side to the top of the snow-covered divide.*

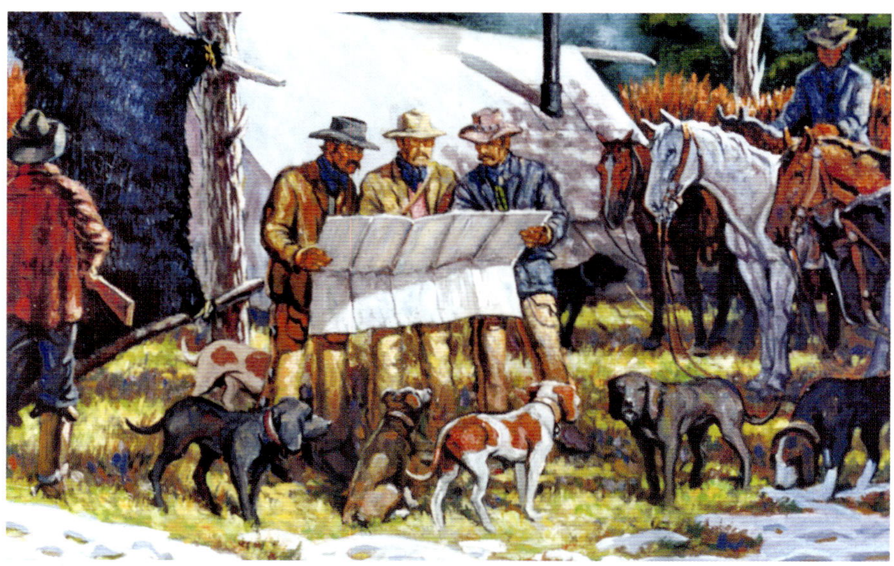

The Hunting Party. Jack Roberts's Roosevelt Series. *W.R. Hall Collection. Courtesy of the Museum of Western Colorado, Grand Junction , Colorado.*

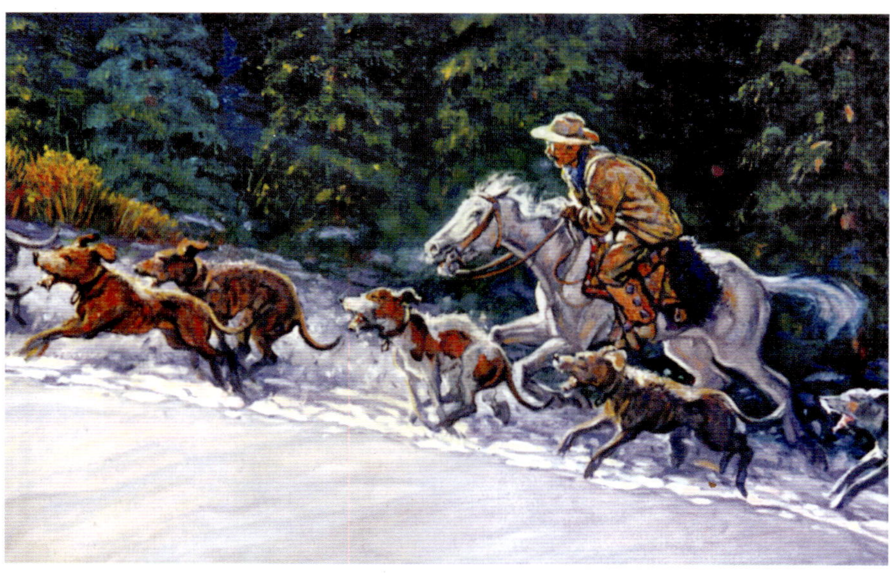

The Hounds. Jack Roberts's Roosevelt Series. *W.R. Hall Collection. Courtesy of the Museum of Western Colorado, Grand Junction, Colorado.*

Opposite, top: Chief Executive. Jack Roberts's Roosevelt Series. *W.R. Hall Collection. Courtesy of the Museum of Western Colorado, Grand Junction, Colorado.*

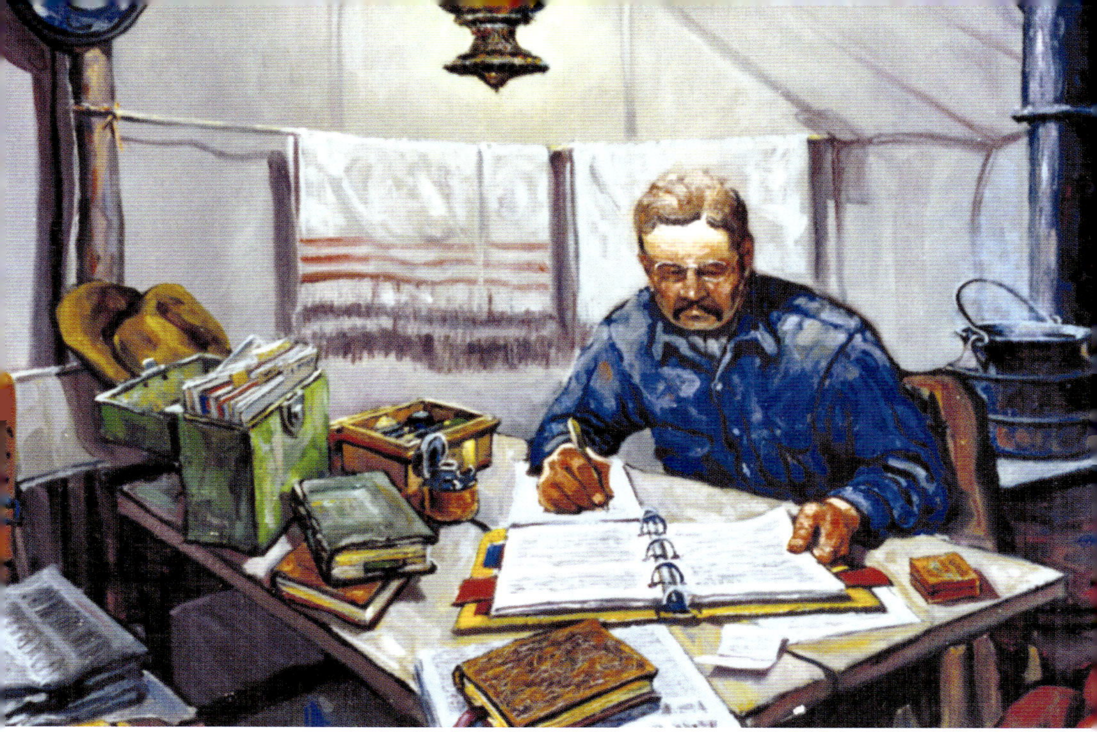

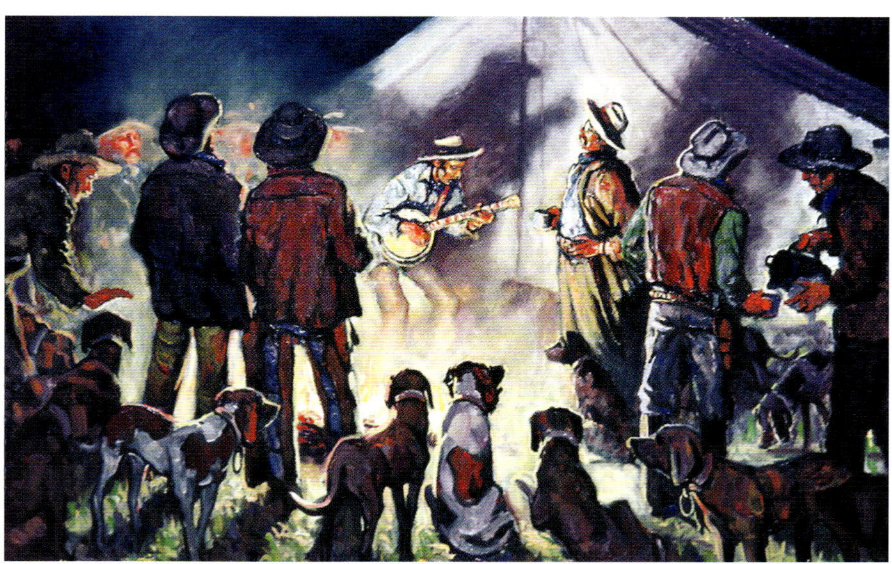

The Banjo Player. Jack Roberts's Roosevelt Series. *W.R. Hall Collection. Courtesy of the Museum of Western Colorado, Grand Junction, Colorado.*

Here the snow was three feet deep in places, and the horses plunged and floundered as we worked our way in single file through the drifts…Opposite us was a high and very rugged mountain-side covered with a growth of pinyon…its precipitous flanks broken by ledges and scored by gullies and ravines.[122]

The hunters saw the bear they had been tracking all morning, surrounded and "worried" by the hounds, on the opposite mountainside. The president described what followed:

It was a hard climb up to where they were, and we had to lead the horses. Just as we came in sight of him [the bear], across a deep gully which ran down the sheer mountain-side, he broke bay and started off, threatening the foremost of the pack as they dared to approach him. They were all around him, and for a minute I could not fire; then as he passed under a pinyon I got a clear view of his great round stern and pulled the trigger. The bullet broke both his hips, and he rolled down hill, the hounds yelling with excitement as they closed in on him. He could still play havoc with the pack, and there was need to kill him at once. I leaped and slid down my side of the gully as he rolled down his; at the bottom he stopped and raised himself on his fore quarters; and with another bullet I broke his back between the shoulders.[123]

The large male bear was one of ten killed during the hunt.

Big Bear Country. Jack Roberts's Roosevelt Series. W.R. Hall Collection. Courtesy of the Museum of Western Colorado, Grand Junction, Colorado.

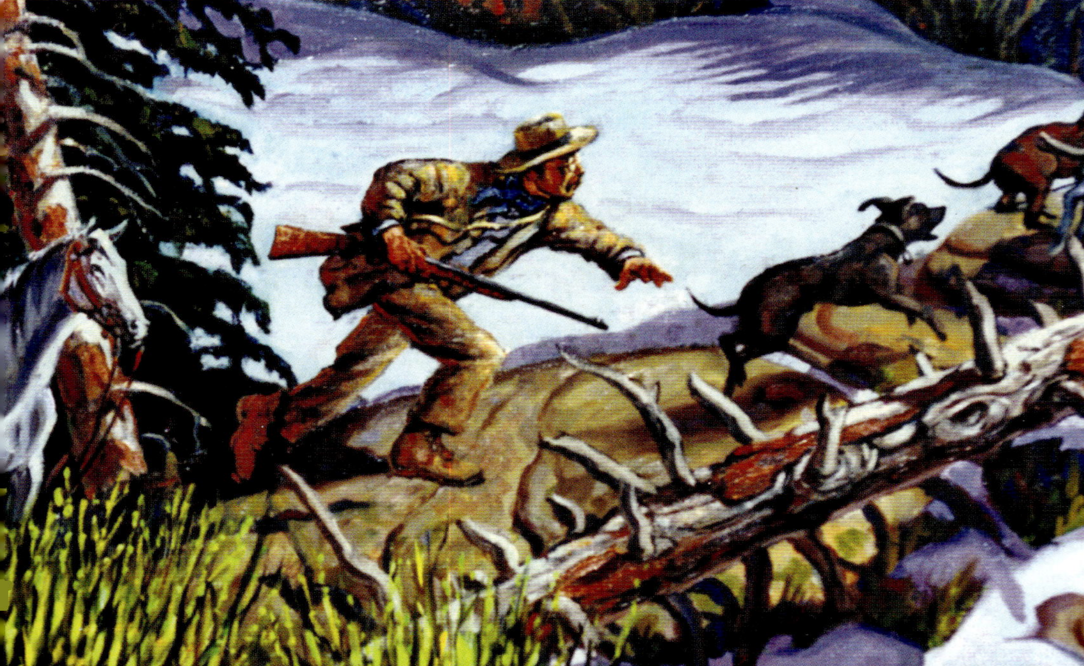

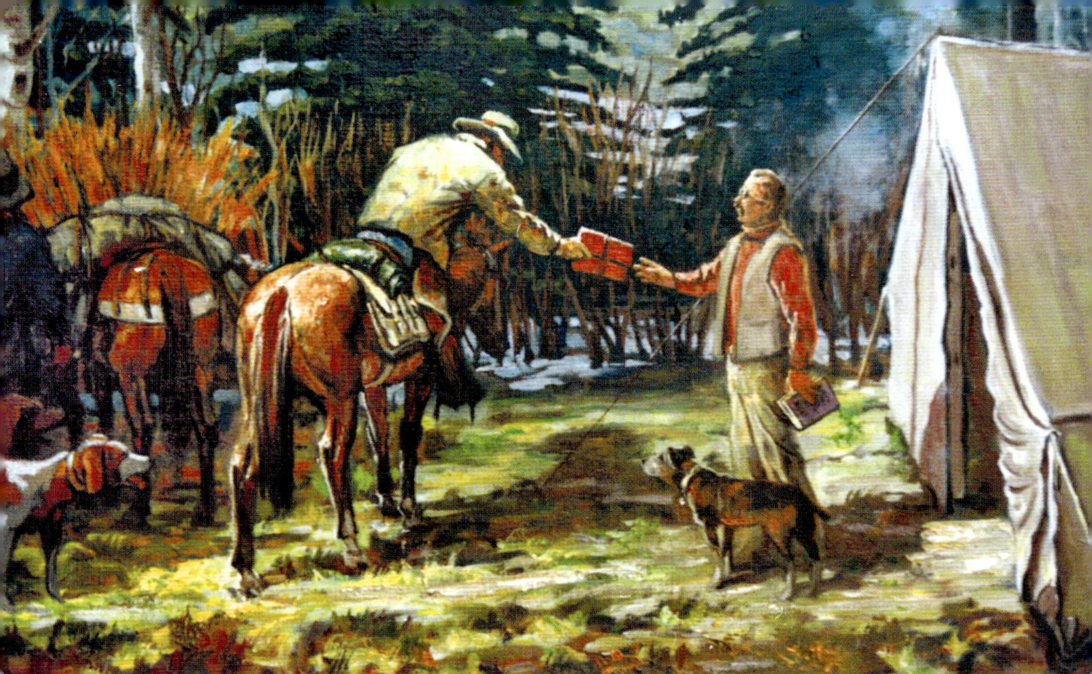

The Courier. Jack Roberts's Roosevelt Series. *W.R. Hall Collection. Courtesy of the Museum of Western Colorado, Grand Junction, Colorado.*

During the three-week hunt, the Hotel Colorado in Glenwood Springs was the "Little White House," where Secretary of State William Loeb set up his office with telegraph service to Washington, D.C. Elmer Chapman, an early day rancher in the Divide Creek region, was selected to be the courier to make daily horseback contact between Loeb and the president. *The Courier* (August) is Jack's representation of that mission.

In *The Headwaters* (September), Jack chronicled a reconnoitering trip to the West Divide area to locate a new campsite. At the new location, *Camp Roosevelt* (October), the president noted:

> *It was a long ride to camp, and darkness had fallen by the time we caught the gleam of the lighted tents across the dark stream…But the days were very enjoyable…It was good fun to be twelve hours in the saddle in such wild and beautiful country, to look at and listen to the hounds as they worked, and finally to see the bear treed and looking down at the maddened pack baying beneath.*[124]

In each of these scenes, Jack's meticulous choice of color, density, light and shadow brought the president's observations to life.

The Little Blue School House (November) records the crowning moment of the president's visit for the people of the area. It was a festive occasion, according to Roosevelt:

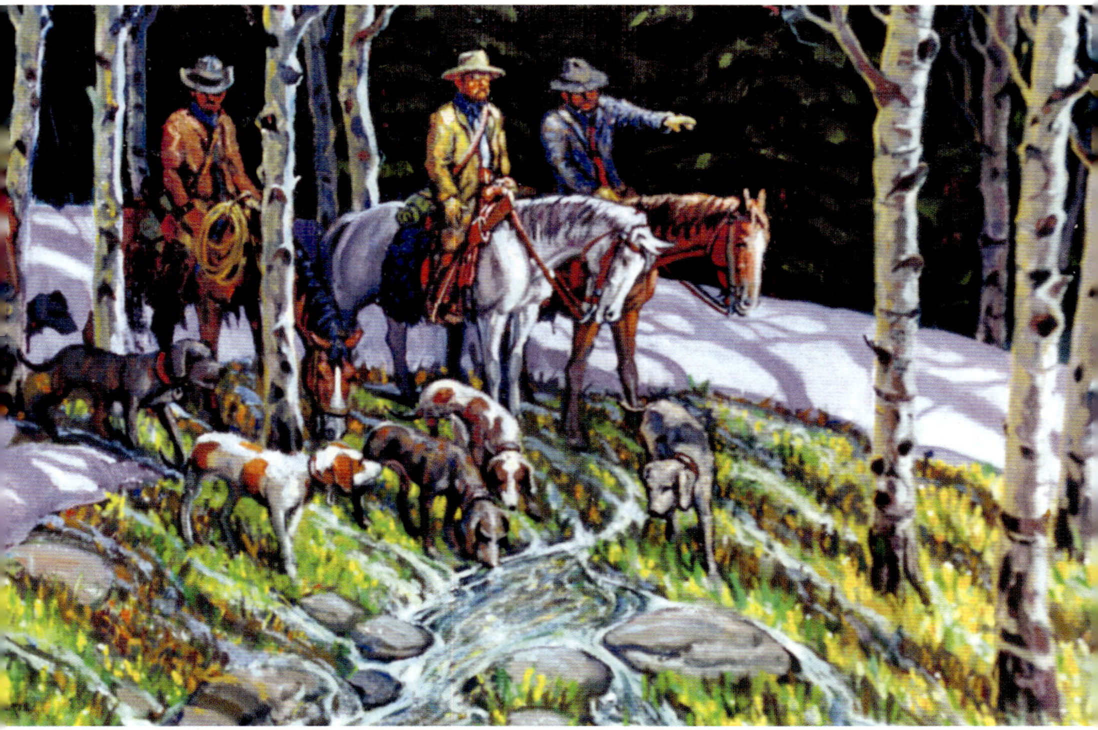

Above:*The Headwaters*. Jack Roberts's Roosevelt Series. *W.R. Hall Collection. Courtesy of the Museum of Western Colorado, Grand Junction, Colorado.*

Below: *Camp Roosevelt*. Jack Roberts's Roosevelt Series. *W.R. Hall Collection. Courtesy of the Museum of Western Colorado, Grand Junction, Colorado.*

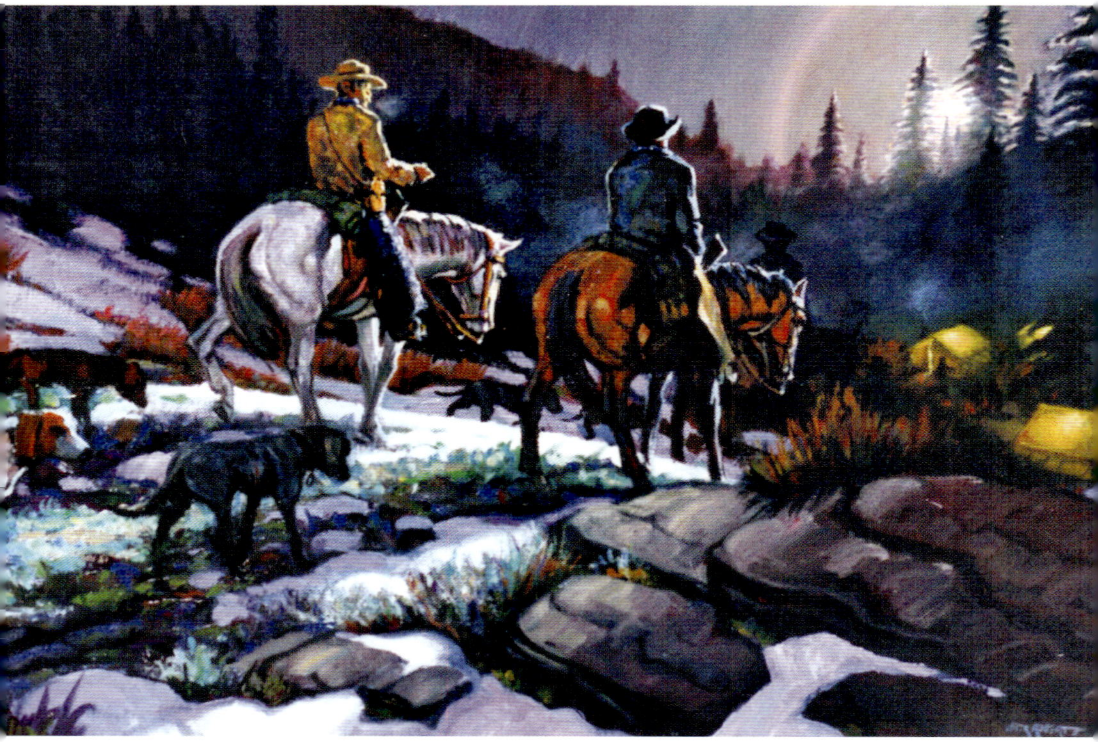

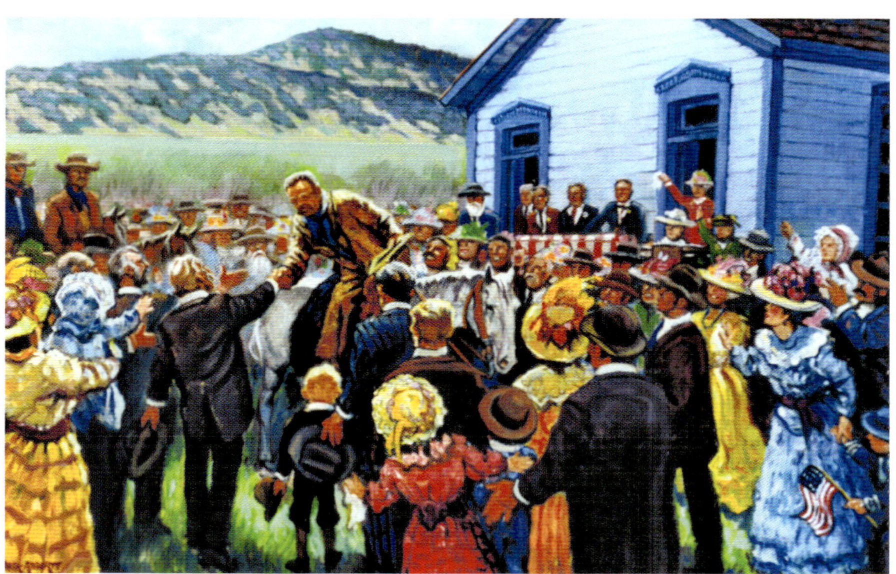

Little Blue School House. Jack Roberts's Roosevelt Series. *W.R. Hall Collection. Courtesy of the Museum of Western Colorado, Grand Junction, Colorado.*

One Sunday we rode down some six miles from camp to a little blue school house [in Raven] *and attended service. The preacher* [Horace Mann, pastor of the Christian Church of Rifle] *was in the habit of riding over every alternate Sunday from Rifle, a little town twenty or twenty-five miles away; and ranchmen with their wives and children some on horseback, some in wagons, had gathered from thirty miles round to attend service. The crowd was so large that the exercises had to take place in the open air, and it was pleasant to look at the strong frames and rugged, weather-beaten faces of the men; while as for the women, one respected them even more than the men.* [125]

As many as 1,400 people attended the event, many of whom spread out blankets on the ground and ate their lunches after Roosevelt spoke. Jack's colorful interpretation of the scene provides a glimpse into the lives of the people of the Grand Valley at the turn of the twentieth century.

The Conservationist (December), the final painting of the series, was for Jack the most important. It portrays the president at the end of the hunt reflecting on conservation as he stands with his little dog, Skip, looking out at the Mamm Peak Range just before his return to Glenwood Springs. Symbolically, it represents the president as the father of national

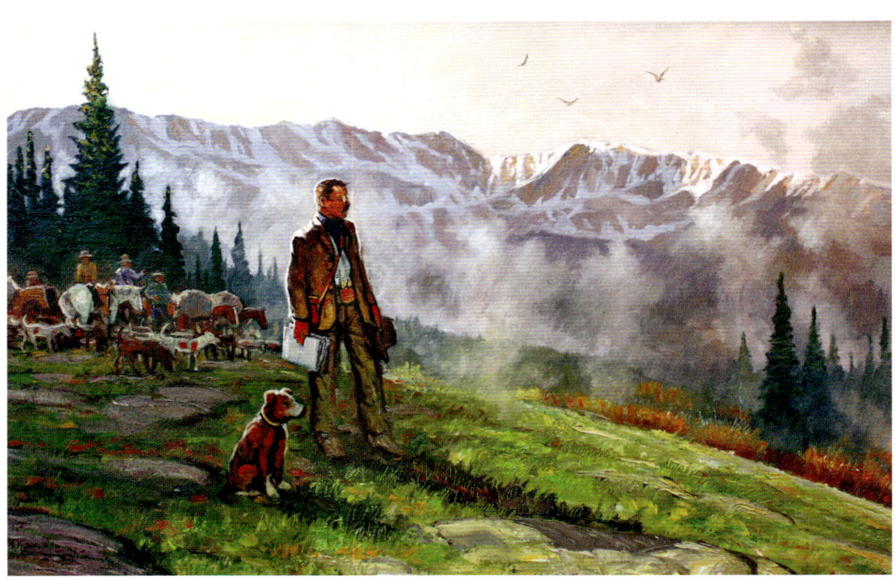

The Conservationist. Jack Roberts's Roosevelt Series. *W.R. Hall Collection. Courtesy of the Museum of Western Colorado, Grand Junction, Colorado.*

conservation. "The more you study history," Jack said in an interview published in the *Rifle Citizen Telegram Centennial Edition* of June 8, 1994, "the more you appreciate Teddy Roosevelt. He was truly a great, great man—a man of integrity and vision."

In an interview with Heather McGregor in 1999, Jack confided that the Roosevelt series was the apex of his career. Although historical accuracy was important in all of his work, it was imperative that his Roosevelt paintings be portrayed with perfection. More than anything, he wanted the paintings to stand the test of time. As with all of his historical paintings, he spent many hours researching and preparing to make sure that in one hundred years, people viewing his work could accurately see how things looked and were at the time, even to the minutest degree. Accuracy and attention to detail make Jack's paintings historical treasures.

Jack and Gary visited the East and West Divide areas in preparation for the *Bear Hunt* series, and Jack took scores of photographs to document the sites that had any association with the event. Over a decade later, he returned to this majestic part of Colorado more for inspiration than historical documentation to prepare himself for a commission to memorialize an event that had become legendary in the folklore of the town of Parachute, Colorado. The event was the train robbery of June 7, 1904.

In 1996, David and Jeanette Truog of Battlement Mesa near Parachute introduced Jack to the story of the famous robbery. They asked him to paint the dynamited train car from a historic photograph. According to Gary, Jack responded with a definitive "No!" A single painting of a photograph would not tell the entire story, he explained.[126] Yet he was intrigued by the subject, and for several days, he could not stop thinking about it. His interest spiked further when local rancher and historian Lee Hayward told him more about the robbery. He learned that the three robbers blew up the wrong train and escaped with very little and that they fled by boat across the Colorado River before riding off on horseback toward the East Divide Creek area south of Silt. The story became even more intriguing to him when he was told that the robber who shot himself with his own gun after being wounded in the shootout with the posse was widely believed to be Harvey Logan, aka Kid Curry, who had been a member of Butch Cassidy's Wild Bunch gang.

Such a tale of romance and high adventure was too much for Jack to resist. After weeks of contemplation, he agreed to paint the train robbery in three paintings instead of one. To do justice to the subject and to document it historically, he argued, three scenes were necessary: the holdup of the train, the crossing of the river by boat and the escape into the night. Each painting was a narrative that together told the story that formed in his mind. The Truogs agreed with the proposal and commissioned him to complete the paintings.

As usual, Jack, along with Gary, did extensive research on the robbery. Still, he could not solve all the mysteries surrounding the famous event, and he painted only what he could document absolutely. Who were these men who robbed the train? Was Kid Curry one of them? How did they learn about the shipment of gold and what train the money was on? Jack puzzled over these and other questions and found unsatisfactory answers for some. He left unanswered the most important question of all: the identities of the three robbers. He did not want to name Kid Curry since he could not positively place him at the scene. At the time of the event, there was no consensus among the authorities concerning the identity of the dead robber, and the body buried in the potter's field section of the Glenwood Springs cemetery was assumed by many to be that of Tap Duncan, another notorious bandit of the time. Subsequently, alleged sightings of Kid Curry

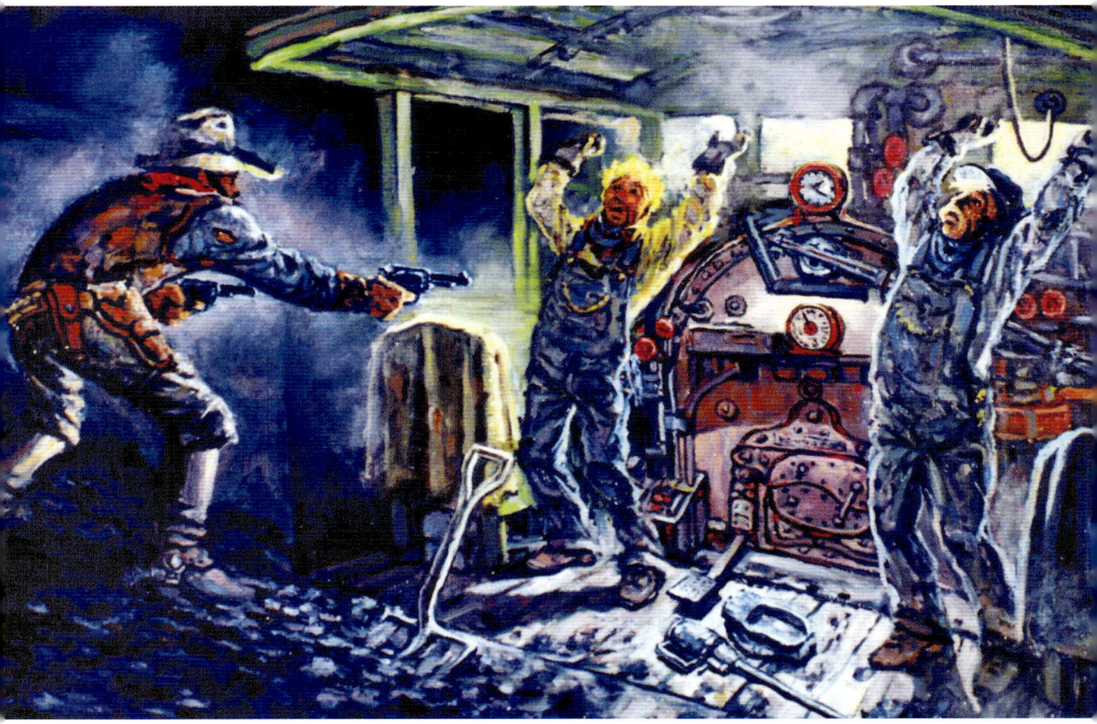

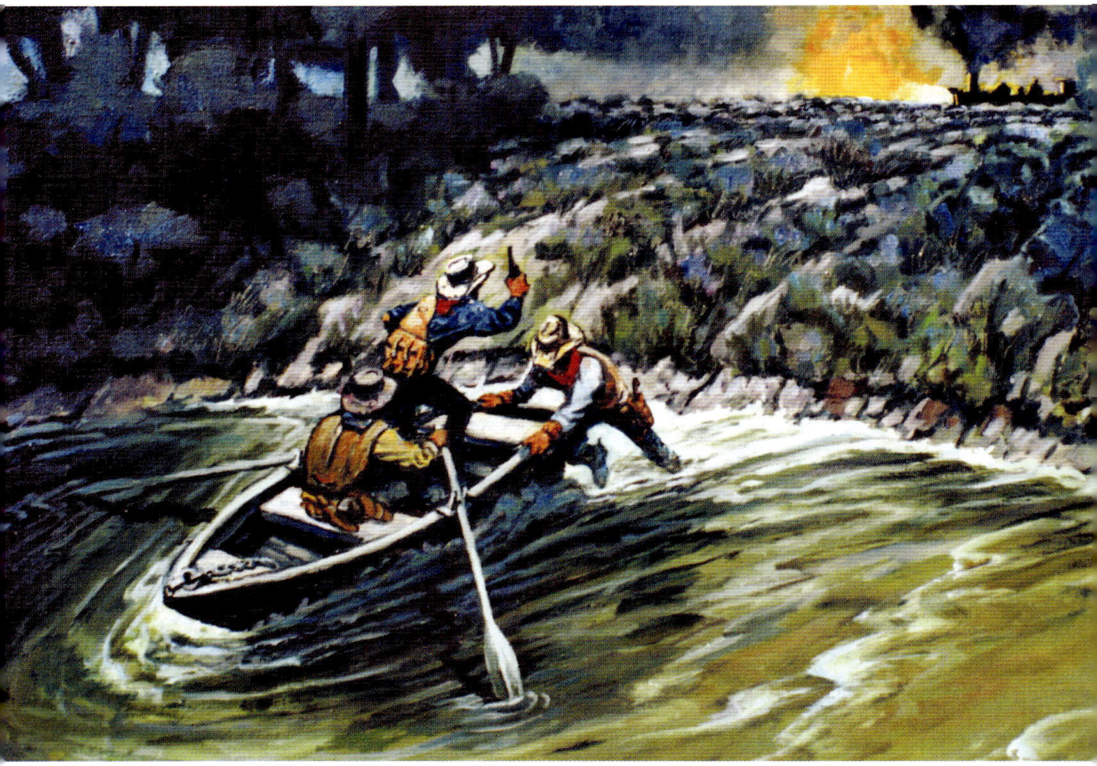

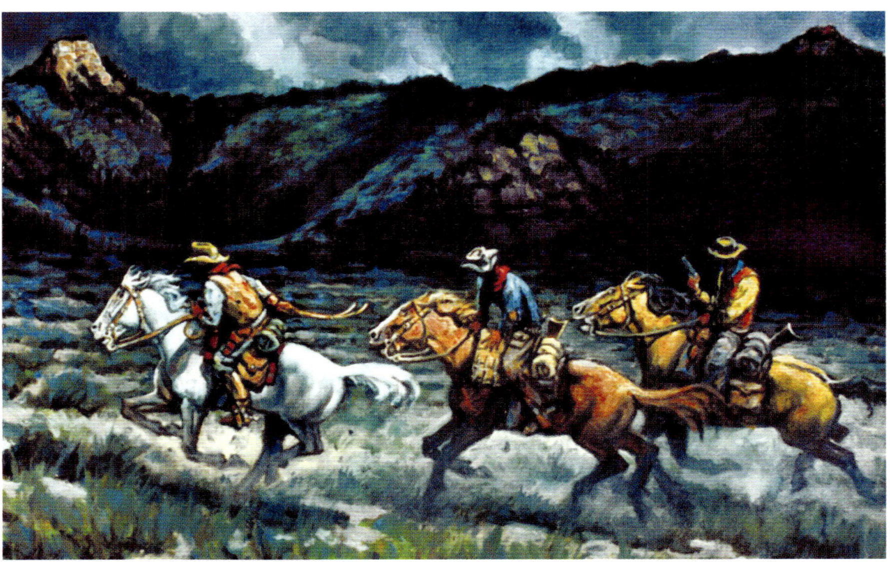

The Getaway. Courtesy of the Grand Valley Historical Society.

Opposite, top: *The Robbery. Courtesy of the Grand Valley Historical Society.*

Opposite, bottom: *The Crossing. Courtesy of the Grand Valley Historical Society.*

in South America strengthened the argument that he was not resting in a Glenwood Springs grave.

With the information he had, Jack was unwilling to give names to the three train robbers, particularly the one who died during the escape. Had he been able to, he probably would have painted a fourth picture in the series depicting the shootout between the fugitives and the posse, which resulted in the suicide death of the outlaw. Indeed, had he had access to the recent compelling evidence that Kid Curry was the "Unknown Bandit" and that the two accomplices who escaped, George Kilpatrick (brother of Ben Kilpatrick) and Dan Sheffield, were occasional members of Butch Cassidy's wild bunch, Jack's vivid imagination might have soared even higher. Surely his commission would have included more scenes depicting this fascinating story of romance and high drama in the old West.

13

SILVER AND SOD

Early Pioneer Life

I t's pretty obvious that I'd rather be living in the pioneer times," Jack remarked to Heather McGregor of the *Glenwood Independent* in 1999. Romanticized stories of the western frontier appealed to his appreciation of simpler times and sparked his curiosity about early events. In depicting the life and times of Lord Gore and Jim Bridger, for example, he imagined that he was with them on their great hunting expedition. Then there were the mountain men trappers and fur traders and their squaw wives, among whom he lived vicariously for a time, and the Indians he welcomed as they arrived at the trading posts to trade buffalo robes and furs for English wares and guns. He picked up his paintbrush to help his Arapaho and Ute friends defend their cultures against the white aggressors. He set the scenes of these adventures in his mind and "lived" and "participated" in all of them before he translated them to his paintings.

"You might say all of my adult life all I've done is compose pictures in my mind and say how nice it would be if the world was really that way," Jack observed in an interview with *Convention Daily* in 1993. "We romanticize quite a bit, we artists do. We portray things we think are very important. I've been very lucky to make a living doing that." He had paid his tribute to the fur traders and Indians, the trading posts and expeditions. Fortunately, there were plenty of other topics to challenge his imagination. In 1982, it was the story of Aspen's early days. Using Henry Staats's journal, Ferdinand V. Hayden's geological survey, historic Aspen newspapers and official records, Jack illustrated the history of Aspen from the discovery of silver in 1879 to the opening of the Wheeler Opera House in 1889. To his knowledge, it was the first time anyone had painted a series based on the history of a mining town.

Jack spent six months researching material for the twelve paintings. Much of the time was in the Aspen Historical Society's archives. "They thought I worked there. I was there for lunch," he told Mary Eshbaugh Hayes in an *Aspen Times* interview. "The real fun of a job like this is digging for the material, and when I read the stories I see a picture in my head." The pictures in his head, Hayes commented, became robust oil paintings on canvas. The "strong and vital" brush strokes depicted "a strong people who settled Aspen."

Jack found the information in Henry Staats's journal to be especially valuable. An inveterate prospector, Staats recounted how as an employee of Henry B. Gillespie, principal owner of the Spar Lode in Aspen, he brought fifteen miners with their provisions on wooden sleds over Independence Pass in midwinter to work the claim. Jack illustrated this story in the painting *The Snow Boats*. Other Staats stories became the basis for three other paintings in the series: *Christmas 1880*, *The Vallejo Whim* and *The Highland Prospector*. Staats's description of the Prospector, "one of the most pathetic sights in this world with his pack animal staked out, his frying pan, coffee pot and little pack of grub, along with his pole pick and shovel," came to life in Jack's whimsical portrait.

Jack also found inspiration for the series in exploring old mine sites. Writing on July 12, 1982, to Mary Webster, who, along with her sister-in-law Lis Sorensen, commissioned the series, Jack noted:

> *I had a wonderful time on Aspen Mountain yesterday and I thought I would drop you a line on the subject. History enhances the beauty and romance of the country. It's a thrill to walk through the flowers and over the rocks knowing that a grand and glorious story evolved on that ground. Men labored and dreamed and schemed and fought and loved and died at the end of labor, and then other generations directed other courses and life goes on. But for those aware of events in history, everything has more meaning and more substance.*

Later in the letter, he expressed his excitement in finding the spot where the Spar Lode was discovered and the sites of the old Vallejo, Aspen, Emma and Conamara mines. "I was surprised to see so much evidence of these old mines, considering that the Little Nell ski slope runs over them. The tailings of the old Aspen Mine are, in fact, right smack in the middle of the Little Nell slope."

In *Parlin's Saloon*, one of the last of this series, Jack strove for humor as well as historic accuracy. The saloon, he explained, was one of the first in town and the one most mentioned by the pioneers. In the interest of simplicity, he told Mary Webster, there should be a "honky-tonk piano" and a central couple on the dance floor to tell the story of the early day rowdy saloon life of the most popular meeting place in old Aspen. The scene would be as follows:

> *One old toothless, grizzled, prospector type whooping it up with a plump saloon girl will tell the story better than a crowd of people on the dance floor. Since women were scarce, it seems unlikely that every old miner would have a dance partner and most of the men would be observing from the bar, and perhaps whooping their approval of the dancers. It takes a lot of thought for the truth to finally work its way to the surface in a painting composition.[127]*

In a subsequent letter, Jack noted that many Old West saloons had at least one painting of a classic nude, "usually copied from Goya's famous reclining nude." It was not incongruous, he added, to have a photograph of Abraham Lincoln on the same wall.[128]

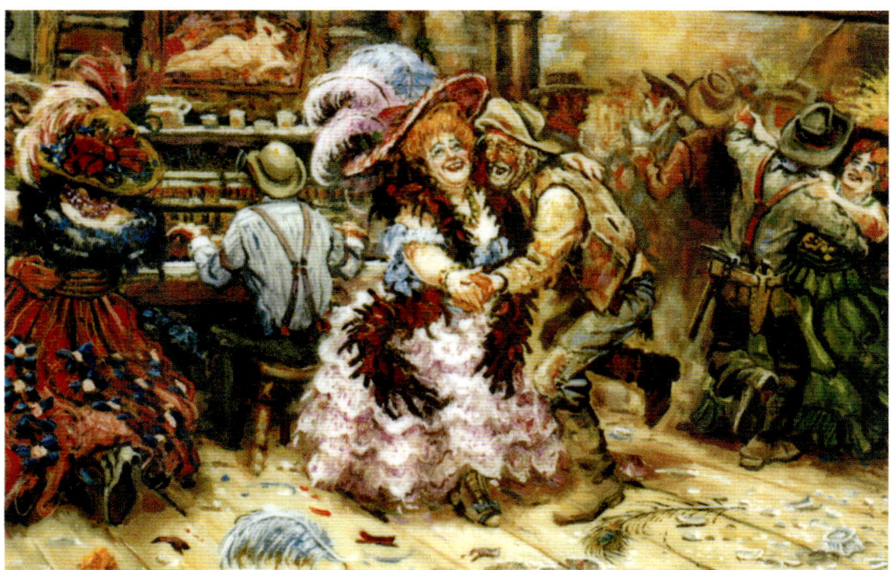

Parlin's Saloon. Bruce Carlson Collection. Courtesy of Bruce Carlson.

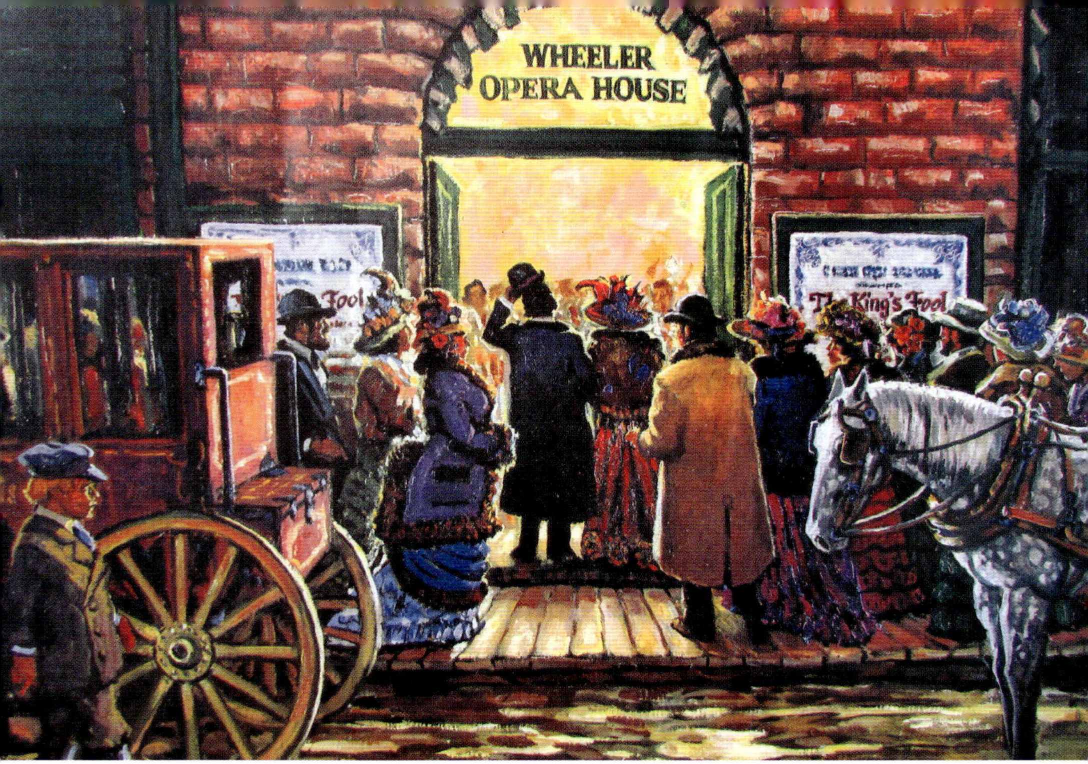

Opening Night. Bruce Carlson Collection. Courtesy of Bruce Carlson.

But early Aspen was more than just a town of rowdy saloons. There was the Wheeler Opera House as well. "Aspen," Jack noted in his interview with Mary Eshbaugh Hayes, "had something going from the very beginning, something that other mining towns didn't have. Culture was always important here." *Opening Night* at the Wheeler was an appropriate way to end the illustrated history of early Aspen.

The Aspen project completed, Jack turned his attention to another historical series set in western Colorado. In April 1984, George McKinley of the First National Bank in Grand Junction approved Jack's sketches for a series of paintings titled *The Grand Junction Pioneers*. In proposing the series, Jack told R.L. Quimby at the bank that he intended "to give this project every grain of salt I have." He planned to focus on the first four years of Grand Junction's history from the breaking of the virgin soil in 1882 to the first bumper crops in 1886. Each of the twelve paintings would portray an aspect of pioneer life that would be easily recognizable to "the most urbanized citizen" and would need no explanation. "Historical accuracy," he told Quimby,

is essential in this job and naturally I plan to make frequent trips to Grand Junction to double check everything. One significant error has already come

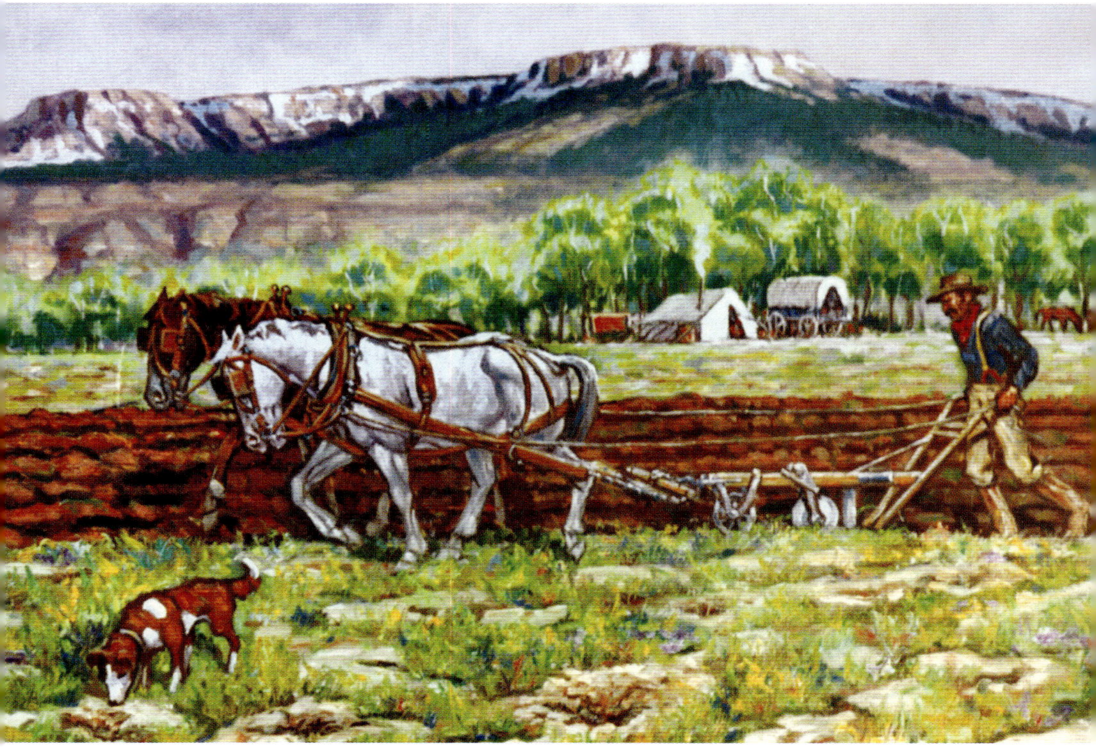

Above: Virgin Soil. U.S. Bank Collection. Courtesy of U.S. Bank.

Below: The Hand Pump. U.S. Bank Collection. Courtesy of US Bank.

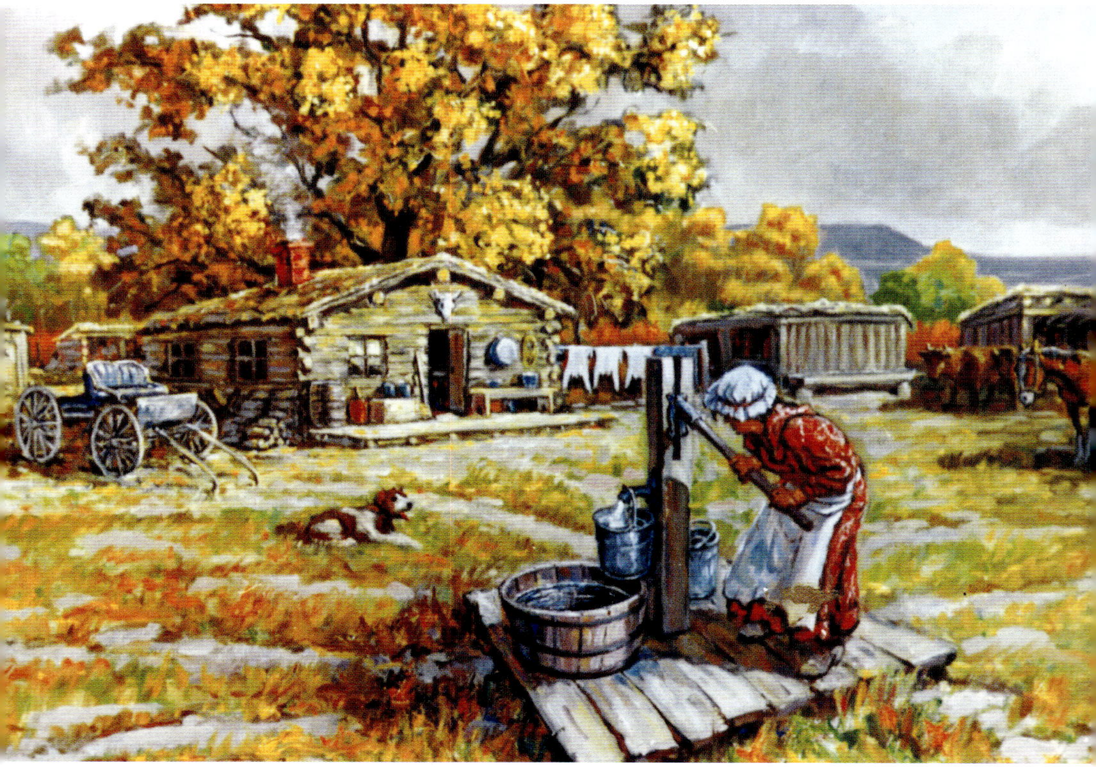

to light and that pertains to my depiction of Orchard Mesa in early history. There was no development in that region until the Orchard Mesa Canal was built around 1895, and so the early history of Grand Junction should focus on the lower valley. The creative process must have a foundation of truth.[129]

The *Pioneers* series strengthened Jack's interest in depicting the various phases of everyday western life. By the late 1980s, he had completed a group of paintings based on this broadened concept of rural living entitled "Visions of Western Colorado." Some of his best scenes were of simple rustic life. A one-room rural schoolhouse (*School Days*), a couple returning home in a wagon (*The Road Home*) and a community dinner during harvest time (*The Harvest Crew*) are representative of this group. Of the latter, Jack explained in handwritten notes on the series:

In those good old days around the turn-of-the-century, neighbors joined forces for the harvest. The women and girls worked in the kitchen and the men worked in the fields. The midday dinner was invariably plain but plentiful and nourishing. This typical dinner consists of pan-fried beefsteak, mashed potatoes and gravy, black-eyed peas, cornbread and good old turnip greens.[130]

As usual in his depictions, the menu items are immediately recognizable.

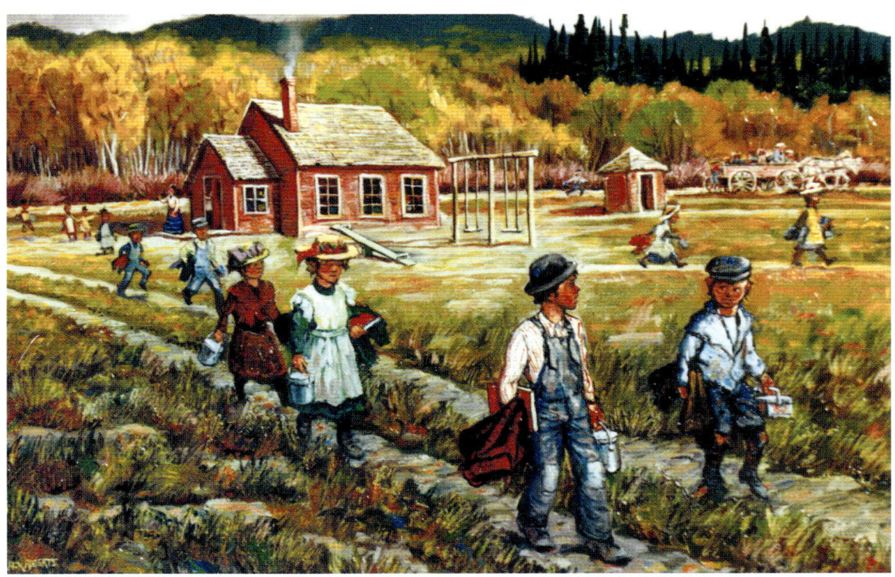

School Days. Courtesy of Gary Miller.

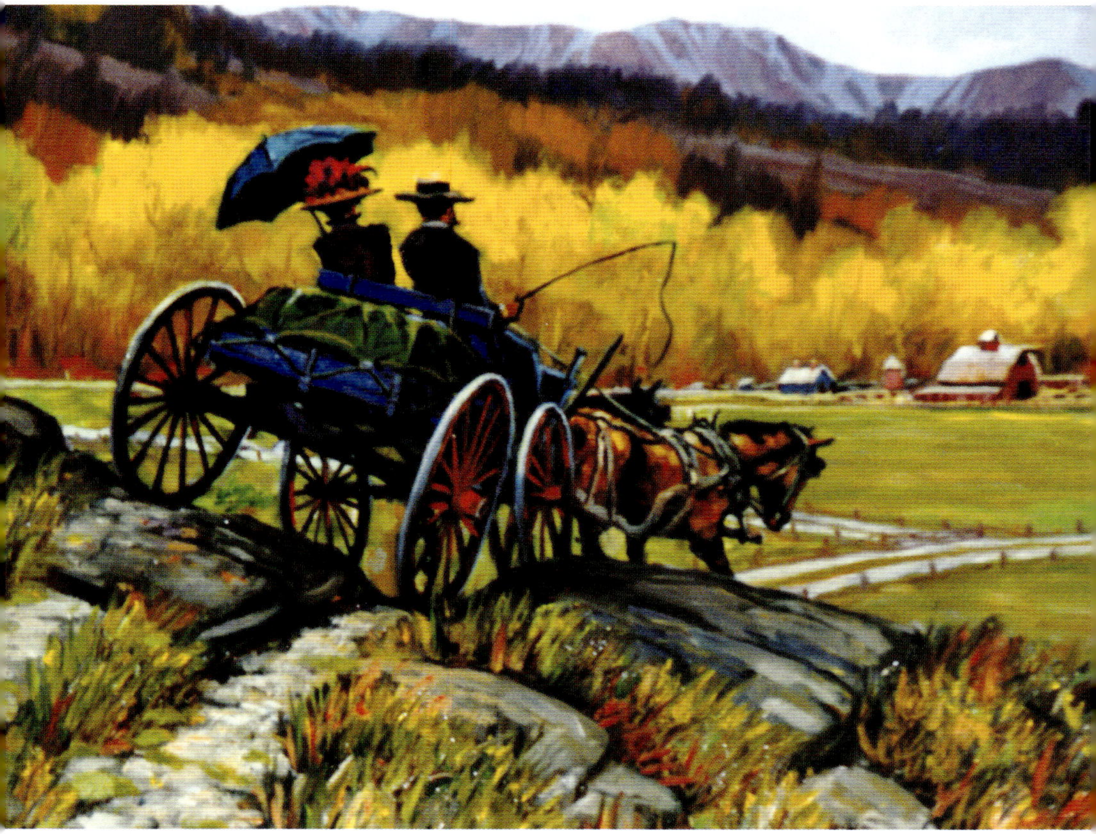

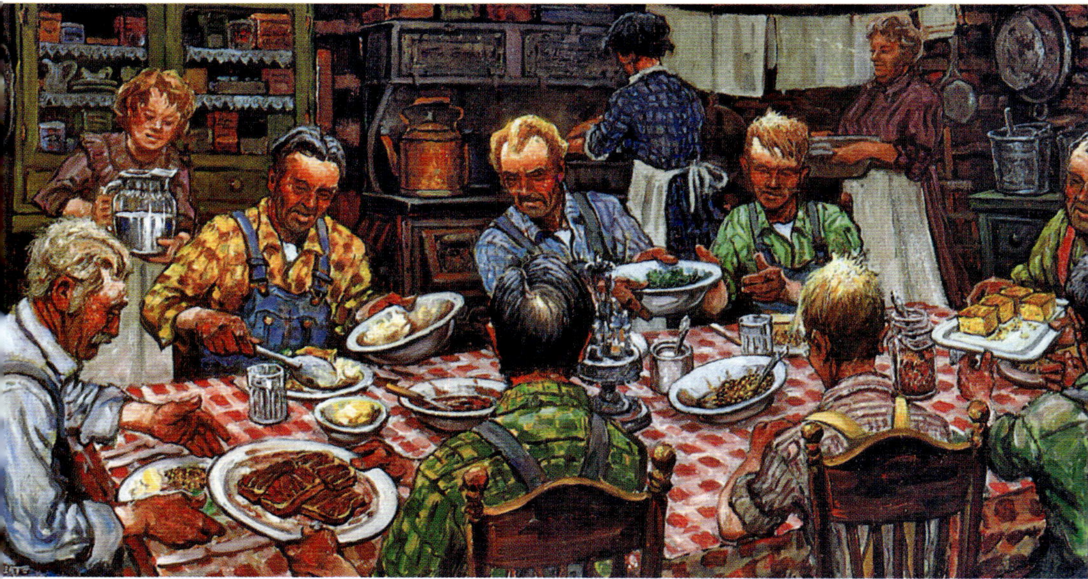

Noteworthy in these paintings, especially *The Harvest Crew*, was their nostalgic Rockwellian quality. They were serious portrayals that eschewed the caricatured and exaggerated figures of many of his earlier humorous works. "I'm representational rather than realistic," Jack told George Kane of the *Colorado Springs Gazette Telegraph*. "I mean, it's all recognizable, but I'm an impressionist. I try to express a certain aspect of cowboy life, rural life; something much broader than just cowboys."

With these paintings, Jack's life and career had come full circle, as he explained in a letter to Suzanne Fowler on June 21, 1989, in which he proposed an exhibit of his works in the Saks Galleries in Colorado Springs:

> *My exhibition could be called a retrospective, since I have essentially returned to the subjects I was painting thirty years ago when Saks began selling my works. My curiosity about Western History has been satisfied and it has brought me back to my beginnings. It seems as though I have made a full circle. I am home again where I belong…where my heart is.*

The exhibit "Jack Roberts: A Retrospective" opened on August 8, 1989. It featured nineteen of Jack's paintings, with *The Harvest Crew* being the centerpiece of the show. After more than a decade, Jack was once again exhibiting in and assigning some of his works on commission to the Saks Galleries. He had come full circle in more than one respect.

Opposite, top: *The Road Home. Courtesy of Gary Miller.*

Opposite, bottom: *The Harvest Crew. Courtesy of Gary Miller.*

14

LAST CALL

A sense of nostalgia during the summer of 1987 took Jack back to the old ditch camp where he had first learned about Colorado. "Last summer I returned to that cowcamp after an absence of thirty years," he wrote to Ed Trumble on February 3, 1988.

> *I took along my son Gary and his wife Monica…and of course my grandson Wade was with us. I was pleased to see that the Forest Service had restricted motorized vehicles beyond the camp. The ranchers of Burns had not hired a rider for that job in many years and the place was vacant…The old way of life is gone forever.*

After the others had left, Jack stayed another week "walking around reminiscing." His old cabin at Stump Park near the confluence of Little Derby and Middle Derby Creeks still existed with the old cookstove still inside, and the vertical-pole outhouse, depicted in many of his paintings, remained in place. The following summer, he returned with Gary, this time with horses, to ride the old trails he had ridden forty years earlier. The experience made him realize more than ever what had been lost.

A year or so later, Gary asked Jack if he was ready to go back to Stump Park. "No," Jack emphatically replied. "I don't ever want to go back up there." Gary was puzzled by Jack's response. "What's the deal with that?" Ruefully, Jack answered, "I want to remember it as it was then, not how it looks today." Thomas Wolfe was right, he lamented. "You can't go home again."[131]

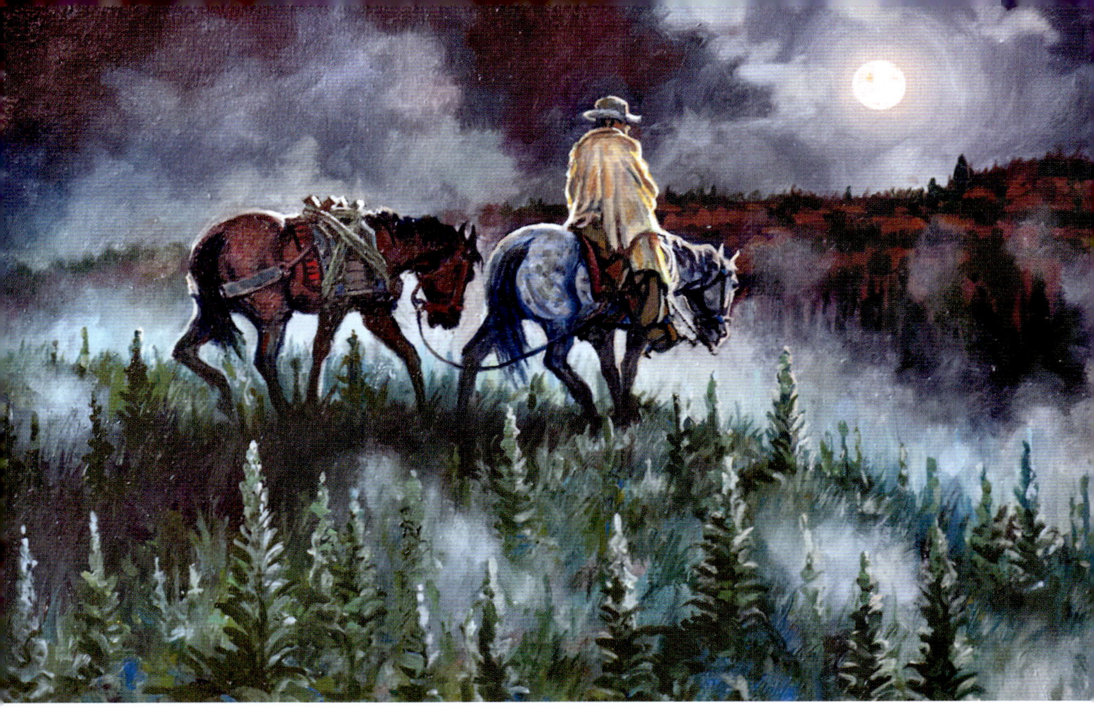

A Long Day's Ride. Gary and Monica Miller Collection. Courtesy of Gary Miller.

Although depressing, his visit to the Burns area inspired Jack to continue painting scenes that reflected his cowboy ditch-riding days. The idea of returning to his old subject matter was exhilarating. It was the things that were stamped on his memory that he wanted to paint. "I still love the old ditch camp and I hope to paint more pictures of the wonderful, wonderful old camp," he confided to Gary.[132] The "Ditch Camp" paintings were in great demand, and Jack had little trouble finding individual buyers. Kurt Wigger, owner of the Buffalo Valley Inn, purchased ten of them to add to his already large collection. *The Ditch Rider*, depicting a lone rider (self-portrait) checking irrigation ditches in the high country, was among this group.

Jack consigned some of the paintings to Gary to sell. As Jack grew older and his relationship with Gary deepened, he relied more on him for advice and companionship. Besides accompanying Jack on research trips and sometimes handling paintings, Gary offered ideas about marketing. Jack, however, did not readily accept all suggestions. He demurred when Gary told him that he should promote his work by having art shows. If someone wanted to have a show, Jack insisted, they could buy his paintings. That was the way it had been done in the past. The Aspen Historical Society, the Colorado Press Association and the Museum of Western Colorado had honored him in such a way. Gary persisted until Jack finally acceded

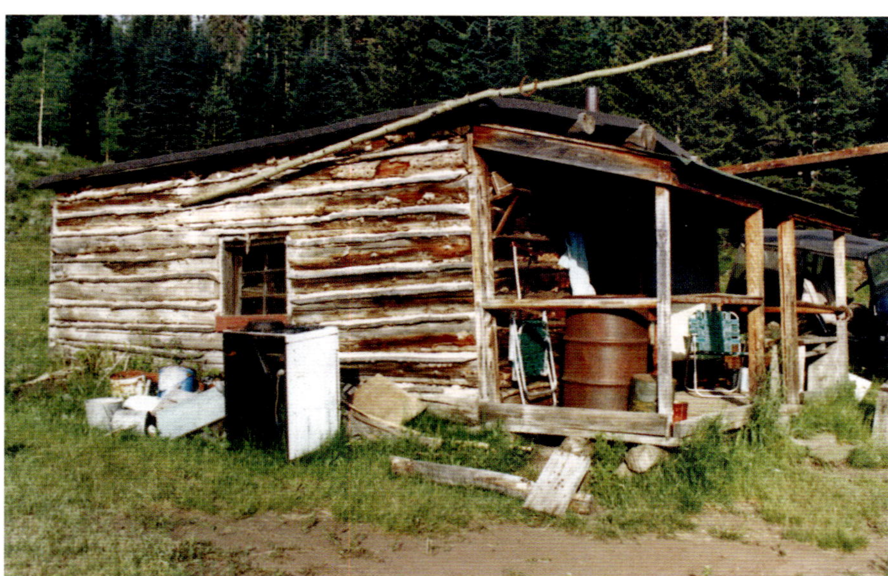

Jack's Stump Park cabin as it was in the late 1980s. *Courtesy of Gary Miller.*

to his suggestion. He did this, Gary admitted, "to placate me."[133] His new approach to marketing would pay dividends in the future.

In June 1994, Gary and Leslie Robinson of the (Rifle) *Citizen Telegram* put together a show of Jack's works as a part of the *Telegram*'s Centennial Celebration. The exhibit featured forty-five paintings and eight prints. Included were paintings from the "Colorado Bear Hunt" collection, Scott and Lori McInnis's "Indoor Life of Outdoor Men" collection and selections from the collections of Gary and Monica Miller and Phil and Joan Anderson. Success brought about a change in Jack's attitude toward shows. "If you want to promote another showing when the "[Train] Robbery" paintings are all done, then let me know," he told Gary. "The Roosevelt series will also be available, as well as the McInnis collection."[134]

These related activities rekindled interest in Jack's paintings and also increased their value. He was in a position to pick and choose from numerous requests for his work. When Susanna Hart of the *Citizen Telegram* asked if he thought about retirement, he answered: "I'm busy. I'm not sitting around watching old John Wayne movies. I always have a painting in the works. I think that's what keeps me in good health…I want to go on as long as I'm able. I'd like to have my work finished when I die." Anyway, he added with a smile, "artists and scientists never retire."

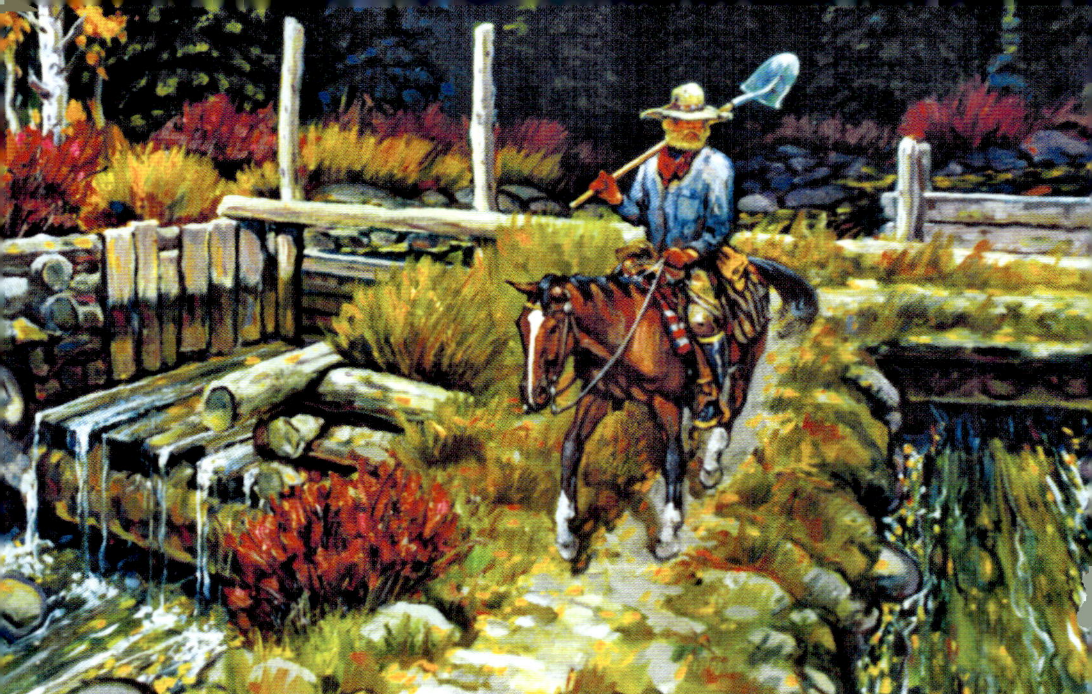

The Ditch Rider. Buffalo Valley Inn Collection. Courtesy of Sue Anschutz Rodgers.

Although busy in 1994 with individual paintings, Jack pursued a major commission he had long sought: a series based on his extensive research of the seasonal migration of the Tabagauche Utes from the area around Montrose, Colorado, to Yampah ("Big Medicine"), the Ute name for the Glenwood hot springs. As he originally proposed, the paintings would depict the history of the Ute summer occupation of the hot springs. Convinced that the topic was of local interest and the theme relevant, he presented his idea to Dr. James Weaver, a member of the Aspen Orthopaedic Associates and of the Glenwood Hot Springs Board. This was a time, he enthusiastically stated in a letter of September 12, 1994, to Dr. Weaver, "when these people [Utes] were developing a splendid way of life" that was "a flawless adaptation to the natural resources."

Weaver was familiar with Jack's work. He took the sketches and proposal to the board and urged the members to commission the series. But they suggested that Jack should broaden the scope of the project to include more contemporary scenes portraying early white settlement in the area and the development of the hot springs. At first, Jack balked at the suggestion. His intention was to tell an Indian story, he insisted, not a history of the hot springs pool. After more discussions with Weaver and some members of the board, however, he became more excited about completing the project. He agreed to add paintings depicting the 1860 Richard Sopris exploration party

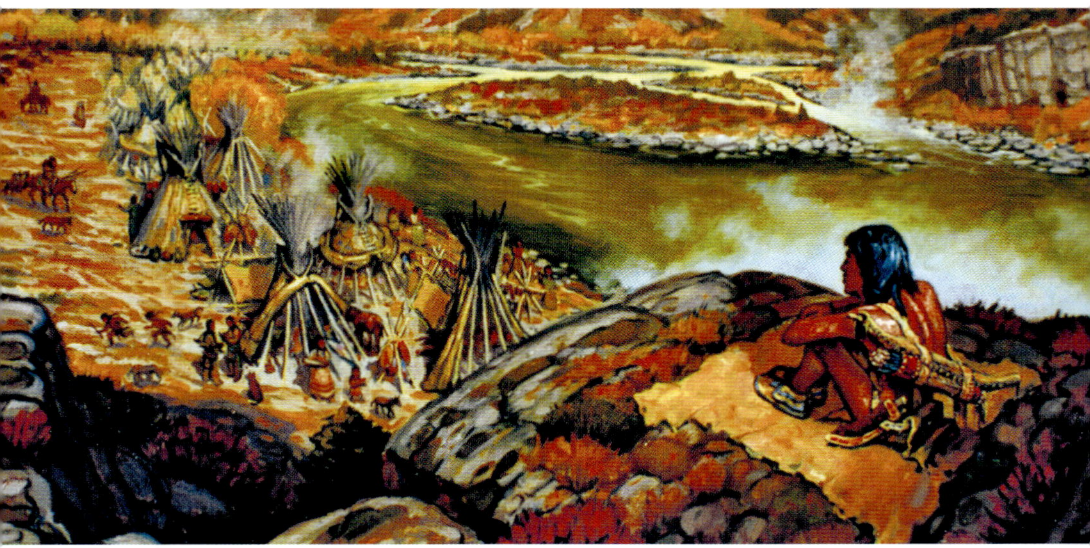

Above: *Indian Summer. Courtesy of Glenwood Hot Springs, Glenwood Springs, Colorado.*

Below: *Natatorium. Courtesy of Glenwood Hot Springs, Glenwood Springs, Colorado.*

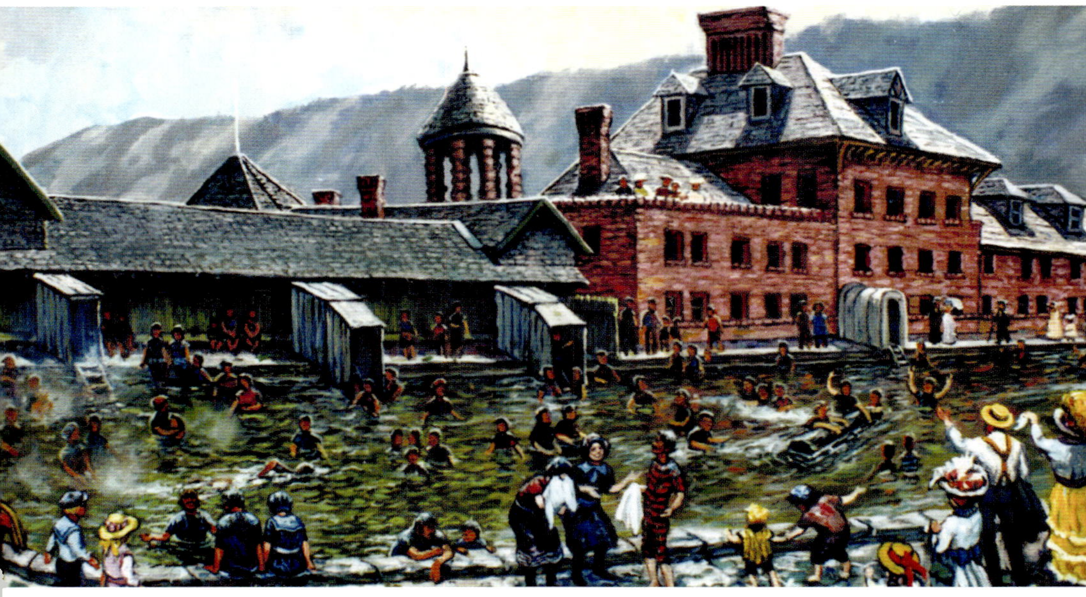

at the springs; the Swan Fountain, one of the attractions at the opening of the 1890 bathhouse; and the natatorium, the hot springs pool filled with bathers. With the addition of these four paintings to six of the proposed

Indian paintings, the board approved the project.[135] It was the last major commission Jack painted.

At the twilight of his career in 1996, Jack was no longer interested in large commissioned projects. Instead, he wanted to explore more personal ideas, especially the subject matter of his early career. On June 4, 1998, he sent photos of two paintings he had recently completed to his dear friend Maxine McElhinney. *The Dining Car*, portraying a gang of bridge men entering the dining car for a hearty lunch, was a tribute to his fellow railroad workers of the 1940s. *An Afternoon with Longfellow* showed the gentle side of an old cowboy in primitive surroundings. "These are good examples of the type of painting I will be doing for the rest of my life," he wrote to Maxine. "Most of my career has been spent in historical illustration and I have thoroughly enjoyed it. Now, in my old age, I am returning to the original events that inspired me in the beginning of my venture into western art. My search in other horizons has led me back to my first horizon."

The images of his personal experiences kept coming back to him again and again, and these were the scenes he painted. He was proud that he had experienced the life they depicted and that he had been able to do the hard work required of the characters he portrayed. Equally as important to him was the balance between toughness and tenderness in the life experiences he re-created. This quality was one he portrayed symbolically in various ways. In particular, the large, often callused hands of his workers and cowboys represented toughness and ruggedness. But those hands also mastered more delicate things like sewing, wrapping packages or writing letters. To Jack, even the most rugged individuals had a softer side.

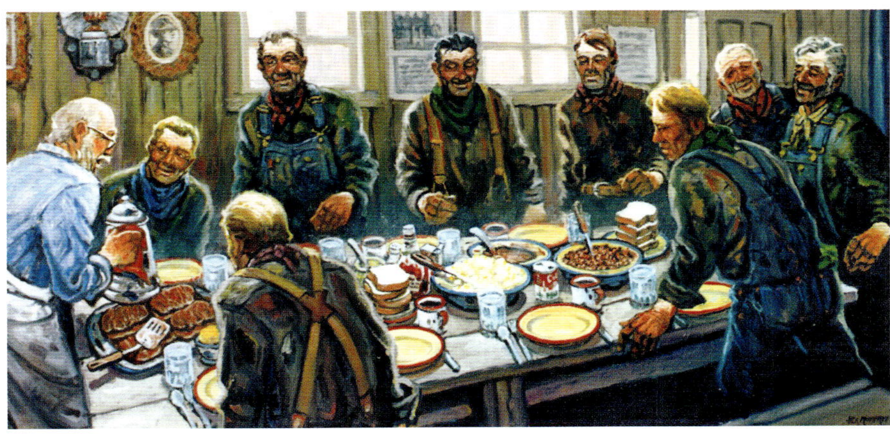

The Dining Car. Courtesy of Mike Waski.

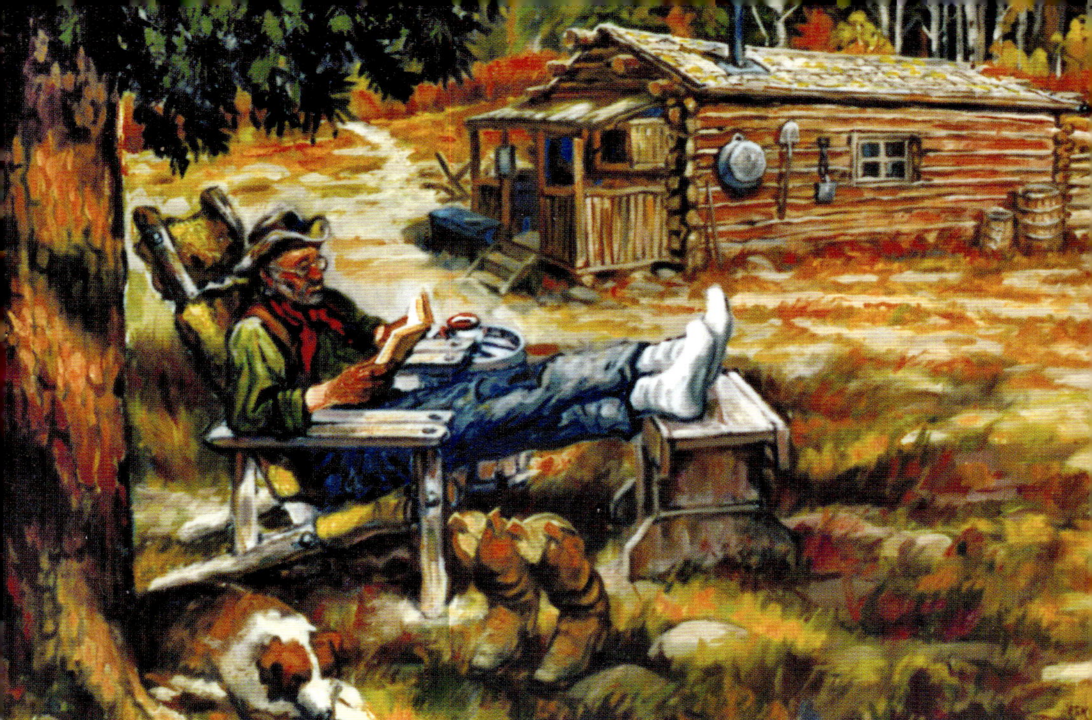

An Afternoon with Longfellow. Courtesy of Kathy and Duane Piffer.

Perhaps Jack's "softer side" contributed to his desire for feminine companionship. By his own admission, he became a "gal chaser" once again after his divorce from Mary Margaret in 1981. His second marriage, like his first, was a failure. His changed view of family life may have prompted him to try marriage again. Certainly he went through a phase when he wanted to be more conventional in his lifestyle—to be more like other people. But for the most part, a conventional life was beyond his reach. Besides, the marriage became a choice of living with Mary Margaret in Missouri for long periods of time while she pursued her own career or returning permanently to Redstone without her. People who knew Jack well were surprised that his marriage to Mary Margaret lasted as long as it did.

With some exceptions, Jack's relationship with women seemed to confirm his need for a sense of viable virility. He went from one "gal" friend to the next in rapid succession until he met Ruth Chacto, the "love of his life." Ruthie, as Jack called her, fit Jack's personality perfectly. She was artistic, vivacious, fun loving and plump, all characteristics Jack admired. He sketched her as the model for the "ladies of the evening" and women at the bar in many of his later paintings. Her shop on the Boulevard in Redstone was one more place to visit when he came to the village. There, he caught up with the latest gossip and enjoyed Ruth's sense of humor. Both had plenty of stories to tell. For many years during the 1980s and early 1990s, they were constant companions who enjoyed each other's company. She was exactly what Jack needed during these waning years of his life.

Jack and Ruth enjoyed traveling together. They toured the Netherlands during three successive springs of 1984, 1985 and 1986. Each time, they visited museums exhibiting paintings by artists of the Dutch Golden Age. Of these Dutch masters, Rembrandt was Jack's favorite. He considered Rembrandt's *The Night Watch* the greatest work of art in all history and the Rijksmuseum in Amsterdam, where the painting was on display, one of the best art museums in the world. Even with the museum visits, there was still plenty of time for the couple to enjoy the countryside by canalboat, car or train. Jack loved every minute of it.

In August 1993, Jack and Ruth made a long-anticipated pilgrimage to South Dakota State University–Brookings to see the collection of Harvey Dunn paintings. Jack was deeply moved when he saw them, many of which he remembered seeing in Dunn's studio during his student days. The trip to South Dakota culminated with a visit to Wall Drug to view the Dunn paintings on display there. To Jack's surprise, he saw his own *Sourdough Flapjacks* hanging in the gallery. Elated by his discovery, he wrote to owner Bill Hustead upon his return to Redstone: "I am indeed flattered to have an example of my work in the same collection of works by Harvey Dunn, Harold Von Schmidt and others."[136]

Jack was curious about the painting's inclusion in the Wall Drug collection. He had sold the painting to Ed Trumble of Leanin' Tree with reproduction rights for the 1982 Christmas card line. In a letter dated September 8, 1993, Hustead informed Jack that the painting had made several stops since its Leanin' Tree days: "I would like you to be aware that your sourdough flapjack painting was on display at the Federal Reserve Bank in Minneapolis during Christmas a couple years ago, and also last year in Helena, Montana at the Federal Reserve Bank, along with approximately thirty other paintings from our Christmas collection." Obviously, Jack approved of its new home.

In April 1999, Jack made another pilgrimage to view Dunn's work. Again accompanied by Ruth, who had returned to Redstone on a visit, he went to the Smithsonian Institution in Washington, D.C., to see Dunn's World War I paintings. Although the public did not have access to the collection, the curator of the Smithsonian Archives arranged a private showing. Given Jack's devotion to Dunn, it was a moving and memorable experience.

Ruth's departure from Redstone in the mid-1990s left a void in Jack's life. Although there were other women, none could take the place of Ruthie.

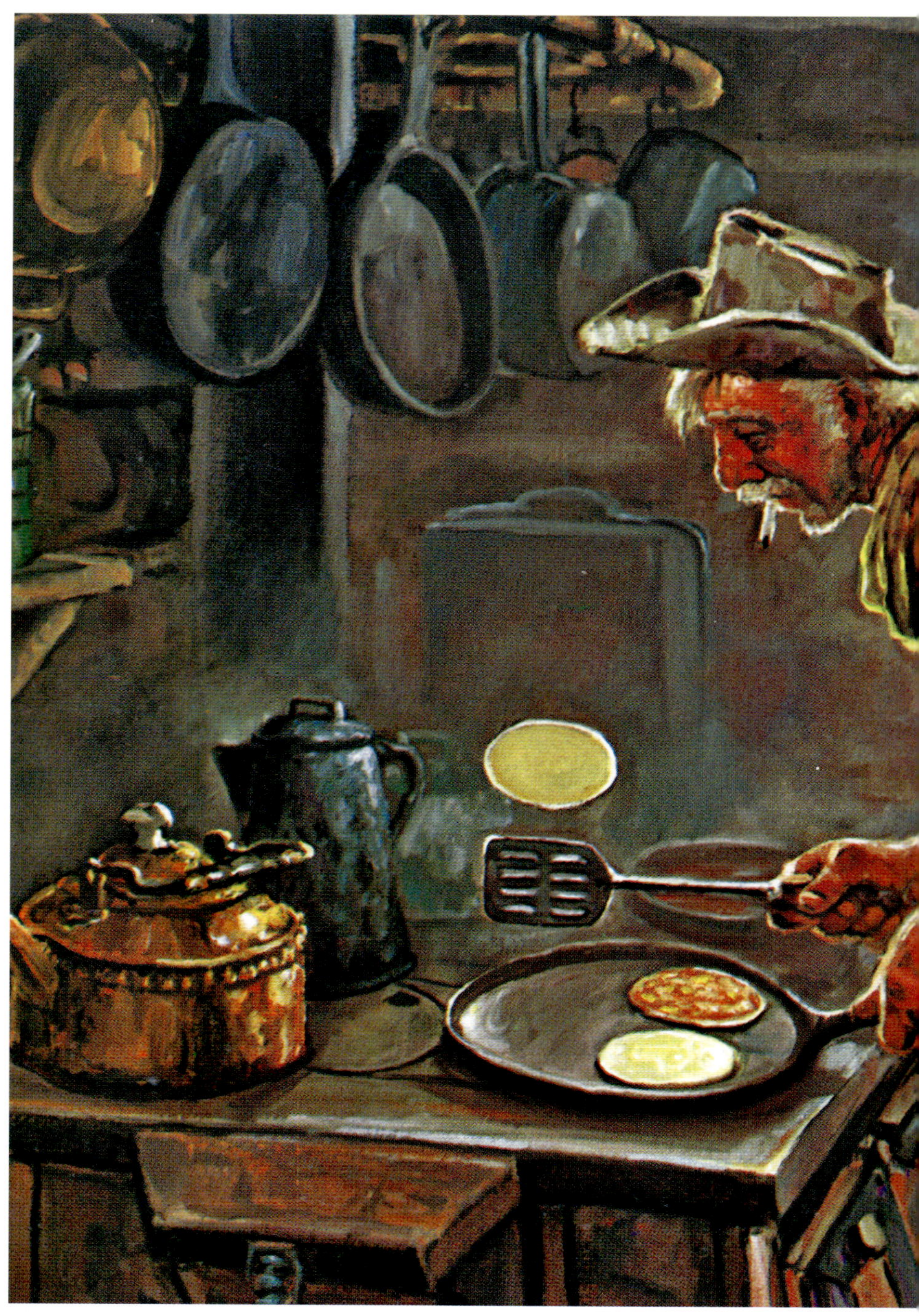

Sourdough Flapjacks. Photo credit: Leanin' Tree Museum and Sculpture Garden of Western Art. Courtesy of Rick Hustead of Wall Drug, Wall SD.

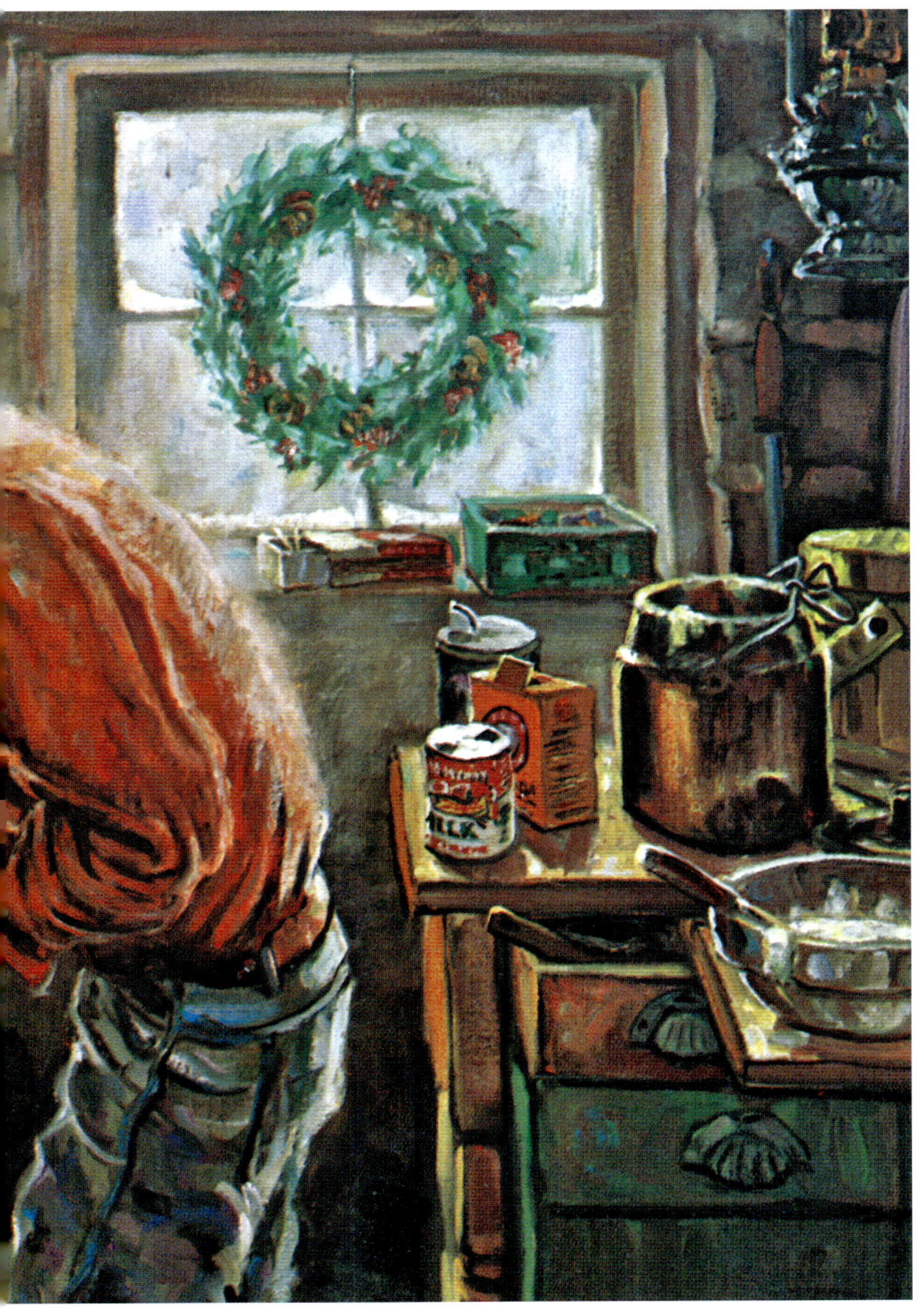

As a consequence, he became more reclusive. "I just don't like loud parties and small talk," he told Maxine McElhinney in July 1996. "I'm always thinking about things I would rather be doing in my studio." He simply wanted to continue his life as historian and artist. The time left for him, he acknowledged, must be spent with his work.

In 1998, Jack complained of slowing down. "I have been going on a few jeep trips and I am enjoying good health," he wrote Gary in July. But, he added, "I have slowed down so much it has got me concerned—it takes me three days to do a day's work." It might be time to consult a doctor, he conceded. He would take a few days off from his painting to do a few illustrations for Angie's book. "I always enjoy that," he added. "I really wish I had lived a hundred years ago. Even then, I would probably wish to have lived in the 18th century."[137]

The book he referred to was *Hope and Hot Water*, Angela Parkison's history of Glenwood Springs from 1878 to 1891. Jack contributed over seventy illustrations depicting the story of Ute Indians, homesteaders, town founders, outlaws, railroaders and other characters who lived during these formative years of Glenwood Springs. He did the illustrations not as a last hurrah, Angie thought, but as a favor to her and a contribution to a family project. He also agreed to paint a rendition of the old Glenwood Hotel for the book, even though his health was declining. It was the last painting he completed.

In his final years, Jack became more contemplative. He talked to Lanny Grant frequently about aging. Slowing down was fine, he conceded, as long as he did not lose his desire to paint. There would be fewer paintings, he told Lanny, but he could not live without painting. While expressing "terrible regrets" about his wasted alcoholic years, he felt fortunate to have been given "a few extra years to make up for that insanity."[138]

He never lost his enthusiasm for painting, but the thought of not being able to finish what he conceptualized left him frustrated. With his mind teeming with ideas, he found it impossible to concentrate on any one of them. "Can't you just begin one painting at a time and finish it?" Gary pleaded. With growing anxiety about his health, that was impossible for him to do.[139]

Although Jack recovered from heart attacks in 1991 and 1995, his doctors told him he had degenerative heart failure. He became extremely depressed as his health continued to deteriorate, and receiving a heart stent did not relieve his anxiety. "Woe is me! I'm going to die," he exclaimed to Joan and Steve Benson time and time again. The Bensons tried to assure him that many people had gone through the procedure, but their assurance was to no avail. Jack feared his heart condition was going to be a constant issue,

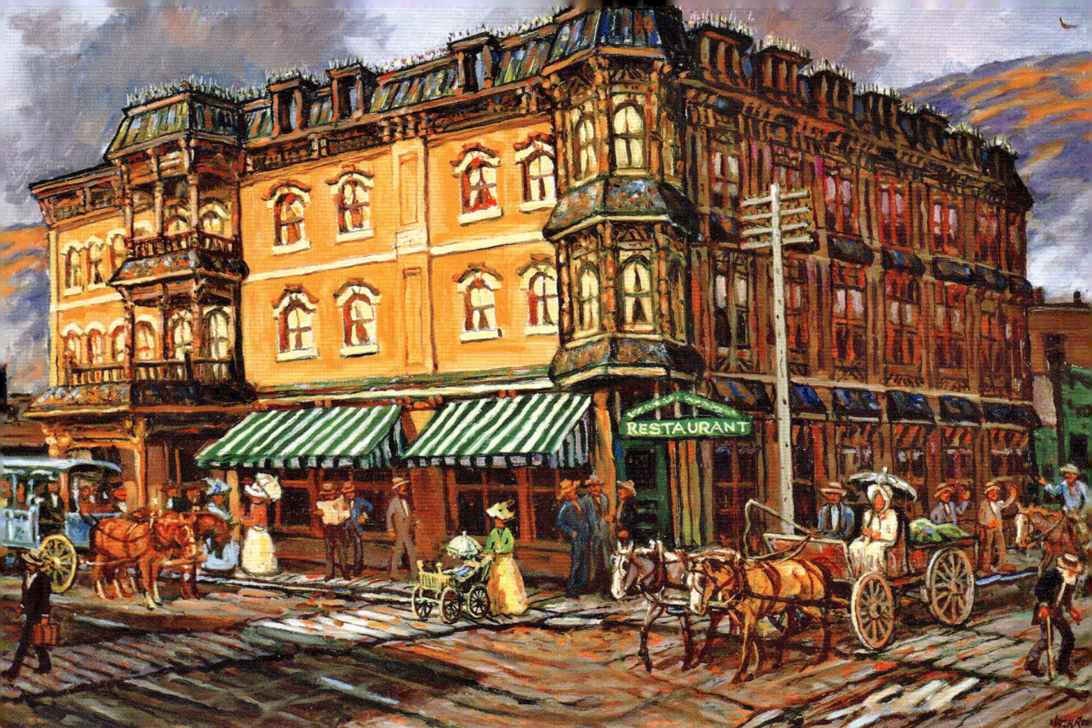

Hotel Glenwood. Courtesy of Angela and Don Parkison.

and he did not want to face that. As he sank deeper into depression, his health deteriorated further. The thought of losing his independence was as intolerable as losing his ability to paint.

"I have so many more pictures in my mind to paint," Jack lamented as Jill Briggs prepared to take him to the hospital on his final trip down valley.[140] But he rallied during the first weeks of his month-long stay at Heritage Park in Carbondale. Many of his friends from Redstone visited him regularly, and he perked up when Gary came in. "What are we going to do today?" he always asked. "Well, you're going to do some physical therapy today," Gary routinely answered. "You're going to do some exercises and some walking with that pretty girl who takes you down the hall." Jack was always delighted to hear that. "But," Gary added, laughing, "it might be a good idea for you to tie the back of your gown before you go."[141]

Gary's visits, as well as the support of Monica and the entire Anderson family, strengthened Jack's will to live. He continued to ask about the progress of Angie's book. He was extremely proud of her for undertaking the project and was delighted that he had been a part of it. Although it was not to be, he anticipated holding a copy of the book in his hands to see again how his illustrations helped tell the story of early Glenwood Springs. But his heart could not wait for the publisher's run.

When he realized that his father was near death, Gary began to talk to him about a living will. At first Jack was confused about the matter, but he eventually agreed to the stipulation that he should not be kept alive by life-support measures. "It'll be like the Indians," Gary told him. "You'll die in a natural state."[142] That satisfied Jack. He was proud that he was debt free and that he had met Harvey Dunn's challenge that only the most dedicated and talented artists could make a living from painting. With Gary at his bedside, the last call came on March 22, 2000. He died peacefully nine days before his eightieth birthday.

Jack had told Joan and Steve Benson that when he died, he wanted to be cremated and that they should go to every McDonald's restaurant they could find and fill the salt shakers with his ashes. Seriously though, he added, he wanted some of them spread on the grounds of the National Gallery. The Bensons wanted to honor his wish but decided it was too risky to carry a plastic baggie filled with ashes onto the gallery grounds in Washington, D.C., at the time of the anthrax scare. Surely Jack would have had a chuckle over their dilemma. Following the memorial service at his studio on Sunday, April 2, a few ashes were placed in his old Willey's Jeep. At least some of Jack got a final ride in the "Whores' Dream," which had delivered him faithfully to so many mountain adventures. It seemed a fitting tribute to a nonconforming artist whose passion for life and devotion to historical truth inspired his paintings and established his reputation as a prominent illustrator of the American West.

NOTES

ABBREVIATIONS

GM: Gary Miller
JR: Jack Roberts
RP: Roberts Papers

CHAPTER 1

1. Bogan, "Roberts Family History," RP.
2. Semrau, "Jack Roberts," 56.
3. Campbell, "Slope Artist"; O'Dwyer, "Jack Roberts."
4. Campbell, "Slope Artist."
5. Ibid.
6. *Denver Post Empire Magazine*, May 30, 1971.
7. Andres, "Harvey Dunn Class Notes."
8. Karolevitz, *Prairie Is My Garden*, 55.
9. Ibid.
10. JR to GM, July 14, 1998, RP.
11. Sheets, "Oils and Sketches; *Airway News*, "Marine Action."
12. *Denver Post Empire Magazine*, May 30, 1971.
13. JR to GM, July 14, 1998, PR.

Chapter 2

14. JR to Scott McInnis, December 7, 1993, RP; Neil, telephone interview.
15. Wurtsmith, telephone conversation; JR handwritten note, RP; Godeski (Daniels's granddaughter) e-mail correspondence.
16. Humphreys, "History of Western Press"; Hedgpeth and Trumble, *Story of Leanin' Tree*, 367.
17. Hayes, "Jack Roberts Recreates Early Days in Aspen."
18. This account from GM in discussion with author, March 6, 2014; McGregor, *Guide*, 16.
19. *Sopris Sun*, "Artists in Our Valley"; McGregor, "After Hundreds of Paintings"; Raabe, "Jack Roberts: Screwball"; Hayes, "Jack Roberts Recreates Early Days in Aspen."

Chapter 3

20. Steve and Joan Benson, interview with author.
21. Velasquez, telephone interview; GM, interview, March 6, 2014.
22. Hopkins, telephone interview, March 26, 2013.
23. O'Dwyer, "Jack Roberts"; Raabe, "Jack Roberts: Screwball."
24. Information for Roberts-Turner friendship is from Grant interview.
25. Turner, "Story of Artist Ben Turner," 14; Hopkins, telephone interview, March 11, 2013.
26. Campbell, "Colo. Artist."
27. O'Connor, telephone interview.
28. Hayes, "Jack Roberts Re-creates Early Days in Aspen"; Pettit, "Jack Roberts."
29. Velasquez, telephone interview.
30. Grant, interview; Brown, interview.
31. Gerbaz and Gerbaz, interview.
32. Parkison and Parkison, interview; GM and Monica Miller, interview, March 6, 2014.

Chapter 4

33. Bershenyi, telephone interview.
34. JR narrative for 1965 Equitable Life Assurance calendar, RP.
35. Ibid.

36. Notes from JR interview with Heather McGregor, April 1999.
37. Campbell, "Indians' Dignity Etched on Canvas."
38. *Sopris Sun*, "Artist in Our Valley"; Saks, "Jack Roberts Exhibit."
39. Roberts, *Amazing Adventures of Lord Gore*, 6–7.
40. Ibid., 7.
41. GM, interview, September 10, 2012.
42. JR to Philip Anschutz, April 27, 1969. RP.
43. Ibid.
44. JR to GM, March 12, 1970, RP.
45. JR to Lemon Saks, November 25, 1970, RP; JR to GM, March 12, 1970, RP.

Chapter 5

46. GM, interview, September 10, 2012.
47. Ibid.
48. Phyllis Miller to Myrtle Rose, September 6, 1966, RP.
49. GM to Myrtle Rose, November 29, 1960, RP.
50. GM, interview, March 6, 2014.
51. Information for the last four paragraphs is from Parkison and Parkison, interview.
52. GM quoted in Hamilton, "Local Artist Leaves Smiles Behind."
53. Barron, e-mail correspondence.

Chapter 6

54. Morrison, interview.
55. Briggs, e-mail correspondence.
56. Semrau, "Jack Roberts," 56.
57. Grant, interview.
58. Information on the Benson-Roberts relationship is from Benson and Benson, interview.
59. Ibid.
60. JR to Lemon Saks, August 15, 1974, RP; Bartlett, interview, October 29, 2012.
61. GM, interview, March 6, 2014.
62. McInnis and McInnis, interview; JR to Bartlett, April 2, 1992, RP.

63. Parkison and Parkison, interview.

64. Grant, interview.

65. Ibid.

66. Ibid.

67. Benson and Benson, interview.

68. Information for this and the next two paragraphs is from the Bensons' interview.

CHAPTER 7

69. JR to Thomas Evans, May 22, 1973, RP.

70. Blue Stroud, letter to the editor, *Sage-Reminder*, April 25, 1973.

71. Michael Kinsley quoting Weixelman and Zakovich in *Glenwood Post*, April 11, 1973.

72. Roberts, "Placita Revisited."

73. GM, interview, September 10, 2012.

74. Durrett, interview; *Valley Journal*, Patrick Noel editorial, April 8, 1976.

75. *Valley Journal*, March 4, 1976; *Glenwood Post*, February 25, 1976.

76. *Valley Journal*, March 11, 1976.

77. JR to Rollie Fischer, February 10, 1976, RP.

78. *Valley Journal*, March 11, 1976.

79. Ibid., March 18, 1976.

80. Helen Kay Ruggero, letter to the editor, *Valley Journal*, April 15, 1976.

81. *Valley Journal*, Patrick Noel editorial, April 8, 1976.

CHAPTER 8

82. JR to Lemon Saks, November 25, 1970, RP.

83. JR to Philip Anschutz, November 25, 1970, RP.

84. JR to Lemon Saks, June 1, 1971, RP.

85. Ibid.

86. Ibid., February 20, 1972, RP.

87. Ibid., May 20, 1972, RP.

88. Lemon Saks to JR, May 22, 1972, RP.

89. JR to Lemon Saks, June 17, 1972, RP.

90. Ibid.

Chapter 9

91. JR to Ed Trumble, February 20, 1972, RP.
92. Pollard, e-mail correspondence.
93. JR to C.J. "Jack" Hire, May 24, 1990, RP.
94. JR to Laurence F. Jonson, May 12, 1981, RP.
95. Jonson to JR, May 18 and June 3, 1981, RP.
96. JR to W.R. Hall, July 3, 1981, RP.
97. DeBruin, "Exhibits Are Western Art Feast"; JR to Laurence Jonson, June 11, 1979, RP.

Chapter 10

98. Trumble, telephone interview; Hedgpeth and Trumble, *Story of Leanin' Tree*, 367.
99. Hedgpeth and Trumble, *Story of Leanin' Tree*, 367.
100. Ed Trumble to JR, November 3 and 27, 1972, RP; JR to Ed Trumble, November 11, 1972, RP.
101. Ed Trumble to JR, November 27, 1972, RP.
102. JR to Ed Trumble, November 30, 1972, RP.
103. Ibid., January 19, 1976, RP.
104. JR to Jane Trumble-Knutson, December 11, 1981, RP.
105. Ibid.
106. Ibid., August 5, 1992, RP.
107. JR to Jan Graham, March 19, 1981, RP.
108. JR to Ed Trumble, February 1982, RP.
109. Ibid., February 3, 1988, RP.
110. Ibid.
111. Trumble, telephone interview.

Chapter 11

112. JR to Ken Johnson, August 19, 1977, and February 11 and April 7, 1978, RP; Ken Johnson to JR, February 16 and April 17, 1978, RP.
113. Ken Johnson to JR, February 20, 1978, RP.
114. Ibid., May 4, 1978, RP; JR to Ken Johnson, May 9, 1978, RP.
115. JR to Ken Johnson, January 7, 1979, RP.
116. Ibid., October 3 and July 21, 1978, RP.
117. Ken Johnson to JR, April 4, 1979, RP.

CHAPTER 12

118. Roosevelt, *Outdoor Pastimes*, 76.
119. Ibid., 76–77.
120. Goff, "Epitome of the Hunt," 543.
121. Roosevelt, *Outdoor Pastimes*, 76, 78.
122. Ibid., 90–91.
123. Ibid., 92–93.
124. Ibid., 104.
125. Ibid., 107–08.
126. GM, interview, September 10, 2012.

CHAPTER 13

127. JR to Mary Webster, August 20, 1982, RP.
128. Ibid., August 28, 1982, RP.
129. JR to R.L. Quimby, March 3 and April 14, 1984, RP.
130. JR, "Visions of Western Colorado," RP.

CHAPTER 14

131. GM, interview, September 10, 2012.
132. JR to GM, June 2, 1998, RP.
133. GM, interview, September 10, 2012.
134. JR to GM, July 17, 1996, RP.
135. Information for this is from Weaver, telephone interview and Mitchell, interview.
136. JR to Bill Hustead, August 27, 1993, RP.
137. JR to GM, July 14, 1998, RP.
138. Grant, interview.
139. GM, interview, March 6, 2014.
140. Briggs, e-mail correspondence.
141. GM, interview, March 6, 2014.
142. Ibid.

BIBLIOGRAPHY

MANUSCRIPTS

Bogan, Pearl Roberts. "Roberts Family History." Typescript. Jack Roberts Studio, Redstone, Colorado.

Jack Roberts Papers. Jack Roberts Studio, Redstone, Colorado.

Roberts, Jack. "Visions of Western Colorado." Typescript. Jack Roberts Studio, Redstone, Colorado.

Turner, Blanche Beach. "The Story of Artist Ben Turner, 1912–1966." Typescript. Jack Roberts Studio, Redstone, Colorado.

BOOKS

Hedgpeth, Don, and Ed Trumble. *The Story of Leanin' Tree: Art and Enterprise in the American West.* Boulder, CO: Leanin' Tree, Inc., 2008.

Karolevitz, Robert L. *The Prairie Is My Garden: The Story of Harvey Dunn, Artist.* Aberdeen, SD: North Plains Press, 1969.

McGregor, Heather. *A Guide to Glenwood Canyon.* Glenwood Springs, CO: Pika Publishing Co., 1993.

Roberts, Jack. *The Amazing Adventures of Lord Gore: A True Saga from the Old West.* Silverton, CO: Sundance Publications, 1977.

Roosevelt, Theodore. *Outdoor Pastimes of an American Hunter.* New York: C. Scribner's Sons, 1905.

ARTICLES

Airview News (Douglas Aircraft Oklahoma City). "Marine Action by Jack Roberts Causes Sensation." June 23, 1945.

Anderson, Steve. "Old West Relived at Local Art Exhibit." *Valley West Dispatch* (Grand Valley/Parachute, CO), March 8, 1989.

Andres, Charles J. "Harvey Dunn Class Notes." http://www.e-pix.com/ArtMuseum/Dunnclassno.html.

Campbell, Robert. "Colo. Artist Puts Entire Effort into Painting Indians." *Daily Camera* (Boulder, CO), July 16, 1971.

————. "Indians' Dignity Etched on Canvas." *Rocky Mountain News*, July 17, 1971.

————. "Slope Artist Attempting to Record American Indian Story 'As It Was.'" *Daily Sentinel* (Grand Junction, CO), July 16, 1971.

————. "Story of the Tabagauche Utes." *Daily Sentinel*, July 9, 1972.

DeBruin, Courtney. "Exhibits Are Western Art Feast." *Daily Sentinel*, October 15, 1985.

Denver Post Empire Magazine. "The Utes' 'Buffalo Culture.'" May 30, 1971.

Dumas, Alan. "Pioneer Impressionist." *Rocky Mountain News*, February 21, 1993.

Equitable Life Assurance Society of the United States. "Life on the Range." 1965 calendar.

Glenwood Post. "Artist Jack Roberts to Paint Five Ute Historical Pictures." January 20, 1971.

Goff, John. "Epitome of the Hunt." *Outdoor Life* 16, no. 1 (July 1905): 541–46.

Hamilton, Theresa. "Local Artist Jack Roberts Leaves Smiles Behind." *Citizen Telegram* (Rifle, CO), March 29, 2000.

Hart, Susanna. "Artist Jack Roberts: A Man with Vision of the Old West." *Telegram Centennial Edition* (Rifle, CO), June 8, 1994.

Hayes, Mary Eshbaugh. "Jack Roberts Re-creates Early Days in Aspen." *Aspen Times*, March 24, 1983.

Humphreys, Kimberly. "The History of the Western Press on Display This Week." *Convention Daily* (Denver), February 12, 1993.

Lustgarten, Abraham. "Roberts a 'Cowboy Poet' with a Paint Brush and a Mission." *Glenwood Post*, September 28–29, 1996.

McGregor, Heather. "After Hundreds of Paintings, Jack Roberts Still Not Satisfied." *Glenwood Independent*, April 21, 1999.

————. "Reliving the Parachute Train Robbery." *Daily Sentinel*, September 5, 1996.

O'Dwyer, Patience. "Jack Roberts: Western Artist." *Glenwood Springs Magazine* 1, no. 2 (Winter 1980): 24–25.

Pettit, Susan. "Jack Roberts: Images of the Old West." *Aspen Times*, January 14, 1982.

Raabe, Steve. "Jack Roberts: Screwball, Girl Chaser, but Mostly Artist." *Weekly News* (Glenwood Springs, CO), July 14, 1982.

Roberts, Jack. "'Placita Revisited'—A Personal Experience." *Valley Journal* (Carbondale, CO), January 29, 1976.

Saks, Lemon. "Jack Roberts Exhibit." Saks Galleries, January 1965.

Semrau, Julie. "Jack Roberts: Paintings from the Briar Patch." *Yippy-yi-yea*, Summer 1992: 56.

Sheets, Nan. "Oils and Sketches by Jack Roberts Now on Exhibit." *Daily Oklahoman*, June 24, 1945.

Sopris Sun (Basalt, CO). "Artists in Our Valley." March 27, 1970.

Webb, Dennis. "Valley Loses Two Creative Legends." *Glenwood Post*, March 8, 1989.

PAMPHLETS

Roberts, Jack. *Aspen Early Days*. Sorensen's Danish Antiks of Aspen. RP, n.d.

———. *The Frontier Press*. Colorado Press Association. RP, n.d.

———. *Grand Junction…A land of Pioneers, Beauty and Hope*. First National Bank, Grand Junction, Colorado. RP, n.d.

———. *The Paintings: Buffalo Valley Inn*. Buffalo Valley Inn, Glenwood Springs, Colorado. RP, n.d.

———. *The Paintings: Fort Vasquez*. Holiday Inn, Greeley, Colorado. RP, n.d.

———. *The Tabagauche Utes*. Buffalo Valley Inn, Glenwood Springs, Colorado. RP, n.d.

INTERVIEWS, E-MAILS AND TELEPHONE CONVERSATIONS

Scott Balcomb. Interview with the author, November 11, 2013.

Mary Barron. Telephone interview with the author, May 22, 2013; e-mail correspondence, July 24, 2013.

Bartlett. Interviews with the author, October 29, 2012; March 6, 2014.

Joan Benson and Steve Benson. Interview with the author, November 16, 2012.

Steve Bershenyi. Telephone interview with the author, February 19, 2013; March 19, 2014.

Kirk Blue. Telephone interview with the author, March 27, 2014.

Jill Briggs. E-mail correspondence, February 8, 2013.

Carole Brown. Interview with the author, February 10, 2015.

Bruce Carlson. Interview with the author, January 28, 2014.

Deanna Musgrave Corn. Telephone interview with the author, February 4, 2014.

Gregory Durrett. Interview with the author, August 29, 2012.

Ernest Gerbaz and Marge Gerbaz. Interview with the author, June 17, 2013.

Keith Gilstrap, Telephone interview with the author, April 22, 2013.

Christy Godeski. E-mail correspondence, September 8, 2013.

Lanny Grant. Interview with the author, June 9, 2013.

Judith Hayward. Telephone interview with the author, February 19, 2014.

Charles Hopkins. Telephone interview with the author, March 11and 26, 2013.

Viola Huber. Telephone interview with the author, April 25, 2014.

Joyce Illian. Telephone interview with the author, November 11, 2013.

Bob Louden. Telephone interview with the author, May 13, 2015.

Mike McBreen. Interview with the author, August 29, 2013.

Kay McElhinney. Interview with the author, April 14, 2014.

Heather McGregor. E-mail correspondence, July 6, 2013.

Lori McInnis and Scott McInnis. Interview with the author, April 1, 2013.

George McKinley. Telephone interview with the author, January 15, 2015.

Gary Miller and Monica Miller. Interview with the author, September 10, 2012; March 6, 2014.

Sherie Milton. E-mail correspondence, June 30, 2013.

Kjell Mitchell. Interview with the author, February 21, 2014.

Sylvia Morrison. Interview with the author, September 10, 2013.

John Neil. Telephone interview with the author, June 13, 2013.

Patrick Noel. Telephone interview with the author, September 3, 2013.

Dennis O'Connor. Telephone interview with the author, December 17, 2014.

Angela Parkison and Don Parkison. Interview with the author, June 12, 2013.

Gloria Pollard. E-mail correspondence, July 1, 2013.

Ed Trumble. Telephone interview with the author, April 11, 2013.

James Weaver. Telephone interview with the author, February 25, 2014.

Scott Werking. Telephone interview with the author, June 22, 2013.

Kurt Wigger. Telephone interview with the author, September 6, 2014.

Eric Williams. Telephone interview with the author, February 13, 2013.

Ben Wurtsmith. Telephone interview with the author, July 11, 2013.

Larry Velasquez. Telephone interview with the author, July 11, 2013.

INDEX

ABOUT THE AUTHOR

F. Darrell Munsell, professor emeritus, West Texas A&M University, is the author of three other books on historical subjects. He received a PhD degree in British history from the University of Kansas and was an exchange scholar at the University of Birmingham, England. Since his retirement from teaching and move to Colorado in 1997, he has divided his time between woodworking and historical research and writing. He has served on the Redstone Historic Preservation Commission and has contributed his time and knowledge to numerous local and state preservation projects. 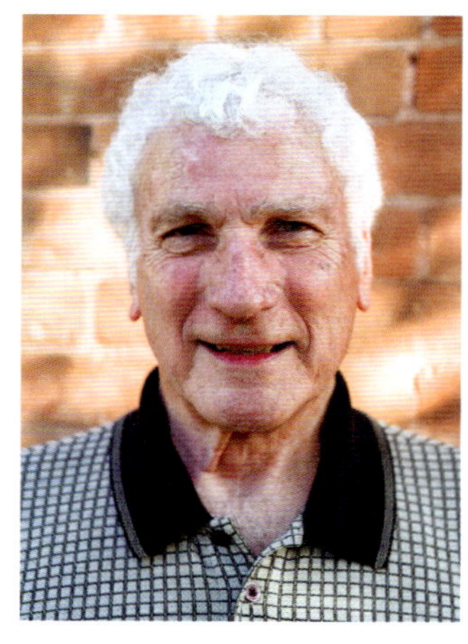
He is actively involved in several area historical societies. He and his wife, Jane, live in the Crystal River Valley south of Carbondale.